Scrap Saver's Gift Stitchery

Scrap Saver's Gift Stitchery

Text and Illustrations by

SANDRA LOUNSBURY FOOSE

Sedgewood™ Press

NEW YORK

Editorial Director, Sedgewood™ Press: *Jane Ross*
Project Editor and Photographic Stylist: *Wendy Rieder*
Managing Editor: *Gale Kremer*
Production Manager: *Bill Rose*

*For
Dean and Tracy,
each a
precious gift*

Photography: *David Arky,* except for pages 144–145, reprinted courtesy Good Ideas from Armstrong.

Credits: Flowers in some photographs, courtesy Madison Flower Shop, Madison, Ct.; page 10, Animal Cozies used by permission from the June 1973 issue of *Good Housekeeping* magazine, © 1973 by the Hearst Corporation; page 105, yarn, courtesy The Sheared Sheep, Essex, Ct.; page 107, china and flatware, courtesy Marlborough Country Barn, Old Saybrook, Ct.; page 129, brass bugle, courtesy Holly Loft Christmas and Gift Shop, Killingworth, Ct.; pages 143–144 and page 152, ornaments and wreaths used by permission from *Good Ideas for Decorating* magazine from Armstrong © 1981 by Armstrong World Industries, Inc.

Distributed by Macmillan Publishing Company, a division of Macmillan, Inc.   ISBN 0-02-496680-0

Library of Congress Catalog Number 83-51240

Manufactured in the United States of America

(10   9   8   7   6   5   4)

Contents

Introduction

Some of the very best gifts I've ever received—a word of comfort, a compliment, a prayer, a hug, a helping hand, a sympathetic ear, a smile, a pat on the back—haven't come to me wrapped in tissue paper and tied with satin ribbons, but they have all been given with love at exactly the right moment.

There are so many happy occasions during the year when we anticipate sharing the presents we've made—the gifts of our hands. We also have daily opportunities to offer well-timed gifts from the heart—love, forgiveness, and understanding. These gifts of the heart cost us little, yet they are of great value and often last forever in the memories of those who receive them.

I hope that this book will inspire you to make and to share gifts of love from your heart and from your hands. All the designs make use of scraps and remnants, but you'll probably need to buy some materials for a few of the larger projects.

Before you buy anything, sort through your scraps. Maybe you have just a handful, but if you've been sewing for very long, I'll bet you'll find at least a bagful stashed away somewhere in the attic, or below the stairs, or under the bed! Perhaps you'll find some pieces left from the pillows you made for your first apartment or the print you used for curtains in the baby's room. Or there might be a few remnants you bought for that quilt you were going to make "someday" and some felt scraps from the costumes you've stitched for your little gremlins.

Why do we save all these scraps? I'm sure we all have our thrifty reasons, but our sentimental reasons are probably much greater. When I sort through the trunk of odds and ends I've saved from all my sewing years, I can see and hold little pieces of the past. It's like looking through an old photograph album. Both experiences are filled with memories that set me to daydreaming of the days gone by and those yet to come. Does that happen to you too? Well, take some of those scrap pieces and the precious memories that go along with them and use this book to create a gift that will make a new special memory for someone you love. Before you begin, however, I suggest that you turn to the "Basic Sewing Supplies, Tools, and Techniques" section at the back of the book for some helpful suggestions.

Gifts
for
Children

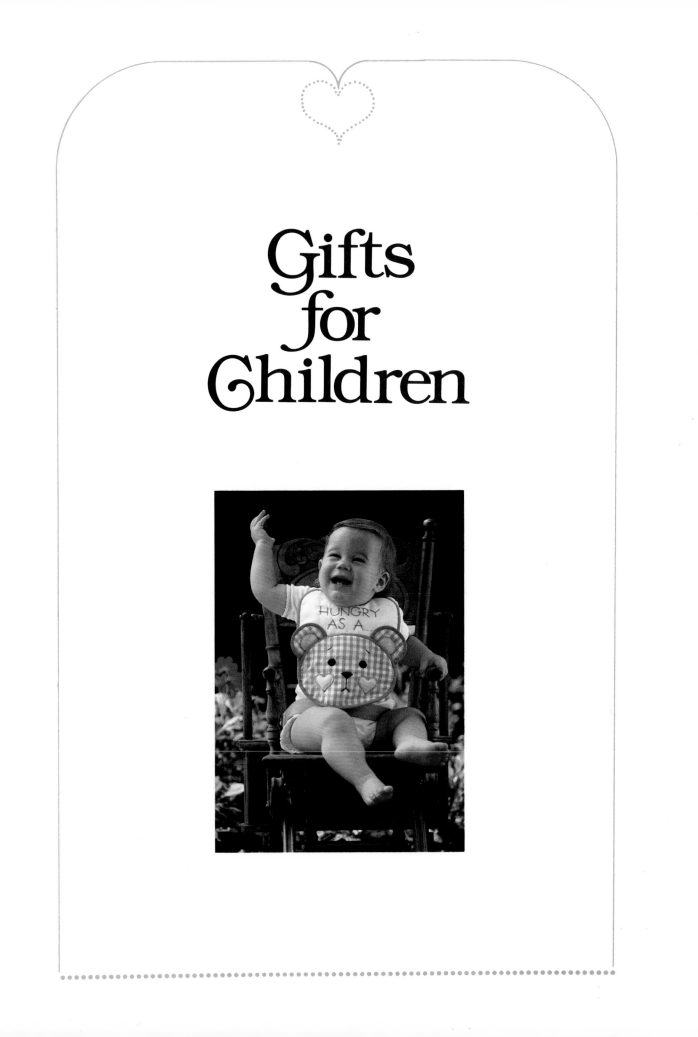

Animal Cozies

Here are my four favorite spring critters—a bunny, a mousekin, a piglet, and a duckling—that can be made to perform a whole gamut of tricks. On Easter morning each one can top an egg cup, peek out of a basket, hide a tiny surprise, or dance on a little hand as a puppet! The light stuffing in the head is optional, so each animal could fit nicely into an envelope as a fuzzy greeting, embroidered with your own special good wishes if you're so inspired.

If you want to use these designs for egg cozies on a daily basis, you'll probably want to consider using polyester felt so you can wash away spots without a worry. I like the "loving hands at home" look of tiny blanket stitches on wool felt, but if you plan to cover your Easter breakfast table with little bunnies and ducklings, I know you'll probably be producing these at the sewing machine. You can save additional time by tacking on felt cheeks and, instead of embroidery, using felt dot eyes cut with a small-hole paper punch.

These little animals are naturals for baby gifts. They look really cute covering trial-sized baby products all snuggled together in a beribboned basket. They can later be used for puppets or participants in a peek-a-boo game. For baby use, don't put any stuffing at all in the heads because they are not stitched closed.

For use as crib toys or tree ornaments for baby's first Christmas, stuff the animals completely, maintaining the flatness, and blanket stitch the bottom edge closed. Remove possible toxins and excess dyes by prewashing the felt that you will use for any baby items, even if you're not making them for toys, because babies have a way of turning everything into a toy. If you are using wool felt, gently dip it into cold water and mild soap suds and rinse well without squeezing or rubbing it. Press out extra moisture between towels and dry the felt flat, away from heat. Wool felt will shrink a lot no matter how careful you are, so by all means wash the felt before you stitch it. For baby's additional safety, stitch on ribbons, ears, wings, etc., extra-securely and omit the ball fringe and braided tails.

Bunny Materials
A 6″ × 11″ pale blue felt scrap
A 3″ × 3″ pale pink felt scrap
6-ply embroidery thread: 18″ dark brown, 1½ yards pale pink, 2 yards pale blue, 18″ medium pink
Polyester stuffing, optional
⅝″- to ¾″-diameter pale pink ball fringe
A 13″ length of ⅛″-wide white satin or grosgrain ribbon

Mousekin Materials
A 6½″ × 10½″ pale green felt scrap
A 2½″ × 5″ pale pink felt scrap
6-ply embroidery thread: 18″ dark brown, 2½ yards pale pink, 2½ yards pale green, 18″ medium pink
Polyester stuffing, optional
A 13″ length of ⅛″-wide yellow satin or grosgrain ribbon

Duckling Materials
A 5½″ × 10″ yellow felt scrap
A 1½″ × 2″ yellow-orange felt scrap
6-ply embroidery thread: 18″ dark brown, 18″ medium pink, 18″ yellow-orange, 2 yards yellow
Polyester stuffing, optional
A 13″ length of ⅛″-wide pale green satin or grosgrain ribbon

Piglet Materials
A 5½″ × 10″ pale pink felt scrap
6-ply embroidery thread: 18″ dark brown, 18″ medium pink, 2½ yards pale pink
Polyester stuffing, optional
A 13″ length of ⅛″-wide pale green satin or grosgrain ribbon

MAKING THE PATTERNS AND CUTTING THE FABRIC FOR ALL THE ANIMALS.

1. Making the patterns—Trace the patterns from the book, transferring all the necessary dots and details and labeling each. All the pattern lines are cutting lines for felt. Cut out the cheeks, eyes, and mouth line to make a template of each body pattern.

2. Marking and cutting the fabric—On the front of the felt, very lightly trace around the patterns with a sharp soft pencil, lightly transferring the facial details and placement dots. Turn the body pattern over to trace the back side in reverse. Cut the ear, beak, or other pieces two at a time from folded and pinned felt.

THE BUNNY

1. Making the pattern and cutting the fabric—Make the pattern and cut out the animals, using pale blue felt for the two ears and two body pieces and pale pink felt for two inner ears. Using one strand of embroidery thread for each color, satin stitch brown eyes and pale pink cheeks on each body piece.

2. Embroidering and assembling the bunny—Pin a pink inner ear in place on each blue ear and,

using two strands of pale pink thread, appliqué them with blanket stitches. Use shallow stitches so they won't show on the reverse side of the ear.

Position and pin an ear on each side of the head using the placement dot as a guide. Using two strands of pale blue thread, appliqué each ear to the head with blanket stitches, then continue edging the entire ear with blanket stitches.

Pin both body pieces together, and, using two strands of pale blue embroidery thread, blanket stitch around the outside edge, except along the bottom. Finish the open bottom edge with blanket-stitching. Stuff the head lightly, if you wish, but keep it flat.

Using one strand of pale pink embroidery thread, satin stitch the nose. Pass the needle from front to back, then bring it to the front by wrapping the thread around the blanket-stitched edge. Repeat, always turning the work from one side to the other so you can guide the needle accurately as you fill in the nose area. Using a single strand of medium pink embroidery thread, back stitch the mouth on the front and back layers, separately.

Stitch ball fringe very securely to the tail area (but omit it for a baby toy).

Tie a white ribbon bow around the neck.

THE MOUSEKIN

1. Making the pattern and cutting the fabric—Make the pattern and cut out the fabric as directed for all the animals, using pale green felt for the two ears and two body pieces and pale pink felt for two inner ears. Using one strand of embroidery thread for each color, satin stitch brown eyes and pale pink cheeks on each body piece.

2. Embroidering and assembling the mousekin—Using two strands of pale pink embroidery thread, pin a pink inner ear in place on each green ear and appliqué them with blanket stitches. Use shallow stitches so they won't show on the reverse side of the ear.

Position and pin an ear on each side of the head using the placement dot on the head as a guide for the bottom point of the ear and tipping the ear tops in different directions for the best look. Using two strands of green embroidery thread, appliqué each ear to the head with blanket stitches, then continue edging the entire ear with blanket stitches.

Pin both body pieces together and, using two strands of pale green embroidery thread, blanket stitch around the outside edge, except along the bottom. Finish the open bottom edge with blanket stitching.

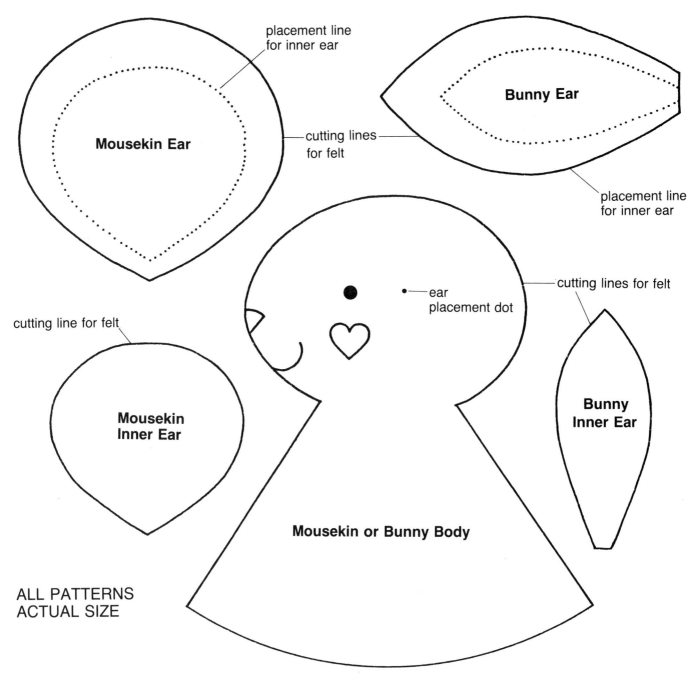

placement line
for inner ear

Bunny Ear

Mousekin Ear

cutting lines
for felt

placement line
for inner ear

cutting lines for felt

ear
placement dot

cutting line for felt

**Mousekin
Inner Ear**

**Bunny
Inner Ear**

Mousekin or Bunny Body

ALL PATTERNS
ACTUAL SIZE

Stuff the head lightly, if you wish, but keep it flat.

Using one strand of pale pink thread, satin stitch the nose. Pass the needle from front to back, then bring it to the front by wrapping the thread around the blanket-stitched edge. Repeat, always turning the work from one side to the other so you can guide the needle accurately as you fill in the nose area. Using a single strand of medium pink thread, back stitch the mouth on the front and back layers, separately.

To make the tail, cut three 12″ lengths of 6-ply, pale pink embroidery thread. One at a time, pull each thread halfway through the lower

back corner at the same spot, removing the needle each time. Braid the strands together, knot the ends and trim away the excess threads.

Tie a yellow ribbon bow around the neck.

THE DUCKLING

1. Making the pattern and cutting the fabric—Make the pattern and cut out the fabric as directed for all the animals, using yellow felt for the two wings and two body pieces and yellow-orange felt for the two beak pieces. Using one strand of embroidery thread for each color, satin stitch a brown eye and medium pink cheek on each body piece.

2. Embroidering and assembling the duckling—Using two strands of yellow-orange embroidery thread, embroider the long curved edge of each beak piece with blanket stitches. Set aside.

Position and pin a wing in place on each body piece. Using two strands of yellow embroidery thread, appliqué each wing to a body section at the top between the dots with blanket stitches, then continue around the wing with blanket stitches, but leave it free.

Pin both body pieces together, inserting a folded-in-half beak piece at each dot, and, using two strands of yellow embroidery thread, blan-

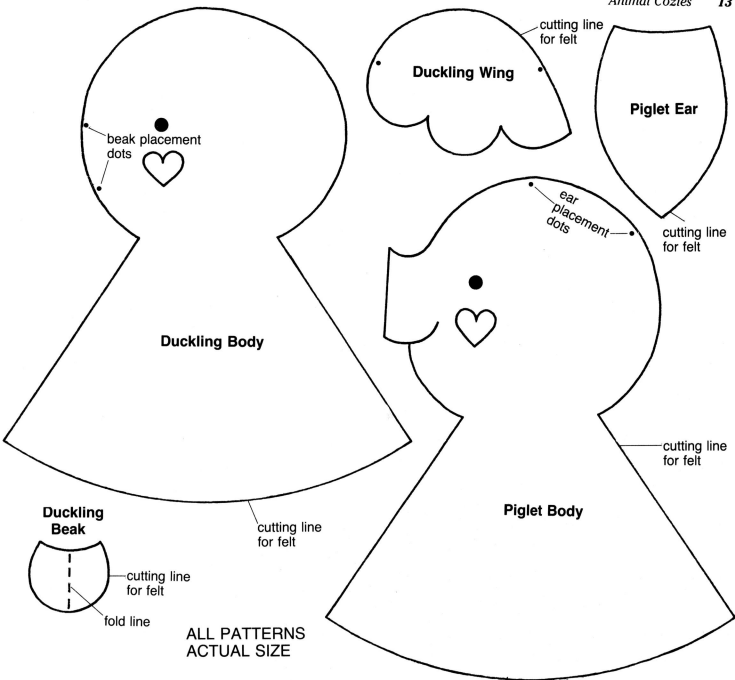

beak placement dots

Duckling Wing

cutting line for felt

Piglet Ear

cutting line for felt

Duckling Body

ear placement dots

cutting line for felt

Duckling Beak

cutting line for felt

fold line

cutting line for felt

Piglet Body

ALL PATTERNS ACTUAL SIZE

ket stitch around the outside edge, except along the bottom. Finish the open bottom edge with blanket stitches. Stuff the head lightly, if you wish, but keep it flat.

Tie a pale green ribbon bow around the neck.

THE PIGLET

1. Making the pattern and cutting the fabric—Make the pattern and cut out the fabric as directed for all the animals, using pale pink felt for the two ears and two body pieces. Using one strand of embroidery thread for each color, satin stitch a brown eye and medium pink cheek on each body piece.

2. Embroidering and assembling the piglet—Using two strands of pale pink embroidery thread, edge each ear with blanket stitches. Pin and baste an ear in place between the dots on the wrong side of each body piece so that the head overlaps the bottom of the ear by ¼".

Pin both body pieces together, and, using two strands of pale pink embroidery thread, blanket stitch around the outside edge, catching the ears, but leaving the bottom open. Finish the open bottom edge with blanket stitches. Stuff the head lightly, if you wish, but keep it flat.

Using a single strand of medium pink embroidery thread, back stitch

the mouth on the front and back layers, separately.

Softly fold down and invisibly tack the ear tips.

To make the tail, cut a ½"- × 2¼"-long felt strip and fold it in half lengthwise. Using two strands of pale pink embroidery thread, blanket stitch along all edges of the strip, then pass the threaded needle invisibly through the length of the two felt layers and pull the thread tightly to pucker and curl the strip. Knot the thread and then stitch the tail securely to the lower corner of the piglet's back side.

Tie a pale green ribbon bow around the neck.

This elephant family of four resides inside its own softly-lined jumbo peanut, which slips into a colorful striped peanut sack for toting. It makes a perfect "church toy" because it produces no clicks, bumps, or crashes when little ones play with it during a quiet time.

The peanut shell alone would make a novel cosmetic bag for a true peanut-butter "nut." You can also turn it into a cuddly piece of soft sculpture by omitting the lining and constructing a zipperless stuffed shell of velour.

Red-and-white bold-striped fabric is most often available as a home furnishing fabric at Christmas time. And, speaking of Christmas, the

Peanut Surprise

baby elephants in this family work equally well as tree ornaments.

If you're very short on time, you can eliminate the label on the bag, or even omit the entire bag and the toy will still have a lot of play value. The soft peanut looks best with its machine-

quilted peanut texture, but you could also save time if you substitute pre-quilted fabric or seersucker.

To speed up the stitchery on the elephants, omit the embroidered heart and star symbols and use pretty red and blue patterned fabrics for the blankets. You can also substitute machine zig-zag stitches in all the places where I've blanket stitched the appliqués, but if you do that, do not add hem allowances to the appliqués.

On the other hand, if take-along stitchery is what you actually prefer, you can cut the elephants from felt, without seam allowances, and then join the fronts and backs together with tiny blanket stitches.

Peanut Bag Materials:
A 17″ × 27″ piece of red-and-white striped fabric, with 1″-wide stripes that are parallel to the 27″-long edge
A 7″ × 7″ blue fabric scrap
A 7″ × 7″ white fabric scrap
6-ply embroidery thread: 1 skein blue, 3 yards each red and golden yellow
White sewing thread

Equipment
White pencil
5″ embroidery hoop

Peanut Materials
A 16″ × 22″ peanut-colored fabric scrap
A 16″ × 22″ white or beige sheer batiste fabric scrap
A 16″ × 44″ piece of thin quilt batting
Peanut-colored thread
7″ peanut-colored nylon or polyester coil-type zipper

A 16″ × 22″ light beige fabric scrap

General materials and equipment for all the elephants
(additional items listed under directions for individual elephants)
White pencil
Sewing thread: red, white, and blue
5″-diameter embroidery hoop
6-ply embroidery thread: blue, red, white, black, golden yellow
Polyester stuffing

Mama Elephant Materials
A 9½″ × 13½″ red-with-white-dot fabric scrap
A 7½″ × 7½″ red-and-white-checked gingham fabric scrap
A 6½″ × 6½″ white fabric scrap
A 6½″ × 6½″ blue fabric scrap
A 9″ length of ⅛″-wide blue satin ribbon

Papa Elephant Materials
A 9½″ × 13½″ blue-with-white-dot fabric scrap
A 7½″ × 7½″ blue-and-white-checked gingham fabric scrap
A 6½″ × 6½″ white fabric scrap
A 6½″ × 6½″ red fabric scrap

Girl Elephant Materials
An 8″ × 10″ red-and-white checked gingham fabric scrap
A 4½″ × 7½″ red-with-white-dot fabric scrap
A 6½″ × 6½″ white fabric scrap
A 6½″ × 6½″ blue fabric scrap
A 9″ length of ⅛″-wide blue satin ribbon

Boy Elephant Materials
An 8″ × 10″ blue-and-white-checked gingham fabric scrap
A 4½″ × 7½″ blue-with-white-dot fabric scrap
A 6½″ × 6½″ red fabric scrap
A 6½″ × 6½″ white fabric scrap

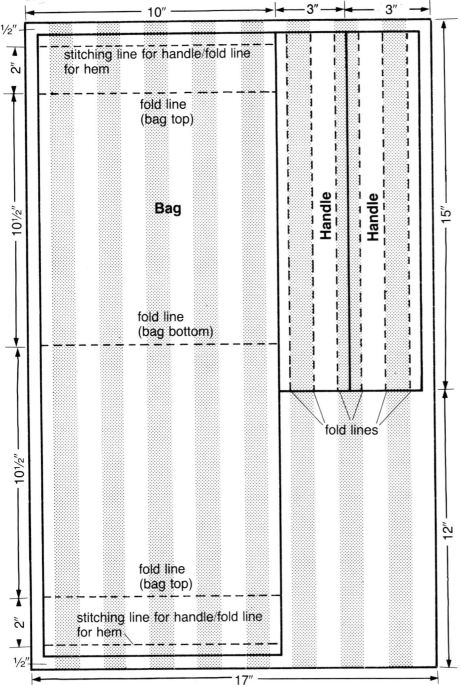

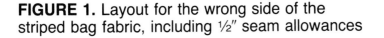

FIGURE 1. Layout for the wrong side of the striped bag fabric, including ½" seam allowances

side down, to the wrong side of the white fabric. Tape the fabric, pattern side down, to a bright window and carefully trace the letters onto the front of the fabric.

Using two strands of blue embroidery thread and working horizontally, satin stitch the word "PEANUTS". Using one strand of golden yellow embroidery thread, chain stitch the shading on the letters.

Using two strands of red embroidery thread, chain stitch the word "FRESH". Using one strand of red embroidery thread, chain stitch "IN THE SHELL".

3. Attaching the label to its border and the bag—Cut out the label adding a ¼" seam allowance. Finger press and baste under the seam allowance. Pin and baste the label in place on the blue label border. Using two strands golden yellow embroidery thread, blanket stitch around the edge.

Cut out the label border adding a ¼" seam allowance. Finger press and baste under the seam allowance. Pin and baste the label in place on the bag, 2¾" from the bottom fold and centered between the side seams. Using two strands of blue embroidery thread, blanket stitch the label border to the bag.

4. Making the bag—Fold the bag section right sides together along the bottom fold line. Stitch the side seams, leaving ½" seam allowances, and trim off the lower corners. Turn the bag right side out and press flat.

To make the handles, press under a ½" seam allowance on each long edge. Then press each handle lengthwise along the center fold line to make a 1"-wide strap. One side will be red, the other white. Machine topstitch each handle lengthwise ⅛" from both edges.

Referring to Figure 2, pin a handle in place on each side of the bag, red side down and right sides together on the top edge of the bag, so that each end of the handle lines up with a red stripe on the bag and the handle top points down toward the bottom of the bag. Machine stitch ½" from the top of the bag.

Fold down 2½" of fabric along the top edge of the bag and raise the handles out of the bag. Align the handles with the stripes on the bag and pin them in place. Tuck under the lower ½" of the seam allowance to make a hem and baste it. Machine stitch ⅛" from the edge of the hem and ⅛" from the top edge of the bag.

PEANUT BAG

1. Cutting the bag fabric—Referring to Figure 1, measure and draw the 10" by 26" bag and two 3" × 15" handle pieces directly on the back of the striped fabric. The measurements include ½" seam allowances. Lightly draw the fold lines. Cut out the pieces and set aside.

2. Lettering the label—Trace the label with its letters and the label border patterns from the book, and cut out both patterns.

Pin the label border pattern to the right side of the blue fabric and trace around its shape with a white pencil, but do not cut it out.

Pin the lettered label pattern, right

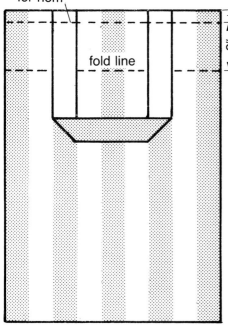

FIGURE 2. Attaching handles to the bag

THE PEANUT

1. Making the pattern—Trace the top and bottom sections of the peanut, and butt and tape them together along the dotted lines to make a complete pattern (see Figure 3, page 19). Use a pen or dark pencil to copy the peanut texture lines on the pattern, and add the dots for the zipper placement. Mark the pattern top and bottom and cut it out on the pattern line.

2. Cutting, backing, and quilting the peanut pieces—To make the outer peanut shell, pin and trace the pattern four times on the wrong side of the peanut-colored fabric spacing the pieces 1″ apart. Cut out the pieces, adding ½″ seam allowances, and set them aside.

Now pin the pattern to the sheer batiste and trace the peanut shape and texture lines directly onto the fabric four times and 1″ apart. *Do not turn or reverse the pattern.* Mark the zipper placement dots on one piece and then cut out all four batiste pieces, adding ½″ seam allowances. Mark the top and bottom of each piece.

To make a backing for quilting the peanut-colored fabric pieces, first pin each batiste piece, wrong side down, to polyester quilt batting, baste ⅛″ from the edges, and cut out each one. Now pin each peanut-colored

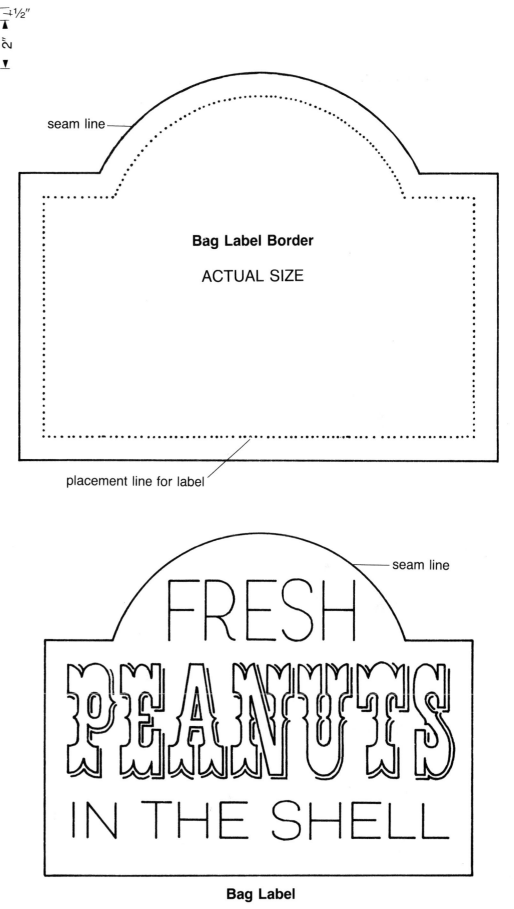

(continued)

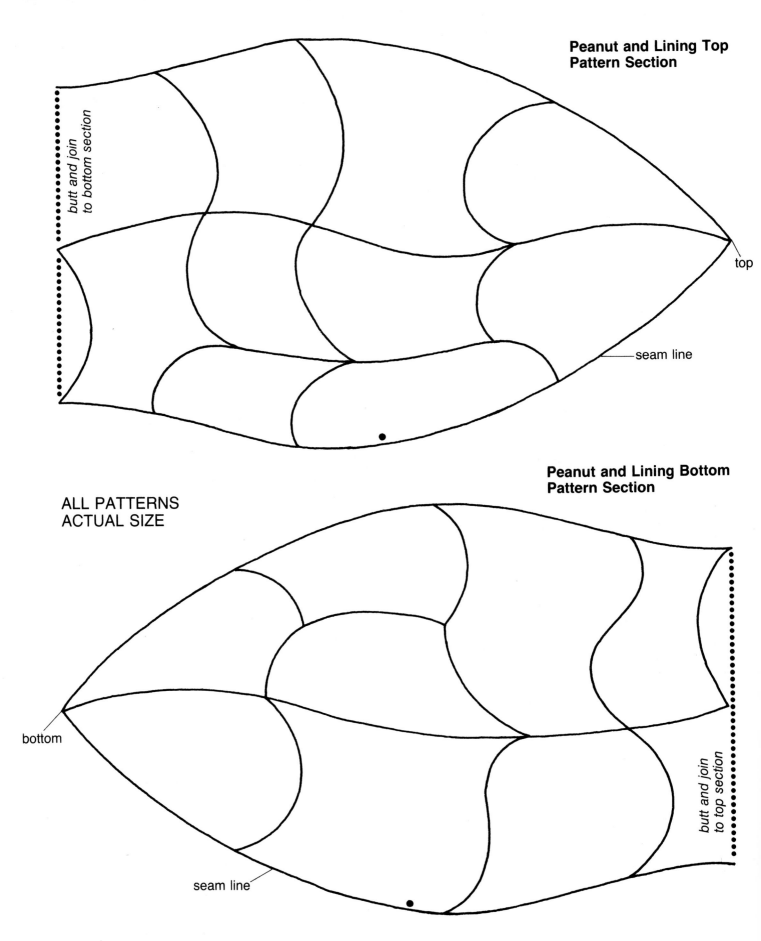

**Peanut and Lining Top
Pattern Section**

butt and join
to bottom section

top

seam line

**Peanut and Lining Bottom
Pattern Section**

ALL PATTERNS
ACTUAL SIZE

bottom

butt and join
to top section

seam line

FIGURE 3. Pattern sections joined
to form complete peanut pattern

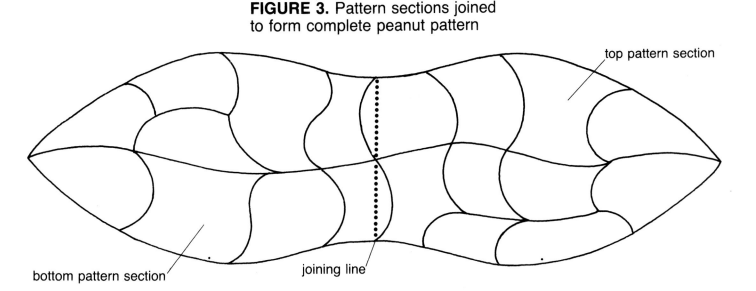

top pattern section

bottom pattern section

joining line

fabric piece, wrong side down, to the batting side of the batiste pieces and baste ⅛″ from the edges.

Using small machine stitches and peanut-colored thread in the bobbin, quilt the peanut texture on the batiste side of each section.

3. Joining the peanut pieces and adding the zipper—Lay out the peanut pieces right sides up so the tops are all headed in one direction (the quilting patterns will be identical on each). Take the section with the zipper placement dots and pin the marked edge to another section, right sides together, to make the peanut front. Machine stitch from each end of the section to the closest dot and backstitch to secure. Then machine baste between the dots. Trim the seam allowances beyond the dots to ¼″. Clip along the trimmed curves but not between the dots and press open the seam allowances.

Center and hand stitch the zipper in place between the dots. Remove the machine basting and open the zipper.

Join the two remaining peanut pieces, right sides together, to make the back. Trim the seam allowances to ¼″. Clip along the curves and press open the seam allowances. Join the peanut front and back, right sides together, making one continuous seam. Clip the seam allowances along the curves, and press them open.

4. The peanut lining—To make the lining, trace the pattern four times and ½″ apart on the wrong side of the beige fabric. Mark the zipper

placement dots on one piece and cut out all four pieces, adding a ¼″ seam allowance to each.

Pin the lining pieces, wrong side down, to polyester quilt batting, baste ⅛″ from the edges, and cut them out.

Stitch the lining piece with the zipper placement dots to another lining piece, right sides together, leaving the seam open between the dots. Join the two remaining pieces, right sides together. Clip the seam allowances along the curves, but not between the dots and press them open. Join both lining units, right sides together, with one continuous seam. Clip the seam allowances along the curves, and press open.

Leave the lining wrong side out and place it inside the outer peanut shell, matching the zipper openings. Turn under the seam allowance on the lining along the opening and invisibly hand stitch the folded edge to the zipper tape.

GENERAL DIRECTIONS FOR ALL THE ELEPHANTS

1. Making the patterns and marking the fabric—Trace the patterns for the elephant body and ear and the blanket and blanket border and cut them out. Cut out the blanket symbol to make a template of it. Add seam allowances when cutting the fabric.

On the wrong side of the chosen body fabric, trace the body, transferring all the placement lines, dots, and details, but do not cut the fabric. Repeat one more time, turning the elephant in reverse to make the opposite side.

Using tiny stitches, transfer the details and placement lines to the front of the fabric. Or, if working in daylight, pin the pattern to the wrong side of the fabric, and then tape them, pattern side down, to a window and very lightly trace the details on the front of the fabric.

Fold the ear fabric, right sides together, pin the pattern along the fold and trace it, transferring the dots and pleat lines; but do not cut it out. Repeat to make the other ear.

2. Making the ears—Using small stitches, machine stitch each ear long the seam lines, leaving an opening between the dots. Trim the seam allowances to ⅛″ with pinking shears, if possible, or trim them with scissors, and clip around the curves. Turn each ear right side out and press it flat. Close the opening with invisible stitches.

Make an inverted pleat on the front of each ear by folding the short lines toward the center and tacking the pleat. Set aside.

3. The blanket—Using a pencil, very lightly trace two blanket border pieces for each elephant on the right side of the blanket border fabric, but do not cut them out. Using a pencil, very lightly trace two blankets and their symbols on the right side of the white fabric, but do not cut them out.

Using two strands of embroidery thread, satin stitch the symbols. Cut out the blankets adding ¼″ seam allowances. Finger press the seam allowances along the sides and bottom of each blanket and baste.

Pin and baste the white blanket

in place centering it on top of the colored blanket border fabric; then using a single strand of gold embroidery thread, blanket stitch along the edge of the white blanket. Cut out the completed blanket with its border, adding a ¼″ seam allowance. Finger press the seam allowance and baste.

Pin a blanket in place on the fabric front of each elephant piece and, using two strands of thread to match the border color, appliqué the edge with blanket stitches.

4. Assembling the elephant—Cut out the elephant front and back, adding ½″ seam allowances. Pin the front and back, right sides together. Machine stitch using very tiny stitches and leaving an opening between the solid dots at the elephant's rear. Trim the seam allowances to ⅛″, clip them along the curves and clip into the V-shaped areas. Clip off the corners at the feet and nose. Carefully turn the elephant right side out and gently pull it into shape using a crochet hook and a sturdy needle. Stuff the elephant lightly but firmly. Close the opening with invisible hand stitches.

Invisibly stitch the ear in place.

5. The features—Using one strand of black embroidery thread, back stitch the mouth. Using two strands of embroidery thread, satin stitch red cheeks and black eyes. Using one strand of white embroidery thread make buttonhole-stitched toes working the stitches from the top, curved edges of the toes so that a ridge of thread is formed across the bottom of the foot.

6. The tail—To make a tail, cut three 6″ lengths of embroidery thread. Using a full 6-ply piece of embroidery thread, stitch through the elephant at the white tail dot; pull the thread about halfway through the fabric and remove the needle. Attach all three lengths of the thread in this way to make six 3″-long thread ends. Divide the thread ends into three sections and braid them to a length of ¾″ for the babies or 1″ for the mama and papa elephants. Knot the thread ends securely and trim the tassel to a ½″ length for the babies or ¾″ for the Mama and Papa elephants.

MAMA ELEPHANT

Follow the General Directions for All the Elephants, making the body of the red-with-white-dot fabric and the ears of red-checked fabric. If desired, fold the ear fabric on the bias. Also make two white blankets and two blue blanket border pieces, satin stitch a red heart on the blanket, make a red tail, and tie a blue ribbon bow on it.

PAPA ELEPHANT

Follow the General Directions for All the Elephants, making the body of blue-with-white dot fabric, the ears of blue-and-white gingham (folded on the bias, if desired), two white blankets, and two red blanket border pieces. Also satin stitch a blue star on the blanket, working the stitches in segments from each tip toward the center, and make a blue tail.

GIRL ELEPHANT

Follow the General Directions for All the Elephants, making a red-and-white gingham body (cut on the bias, if desired), two red-with-white-dot ears, two white blankets, and two blue blanket border pieces. Also, satin stitch a red heart on the blanket, make a red tail, and tie a blue ribbon bow on it.

BOY ELEPHANT

Follow the General Directions for All the Elephants, making a blue-and-white gingham body (cut on the bias, if desired), two blue-with-white-dot ears, two white blankets, and two red blanket border pieces. Also, satin stitch a blue star symbol on the blanket, working the stitches in segments from each tip toward the center, and make a blue tail.

ALL PATTERNS
ACTUAL SIZE

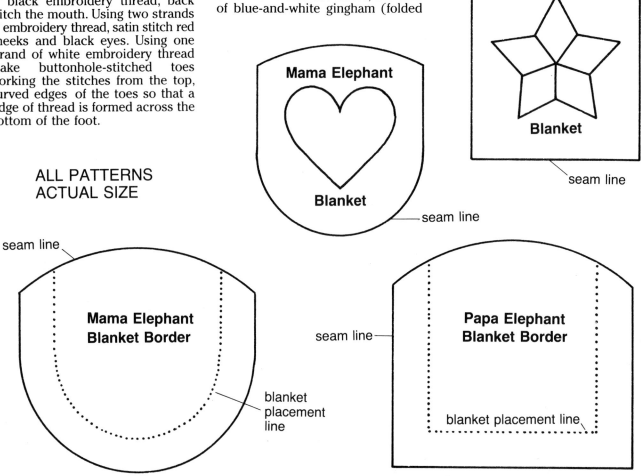

Mama Elephant — Blanket — seam line

Papa Elephant — Blanket — seam line

Mama Elephant Blanket Border — seam line — blanket placement line

Papa Elephant Blanket Border — seam line — blanket placement line

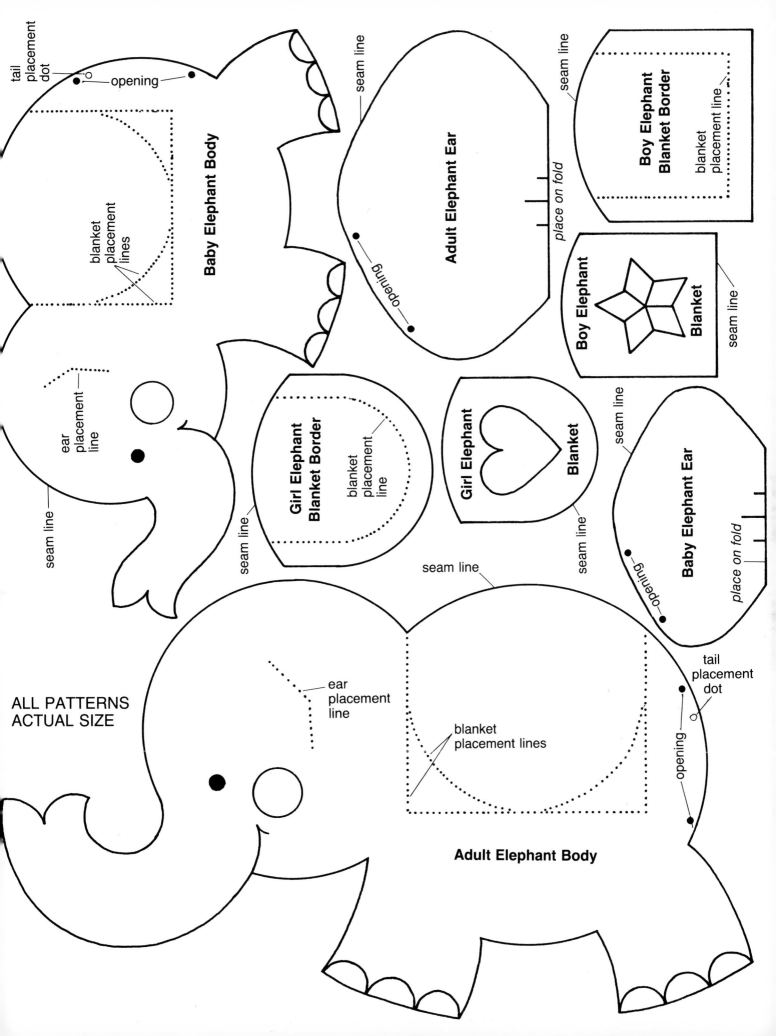

tail placement dot

opening

Baby Elephant Body

blanket placement lines

seam line

ear placement line

seam line

ALL PATTERNS ACTUAL SIZE

seam line

Adult Elephant Ear

opening

Girl Elephant Blanket Border

blanket placement line

seam line

Girl Elephant **Blanket**

seam line

seam line

Boy Elephant Blanket Border

blanket placement line

Boy Elephant **Blanket**

seam line

seam line

place on fold

seam line

Baby Elephant Ear

place on fold

opening

tail placement dot

ear placement line

blanket placement lines

seam line

opening

Adult Elephant Body

Teddy Bear Boutique

You can make this Hungry Bear Bib entirely by hand, which I did to make use of some of my traveling time. Prepare your own stitchery kit by filling your sewing bag with all the marked and cut fabrics and quilt batting, the proper threads, bias tape, scissors, a tape measure, and an embroidery hoop. With the help of a photo copier, you can even make portable directions.

Hungry-As-a-Bear Bib

If you're worried about food stains spotting a pastel and white creation, opt for a bright fabric alternative. Use deep blue (not navy) for the bib fabric and embroider white letters on it. Then use red-and-white gingham for the bear, red binding, and plain red for the cheeks and inner ears. All the other embroidery should then be done in deep blue. Packaged with a baby food grinder, a baby food cook book, a dish, or a fork and spoon, the bib would make a thoughtful and fun gift for a new Mom.

Materials

An 11½″ × 13″ white piqué or pop-lin fabric scrap

6-ply embroidery thread: 5 yards blue, 3 yards dark brown

A 9″ × 11½″ white terry cloth scrap or a washcloth

A 4½″ × 5″ pink fabric scrap

A 7½″ × 12″ blue-and-white ¼″ gingham fabric scrap

An 8½″ × 9½″ piece of very thin quilt batting, optional

2½ yards of ¼″-wide blue double-fold bias tape

1. Making the pattern—Trace the bib top and bottom sections including the letters, and join them together along the heavy dotted line to make a complete pattern. All pattern lines are cutting lines for the fabrics in this project.

On folded paper, trace the pattern for the bear's head, copying all placement lines, dots, and facial details, but don't trace the placement line for the bias tape. Trace the ears, inner ears, and cheeks, copying all the details, except for the tape placement lines.

2. Marking and cutting out the bib front—Using a sharp, soft pencil, draw over the letters on the reverse side of the bib pattern. Pin the pattern to the front of the white fabric, and rub the letters to transfer them to the fabric. Draw the bib outline. Remove the pattern, and mark over the letters again on the fabric.

Use two strands of embroidery thread for all the embroidery in this project and an embroidery hoop, if you have one. Chain stitch blue letters and make French knots for the dots. Cut out the bib.

Pin the bib, right side up, to the terry cloth, and baste them together ¼″ from the bib edge. Trim the terry cloth to match the bib front and set aside.

3. The cheeks and inner ears—Using a soft pencil, darken the stitching lines on the cheek and inner ear patterns. Place the patterns penciled side down on the back of the pink fabric and trace the outlines. Rub the stitching lines to transfer them. Trace and cut out two cheeks and two inner ears.

Using tiny stitches, transfer the stitching lines to the fabric front. Clip the seam allowance completely around the cheeks. Clip around the inner ears, but not along the lower edge since the head will overlap it. Finger press along the stitching lines,

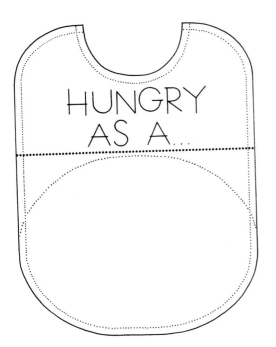

FIGURE 1. Bib with pattern sections joined

turning under the seam allowances, except along the lower edge of the inner ear. Baste. Back the pieces with batiste if they're too sheer. Set aside.

4. The bear—Cut the eyes, nose and cheeks out of the head pattern to make a template. Pin the pattern to the right side of the blue-and-white checked fabric, trace around it, and also draw the features. Mark the ear placement dots with stitches. Pierce the pattern with a needle and mark the eyebrows and mouth with pencil dots. Before cutting out the head, chain stitch brown eyebrows and a brown mouth, and make brown padded satin stitches (see *Embroidery Stitches*) for the bear's eyes and nose.

Pin and baste the cheeks in place on the head and appliqué them using blue blanket stitches. If you wish, remove the bastings just before you've finished and push in a little polyester stuffing to puff out the cheeks.

(continued)

Upper Bib Pattern Section
ACTUAL SIZE

cutting line

placement line for tape

butt to lower section

HUNGRY AS A...

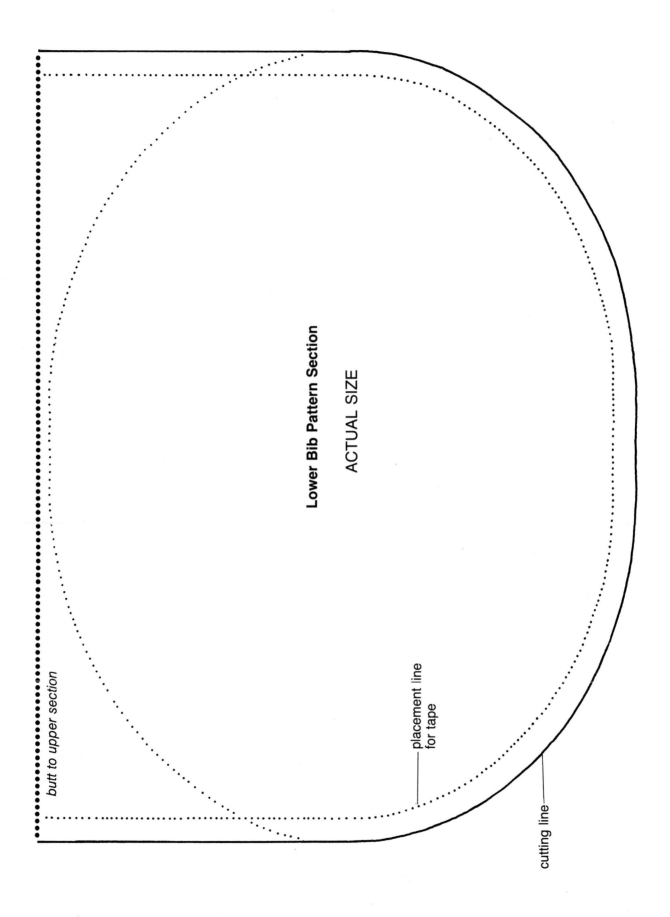

Lower Bib Pattern Section

ACTUAL SIZE

butt to upper section

placement line
for tape

cutting line

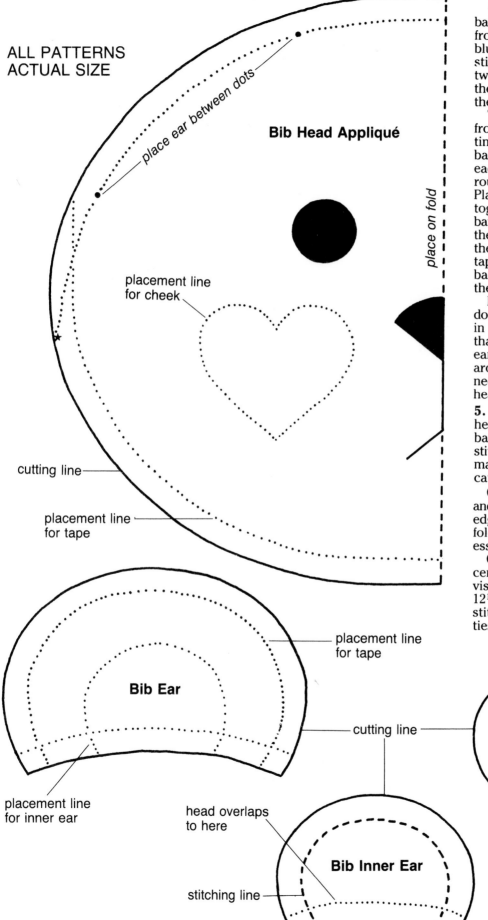

**ALL PATTERNS
ACTUAL SIZE**

place ear between dots

Bib Head Appliqué

place on fold

placement line
for cheek

cutting line

placement line
for tape

Bib Ear

placement line for tape

placement line
for inner ear

head overlaps
to here

Bib Inner Ear

stitching line

cutting line

Bib Cheek

stitching
line

Cut out the head and pin it to quilt batting. Baste the layers together ¼" from the edge. Cut a 13" length of blue double-fold bias tape and hand stitch it around the head top between the stars, tapering the tape to the stars by pushing the excess to the back of the head.

To make the ears, cut two each from the piqué or poplin, the batting, and the checked fabric. Pin and baste a pink inner ear in place on each checked ear and appliqué the rounded edge with blanket stitches. Place a white ear and a checked ear together, right sides out, inserting a batting ear between them, and baste the three layers together ¼" from the edge. Cut a 7" length of the bias tape and hand stitch it, front and back, along the top curved edge of the ear. Repeat for the other ear.

Pin the ears in place between the dots on the head back. Hold the head in position on the bib to make sure that there will be ¼" between the ear and bib edge to stitch bias tape around the bib. Adjust the ears, if necessary, and baste them to the head.

5. Assembling the bib—Pin the head in place on the bib front, and baste ¼" from the edge. Invisibly stitch the bound head top to the bib, making stitches deep enough to catch the terry cloth layer.

Cut a 31" length of the bias tape, and invisibly stitch it along the outer edge, not the neck edge, of the bib, folding the ears forward when necessary.

Cut a 32" length of the bias tape, center it on the neck edge, and invisibly stitch it in place, leaving a 12½"-long tie at each end. Invisibly stitch along the open edges of the ties to close them. Knot the tie ends.

Let these bear-shaped wash mitts encourage your little cubs to scrub their paws clean while you take care of the rest of the job. The cub mitt is large enough (6½″ × 6¾″) for a six-year old's hand, and the bear mitt is roomy enough (8½″ × 9¼″) for Mom or Dad to use, depending on who has bath duty.

The mitts are very easy to make, using either a borderless guest towel or two borderless wash cloths for each. When purchasing supplies, look for a sale on "irregulars" to make the project

Bear and Cub Wash Mitts

easier on your pocketbook. The velour side of the cloth is nicest for the front because it feels so soft and cuddly

and the velvety nap is easier to embroider than the terry side. Use the terry side for the back if you want a good scrubbing surface. Also make sure to topstitch around the edge of the mitt for added strength and sharper definition of the shape.

In or out of the tub, these little hand-puppet mitts can provide some happy moments of parent-child playtime. At our house they've sometimes even helped to settle a difference of opinion, and, at times, they have changed shouts and tears to giggles and bear hugs!

Materials for One Mitt

2 tan velour borderless washcloths or 1 tan velour 11″ × 18″ borderless guest towel
6-ply embroidery thread: 1 yard each of dark brown, medium pink, and blue
Tan sewing thread

Equipment

Laundry marking pen

1. Making the patterns—Trace each pattern on a piece of folded tracing paper, as indicated on the drawing, and cut it out. The pattern lines are stitching lines for this project. For each pattern, cut out the eyes, nose, and cheeks and pierce the mouth and tie line with a needle.

2. Cutting out and embroidering the mitt fronts—For each mitt front, pin the pattern to the terry side of a washcloth or guest towel, placing the lower edge of the pattern along the finished edge of the fabric. Trace the pattern outline with a laundry pen. Baste around the outline to transfer the bear shape to the velour side of the cloth. Cut out the bear, adding a ¼″ seam allowance around the edges.

Pin the pattern to the velour side of the cloth, placing it within the basted outline, and, using a sharp soft pencil, mark the facial details with lines of dots. Embroider the facial details as follows. For the bear and cub, use one strand of brown embroidery thread to chain stitch the mouth and to satin stitch the eyes and nose. Using one strand of pink embroidery thread for the cub and two strands of thread for the bear, satin stitch the cheeks. Using two strands of blue embroidery thread for the cub and three strands of thread for the bear, chain stitch the tie.

3. Finishing the mitts—Lay each embroidered mitt front face down on the velour or terry side, whichever you prefer, of a second wash cloth or remaining portion of guest towel, aligning the finished edges along the bottom. Pin together and machine stitch along the outline, leaving the bottom open.

Trim the seam allowances to ¼″, then grade the seam allowances by trimming one to ⅛″. Clip around the curves and deeply into the V-shaped areas.

Turn each mitt right side out, pushing out the curved areas. Hand press each mitt flat, and pin the front and back together to maintain the bear's shape. Topstitch around the edge of each mitt, leaving the bottom open. Define the head shape by topstitching a line along the base of the ears that continues the curve of the head.

In their dual role of scrubber and hand puppet, Bear and Cub Wash Mitts make any bath more fun.

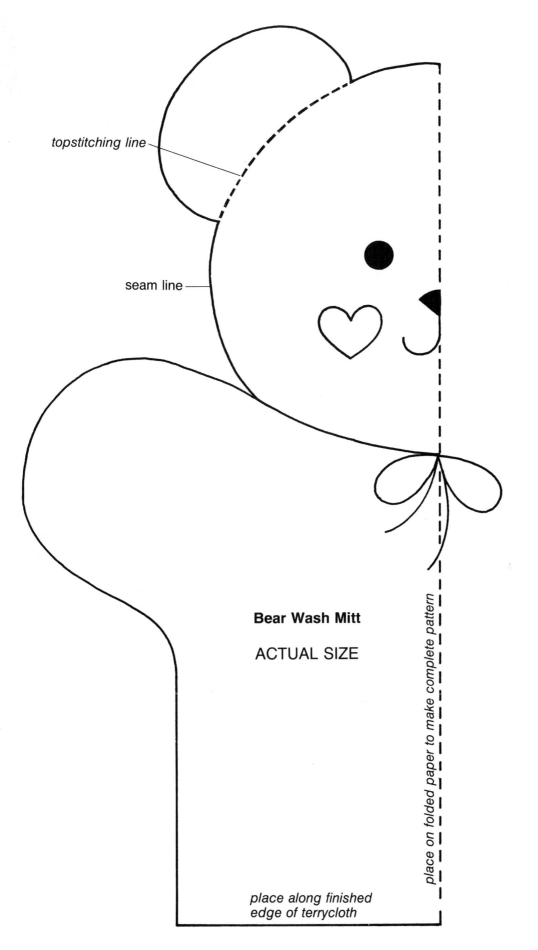

topstitching line

seam line

Bear Wash Mitt

ACTUAL SIZE

place on folded paper to make complete pattern

*place along finished
edge of terrycloth*

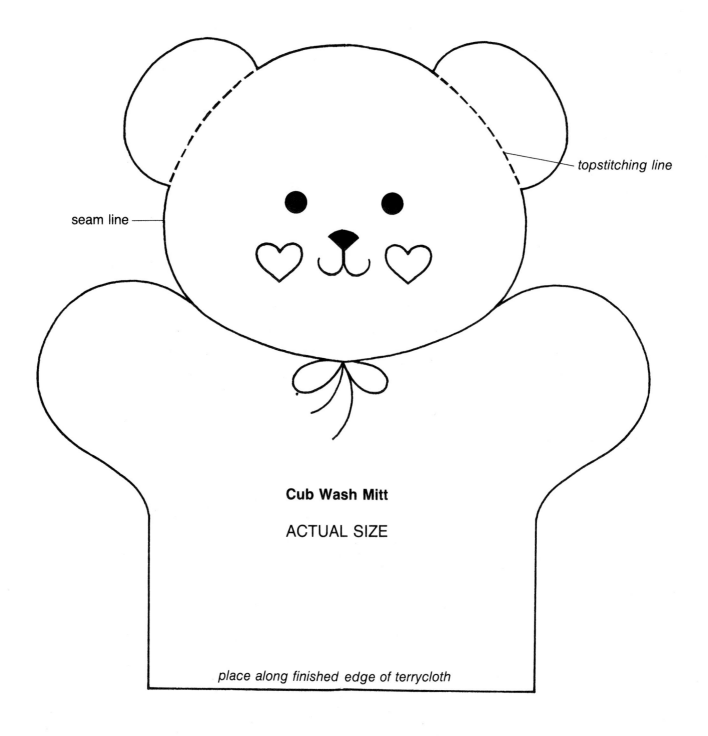

topstitching line

seam line

Cub Wash Mitt

ACTUAL SIZE

place along finished edge of terrycloth

This tiny teddy purse and the bearettes are other quick-to-stitch bear accessories.

Corduroy or furry fabric would make a cute alternate fabric choice for the purse, but this design is especially fast to make if you omit the lining and batting and use reversible quilted fabric. For an older child, you can save a little more time by substituting shiny brown buttons for the embroidered eyes. The bias tape shoulder strap ties at the top for easy adjustment to the proper length.

The purse is just the right size (6″ × 7¾″) to hold a comb, some tissues, and a few other surprises as well. On various occasions I've reached inside and found fuzzy raisins, limp dande-

Tiny Teddy Purse and Bearettes

lions, an assortment of rocks and even a vacated locust shell. Perhaps "purse" is a misnomer. For a child of four or five, this is really a carryall.

To make the teddy "bearettes," first check your supermarket or variety store for a card of very small plastic

barrettes. The best card I purchased contained five colored sets of various shapes, including a perfect set of white ones. On the card back was written: "Kiddie Barrettes with teeth and wire clasp."

The bears can be made with or without clothes, and they need not all be barrettes. Instead, you can stitch a very small safety pin to the back to make a cute lapel pin. Or omit the pin and the barrette and dress the back as well as the front, and you'll have a two-inch teddy toy that never needs to stay at home. Please remember, however, that this miniature 1½″ × 2″ bear is too small a plaything for a child under three.

TINY TEDDY PURSE

Materials

An 8″ × 16″ tan-with-white dot fabric scrap, or substitute a piece of reversible quilted fabric for this as well as the batting and gingham fabric that follow
6-ply embroidery thread: 2 yards dark brown, 1½ yards tan
A 2½″ × 7½″ pink fabric scrap
Polyester stuffing, optional
An 8″ × 14″ piece of thin quilt batting
2⅞ yards of ¼″-wide tan double-fold bias tape
An 8″ × 12″ pink 1/16″ gingham check fabric scrap
A 14″ length of ⅝″-wide blue gingham ribbon, optional

Equipment
Small embroidery hoop, optional

1. Making the patterns—Trace patterns for the head, ears, inner ears, and cheeks on page 33, copying all placement dots and facial details, but omitting the dotted placement lines for the bias tape. Cut the eyes, nose, and cheeks from the head pattern to make a template. All pattern lines are cutting lines for the fabrics in this project.

2. Marking and cutting out the fabric—Pin the head pattern to the front of the tan dot fabric, trace around it and around the cut-out features. Mark the ear placement dots with stitches on the fabric. Piercing the pattern with a needle, mark the mouth with dots. Remove the pattern, and place the fabric in an embroidery hoop, if you have one. Using two strands of brown embroidery thread, chainstitch the mouth and use padded satin stitches to make the eyes and nose.

Using a soft pencil, darken the stitching lines on the cheek and inner ear patterns. Place the patterns penciled side down on the back of the pink fabric, trace the edges, and rub the stitching lines to transfer them. Trace and cut out two cheeks and two inner ears.

Using tiny stitches, transfer the stitching lines to the fabric front. Clip the seam allowances completely around the cheeks. Clip around the inner ears, except along the lower edge which will be covered with bias tape. Finger press along the stitching lines, turning under the seam allowances, except along the lower edge of the inner ear, and baste them in place. Back the pieces with batiste if they are too sheer.

3. Finishing the cheeks and ears—Pin and baste the cheeks in place on the head and appliqué them, using two strands of tan thread and

Tracy, the author's daughter, loves to wear her Tiny Teddy Purse with a Teddy pin on its strap. She also clips a "Bearette" into each braid.

blanket stitches. If you wish, remove the bastings just before you've finished and push a little polyester stuffing under the cheeks to puff them out. Cut out the head front as well as a plain head back from the tan dot fabric. Set aside.

Cut four ears from the tan dot fabric and two from the batting. Pin and baste each inner ear in place on a dot ear, and appliqué it along the rounded edge using two strands of tan thread and blanket stitches. Place an ear/inner ear piece on top of a plain ear, wrong sides together, insert a batting ear between them, and baste the layers together ¼" from the edge. Overcast the edges. Cut a 10" length of tan bias tape and hand stitch it all around the ear, mitering the corners. Repeat on the other ear. Put aside.

4. Lining and finishing the head sections—Pinning the head pattern to the pink gingham, trace it twice. Pin the gingham to the batting, and baste them together ¼" inside the outline of each head shape. Cut out the gingham and batting together. Pin and baste a tan head piece, right side up, to the batting side of each pink head piece. Overcast the edges.

Cut two 11" lengths of tan bias tape and handstitch one along each head top between the side stars. Taper the binding to the stars, pushing the excess to the lining side of the head.

Pin and baste an ear between each pair of dots on the lining side of the head front. Invisibly stitch the head top binding to the ear on the head front. On the lining side, stitch the lower edge of the ear binding to the lower edge of the head binding.

5. Joining the sides and finishing the purse—Pin the head front and back lining sides together, matching the side stars. Baste together and overcast the edges. Cut a 60" length of bias tape and mark the center point with a pin. Place the center point at the bear's chin and invisibly stitch the binding in place along the lower edge of the head and up along the sides to the lower edge of the ears. Then continue invisibly stitching along the open edges of the binding to close it and create a shoulder strap at each end. Knot the ends of the tape, and adjust the strap length to the child by tieing a bow at the shoulder.

To decrease the size of the purse opening, stitch the binding along the back head top to a point midway along the back lower edge of the ear.

Tie the ribbon into a bow, trim the ends, and stitch it to one ear.

ALL PATTERNS ACTUAL SIZE

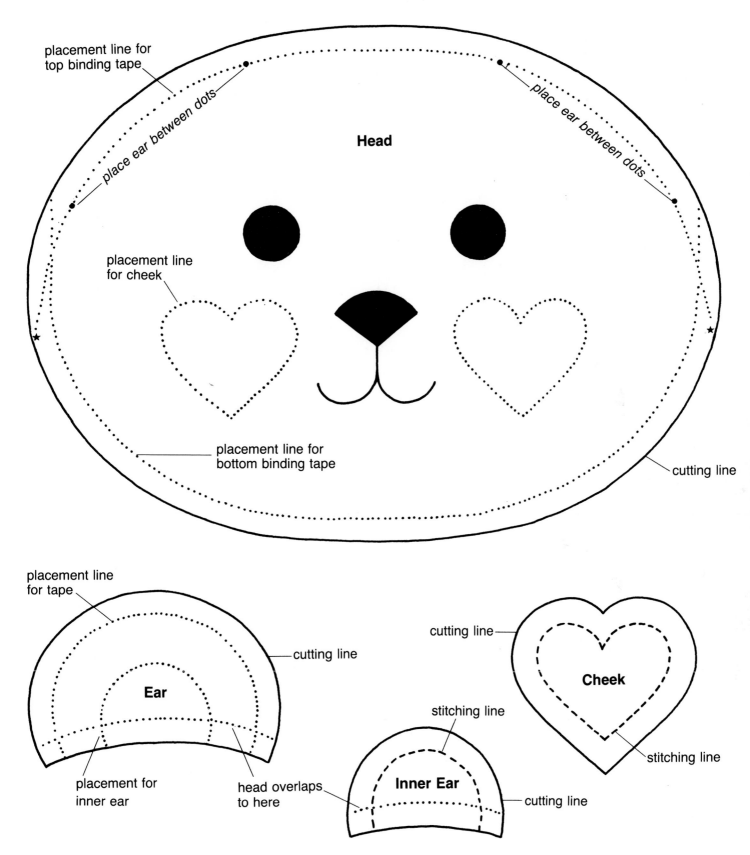

placement line for
top binding tape

place ear between dots

place ear between dots

Head

placement line
for cheek

placement line for
bottom binding tape

cutting line

placement line
for tape

cutting line

Ear

placement for
inner ear

head overlaps
to here

stitching line

Inner Ear

cutting line

cutting line

Cheek

stitching line

A Teddy "Bearette" can be dressed in a vest and bow (top) or in a dress and bow (bottom). It even looks cute wearing only an embroidery-thread bow (center).

TEDDY BEARETTES

Materials for One Bear Body

A 2½" × 4" tan felt scrap
6-ply embroidery thread: 18" each of dark brown, pink, and tan
Polyester stuffing
A flat, ⅜" × 1½" or smaller barette with a wire clasp

Bare Bear Tie

An 8" length of embroidery thread

Vest Materials

A 1" × 1½" blue felt scrap
6-ply embroidery thread: 18" each of white and blue, 8" of pink

Dress Materials

A 2" length of ¼"-wide, or less, white lace
A 2" length of ⅝"-wide pink rayon gingham ribbon
A 6" length of 6-ply blue embroidery thread

Equipment

X-acto knife
Short sharp needle, such as a #8
Small, sharp scissors
Emery board
White glue

1. Making the body pattern— Trace the bear front/back pattern with the features and cut it out. Use an X-acto knife to cut out the eyes, nose, and cheeks. Pierce the pattern with a pin to mark the mouth.

2. Cutting and embroidering the fabric— Cut the tan felt into two 2" × 2½" pieces. Pin the pattern to one and trace around the outside edge and the features, but don't cut it out. If you can't mark felt well with pencil lines, make dotted lines instead by pushing and twisting a pencil against the felt all around the pattern.

Using one strand of embroidery thread for all the embroidery, satin stitch the cheeks pink and the eyes and nose brown, and straight stitch a brown mouth line.

Pin the embroidered bear front to the plain back piece and cut out both layers together along the pattern lines.

3. Stitching and finishing the body— Starting at the neck, blanket stitch around the head and ears. To keep stuffing out of the ears, make tiny running stitches along the head line, as indicated on the pattern, turning the work from front to back to make even stitches. Stuff the head lightly and close the neck with tiny running stitches.

Blanket stitch and stuff each arm, then close it off with tiny running stitches along a line from the neck to the underarm, as indicated on the pattern.

Stitch and stuff the body and legs, pushing in the stuffing as you work. When the blanket stitching and the stuffing is completed, make a line of running stitches at each leg top to define the leg.

Roughen the smooth plastic top of the barrette with an emery board. Glue the barrette to the back of the bear's arms. When dry, stitch the barrette to the bear.

4a. Bare bear—If you are leaving the bear as is, tie a bow of blue embroidery thread around its neck and knot the ends.

4b. The vest and bow—Trace the vest pattern, cut it out, and pin it to the blue felt. Trace around the outside edge and transfer the button dots. Cut out and pin the vest to the bear front, which has been embroidered and cut out following directions for the body. Blanket stitch all around the outside edge. Embroider white French-knot buttons.

Complete the body following the directions given, but don't stitch the leg tops.

Tie pink embroidery thread around the neck, make a very small bow, knot the ends at a length you like and trim away the excess thread below the knots.

Attach the bear to a barrette, as explained under Step 3 of the directions for making the bear body.

4c. The dress and bow—Complete the bear body as directed, but do not attach it to a barrette. Then invisibly stitch narrow lace to one long edge of the pink gingham ribbon. Fold under $\frac{1}{8}''$ at each end of the ribbon and hem. Make tiny running stitches along the untrimmed edge of ribbon and pull the thread to gather the ribbon.

Tie the thread tightly around the bear's neck and invisibly stitch the gathered edge of the ribbon to the neck. Invisibly stitch the hemmed edges of the ribbon to the bear's front along the arm lines at the sides.

Tie a length of blue embroidery thread into a very small bow. Knot the ends at a length you like and trim away the excess thread below the knots. Stitch the bow to the head top.

Attach the barrette as explained under the directions for the body.

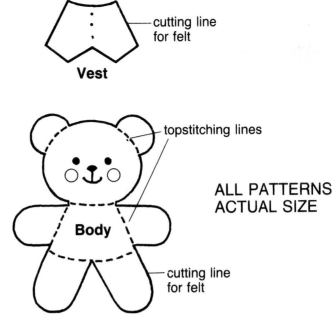

Vest

cutting line for felt

topstitching lines

Body

ALL PATTERNS ACTUAL SIZE

cutting line for felt

Wearing a boy and girl "Bearette" together makes them all the more fun.

Here's a Teddy Tote that can be made very quickly if you omit the lining and use reversible quilted fabric. I used single-faced quilted fabric with a lining because I couldn't find a good pink and blue reversible combination.

I intended this tote to be used by a toddler or a young child as a travel bag. The bear and his paw pockets can be filled with books, fa- vorite games, and toys, or the bag can be stuffed with a folded towel or small blanket

Teddy Tote

to make a nice cozy Teddy pillow for your sleepy little traveler.

The bag is also useful as a tie-on tote for the pram and stroller set. It's actually quite small (2¼″ deep, 9¾″ across, and 12″ high, excluding the handle), but it will hold a change of clothes, a diaper or two, and a toy for short neighborhood outings with that darling baby!

Materials

A 17″ × 35″ piece, or ½ yard, of quilted blue and white ¼″ gingham fabric

A 17″ × 35″ piece, or ½ yard, of pink fabric with white dots

A 5″ × 6″ pink fabric scrap

6-ply embroidery thread: 3½ yards blue, 3½ yards brown

6½ yards of ¼″-wide blue double-fold bias tape

Blue sewing thread

1. Making the patterns—Trace patterns for the upper and lower front/back sections on pages 38 and 39, copying all the features, dots, squares, and stars, but not the bias tape placement lines. Join the two sections together along the heavy dotted line to make a complete pattern (see Figure 1, page 40). All pattern lines are cutting lines for the fabrics in this project. Cut out the eyes, nose, and cheeks, and pierce the mouth and eyebrow lines with a needle to make a template.

Trace patterns for the ear, inner ear, paw, and cheek, page 41, including all details.

2. Cutting the fabric—Referring to Figure 2, page 40, draw two 2″ × 34″ handle/side/bottom pieces directly onto the wrong side of the blue and white gingham fabric. Repeat on the pink polka dot fabric for the lining. Mark the stars, squares, and dots on all the pieces at the intervals indicated on the drawing, then cut out the pieces and set aside.

From the blue-and-white gingham, also cut one piece for the bag front, one piece for the back, and four ears. Cut one paw and then flip the pattern over and cut another paw in reverse. Transfer the features and all details onto the front piece only, but transfer all other markings to all pieces. Machine stitch around all the pieces, about ³⁄₁₆″ from the edges to secure the quilting stitches.

From the pink-and-white dot lining fabric, also cut one bag front and one bag back, transferring the dots and stars.

Using a soft sharp pencil, darken the stitching lines on the cheek and inner ear patterns. Place the patterns, penciled side down, on the wrong side of the pink fabric and trace around the outside edges. Rub the stitching lines to transfer them to the fabric. From the pink fabric cut two cheeks and two inner ears. Transfer the stitching lines to the front of the fabric with small basting stitches.

3. Finishing the features—Clip the edges of the curved cheek and inner ear seam allowances. Finger press to fold the seam allowances under, except at the lower edge of the inner ear, which will be bound. Baste and set the pieces aside.

Using two strands of brown embroidery thread and padded satin stitches (see *Embroidery Stitches*), stitch the eyes and nose on the bag front. Draw a vertical center line on the nose, dividing it into two sections for easier horizontal stitching on the first layer of stitches. Using

two strands of brown embroidery thread, chain stitch the eyebrows and mouth.

If the pink fabric is sheer, back the cheeks and inner ear pieces with batiste. Pin and baste the cheeks in place and, using two strands of thread, appliqué along the edges with blue blanket stitches. If you wish, push in a little stuffing to puff out the cheeks before completing the stitching.

Pin and baste each pink inner ear in place on the right side of a gingham ear, and appliqué them together using blue blanket stitches. Then pin and baste each ear/inner ear unit to a plain gingham ear, right sides out, and join, stitching ¼″ from the edges. Cut two 13½″-long strips of bias binding, and stitch a strip completely around each ear, mitering the binding at the corners.

4. Finishing the front and back — Pin and baste each quilted gingham front/back piece to a pink dotted front/back piece, right sides out. Baste ¼″ from the edges to provide a guideline for the trimming. Cut a 16″-long strip of bias tape and bind the top of the bag front, tapering the binding to the squares and pushing the excess tape to the lining side. Repeat to bind the top edge of the bag back.

5. The paws—Using two strands of thread, chain stitch the brown paw lines on the front of each paw. Cut two 10½″-long strips of bias binding, and stitch one piece to each paw along the curved edge only, as in-

(continued)

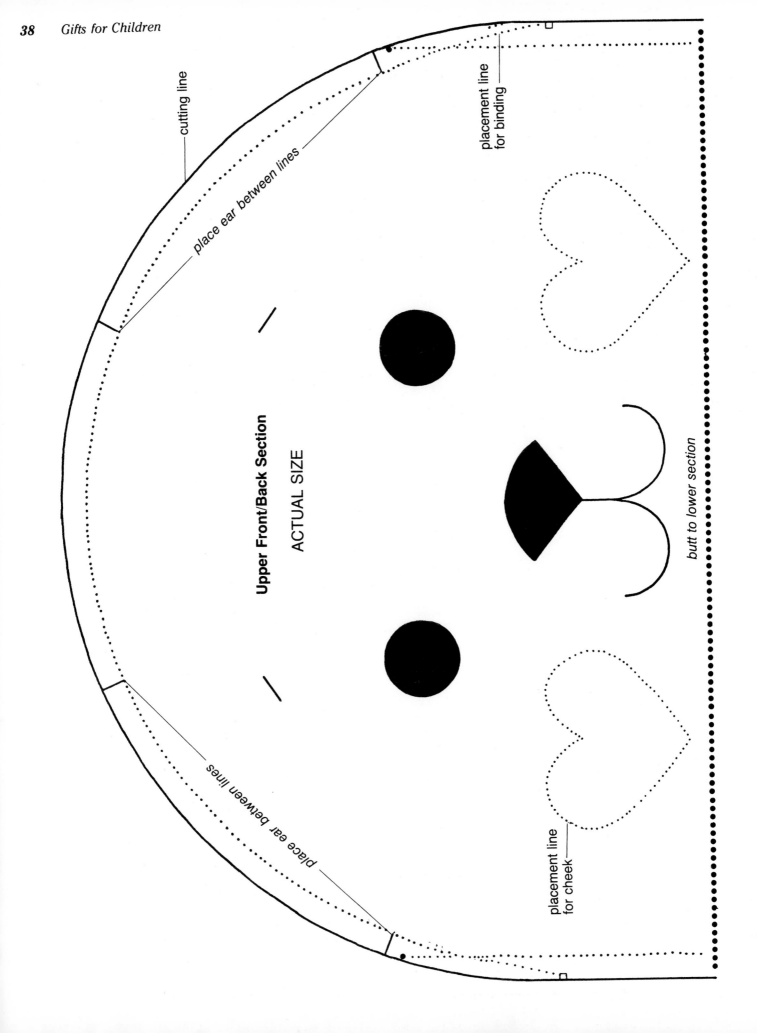

cutting line

place ear between lines

placement line
for binding

Upper Front/Back Section

ACTUAL SIZE

butt to lower section

place ear between lines

placement line
for cheek

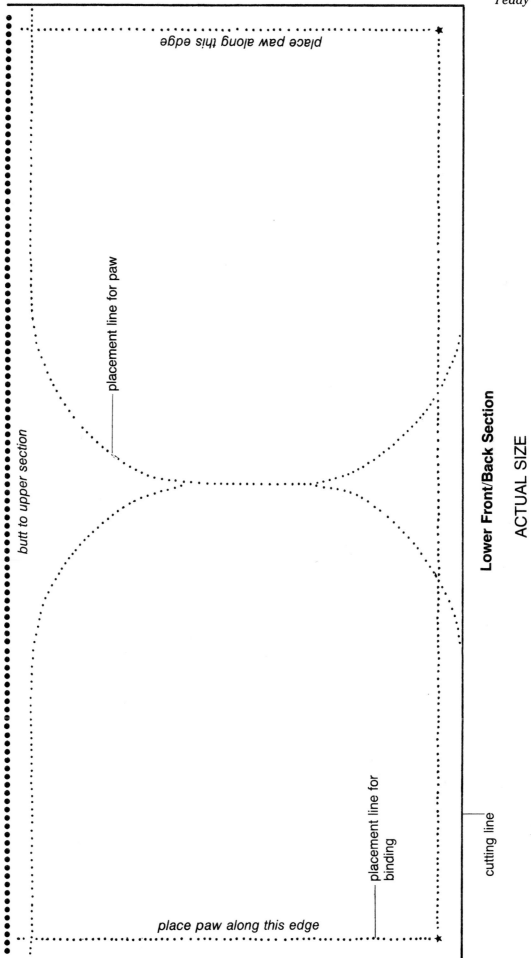

place paw along this edge

placement line for paw

butt to upper section

Lower Front/Back Section

ACTUAL SIZE

cutting line

placement line for
binding

place paw along this edge

FIGURE 1. Pattern sections joined to form complete front/back pattern

FIGURE 2. Dimensions of side/handle/bottom piece

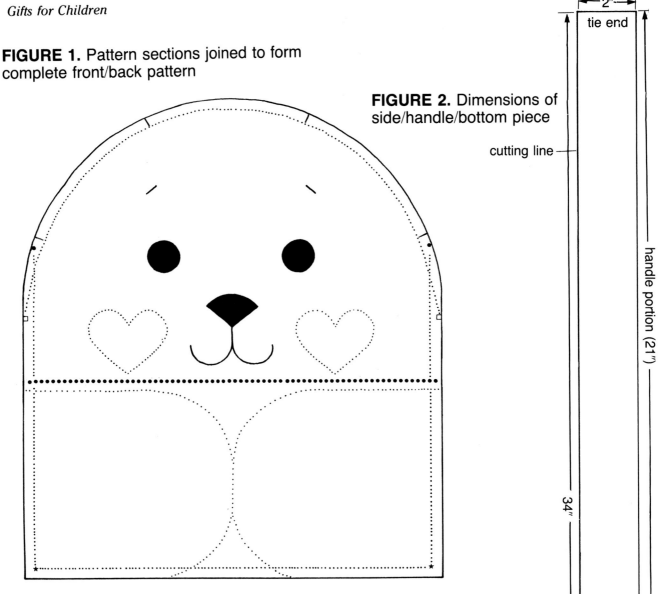

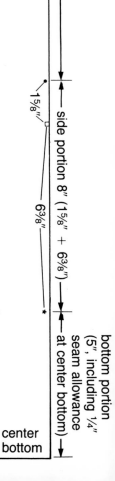

dicated on the pattern, tapering the binding to the square on the front and pushing the excess to the back. Pin the paws in place on the front section, aligning the side and bottom edges, and invisibly hand stitch them together along the bottom and up the sides to the top paw line to form pockets.

6. Assembling the tote—Right sides together, pin and stitch both gingham handle/side/bottom pieces at the center bottom. Right sides together, pin and stitch both pink dotted handle/side/bottom pieces at the center bottom. Press open the seam allowances.

Pin the gingham handle/side/bottom piece to the matching pink dotted piece, wrong sides together. Machine stitch them together about ³⁄₁₆″ from the edges. Clip to the stitching line at each of the four star markings.

Pin the handle/side/bottom strip to the bag front and back sections so the seam of the strip is at the center bottom and the dots and squares on the head sides match the dots and squares on the strip. Match the stars on the strip to the bag corners. Join the strip to the front and back by machine (essential), starting at a dot on one side of the head and finishing at the dot on the opposite side of the head and stitching about ³⁄₁₆″ from the edge all around the tote. Pivot at the star markings on the bottom corners.

Encase all unbound edges of the bag and handle in bias binding, mitering it at the corners.

Pin the ears in position between the lines marked on the head top, adjusting to allow room for the strip, if necessary. Invisibly hand stitch them in place, front and back.

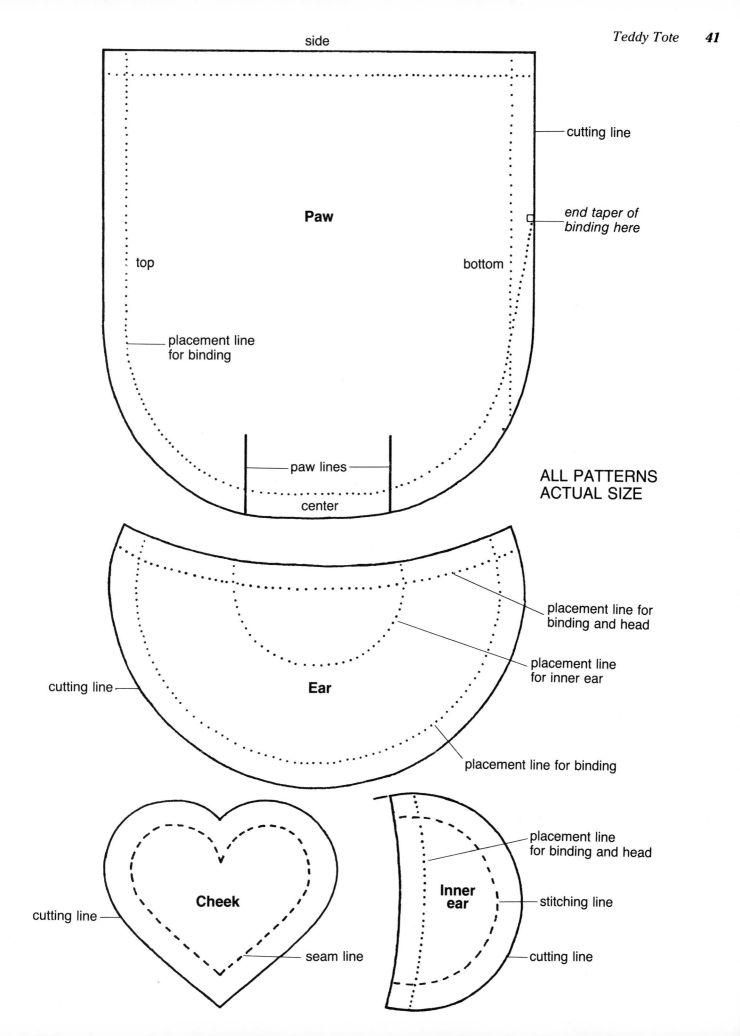

side

cutting line

end taper of binding here

Paw

top

bottom

placement line
for binding

paw lines

ALL PATTERNS
ACTUAL SIZE

center

cutting line

Ear

placement line for
binding and head

placement line
for inner ear

placement line for binding

Cheek

cutting line

seam line

placement line
for binding and head

Inner ear

stitching line

cutting line

cutting line

Originally this project was going to provide a one-size pattern suitable for a little three- or four-year old child, but as I sat and sketched the mouse apron, my six year old peered over my shoulder and said, with a sigh, "Mom, I would love that!" Because of that wistful comment, you can now make any of these aprons for all your small (2 to 3), medium (4 to 5), and large (6 to 6x) girls! The basic apron patterns can be used to make plain denim or ticking cover-ups for the little chefs at your house, too. Customize your patterns, if necessary, by adding length to the bottom or width to the sides. Replace the button and ball fringe trims with embroidery if the recipient is under three.

Pocket Toy Aprons

I must admit that I didn't use my scraps for these aprons, because some nice, expensive, reversible, quilted material caught my eye in a fabric store. I couldn't resist

and bought a half yard of each of four colors. Although I've specified ⅝ yard for safety's sake, the large size apron is exactly 18″ long, so you can actually cut two of them from just half a yard if the yardage is cut as accurately and generously as possible! A ⅜ yard piece is really enough for two of the small-size aprons.

Quilted fabric isn't required, but do use something fairly sturdy. To add a pretty touch, back the apron fabric with the same print that you use to make the toy. If you're thinking about Christmas, keep in mind that the animals are just the right size to pop out of a stocking and become cuddly companions for a baby, a toddler, or even a six year old.

Fabric Quantities for the Aprons

Size	Fabric for 1 apron	Fabric for 2 aprons	Yards of Bias Tape
Small:	A 13½″ × 17″ fabric scrap	⅜ yard 44″-wide fabric	3¾
Medium:	A 16½″ × 18″ fabric scrap	½ yard 44″-wide fabric	4
Large:	A 17″ × 19″ fabric scrap	⅝ yard 44″-wide fabric	4¼

Equipment for All the Aprons

An 11″ × 14″ piece of tracing paper for each apron appliqué and toy

Tracing paper for the size apron you are making: small, 8½″ × 14″; medium, 9″ × 16½″; and large, 10″ × 19″

GENERAL DIRECTIONS FOR MAKING ALL THE APRONS
(to be used with specific directions for each different design)

1. **Making the apron pattern and cutting the fabric**—Make a grid of 1″ squares to match the grid on page 44. Select the size of the apron you want to make and enlarge the half

pattern in the book on your grid, following the directions in the *Sewing Techniques* section on page 163. Pin the half pattern on the folded apron fabric and cut it out along the pattern line without adding seam allowances. Mark the vertical center line of the apron with long basting stitches. If you are using quilted fabric, machine stitch around the apron ¼″ from the edge to secure the quilting stitches.

2. **Attaching the apron binding**—Bind the top edge of the apron with bias tape according to the directions on the package, cutting the tape to the appropriate length as follows: small, 6½″; medium, 7¼″; and large, 8½″. Trim off the excess.

Use another strip of the bias tape to bind the straight sides and lower edge of the apron, cutting the tape to the appropriate length as follows: small, 36½″; medium, 40″; and large,

43½″. Trim off the excess.

Cut two additional pieces of the bias tape to bind each curved underarm edge of the apron as well as create ties for the neck and waist as follows: small, 45″ each; medium, 47″ each; and large, 49″ each. Each neck and waist tie will be 18″ long, regardless of the apron size, so place a pin on each piece of tape at that distance from both ends to help you center the section that will bind the underarm edge. Clip the seam allowances of the tape along each section that will bind the curved underarm edge of the apron, and attach a strip of tape to each side of the apron. Stitch closed the open edges of the tape that will be used as ties at both ends.

Trim the ties to 18″. Tuck under and stitch the cut ends of tape or knot them.

3. Making the pocket and toy patterns—Trace, label, and cut out patterns for the appliqué pockets and toys from the book, making sure to copy all dots, facial features, and trim placement lines onto the patterns.

When indicated, trace toy patterns on folded paper to make complete patterns. The patterns for the toys and pockets are the same for all sizes of aprons.

4. Cutting and attaching the appliqué and pocket—Pin the appliqué and pocket patterns to the wrong side of the appliqué/pocket fabric and trace each outline. Cut out the pieces, adding ¼″ seam allowances around the edges, when indicated. If necessary, back the pieces with batiste to make them opaque. Refer to the specific directions for each apron to attach the appliqué, if used. Pin the pocket in place on the appliqué and machine stitch close to the edges along the sides and bottom, leaving the pocket top open.

5. Marking, stitching, cutting and stuffing each toy—Fold the fabric for the toy in half, as indicated, right sides together. Trace around the patterns and features with a soft sharp pencil on the wrong side of the fabric. Open the fabric and place it wrong side down against a bright

window. Transfer the facial features to the fabric front by drawing over them lightly with a pencil. (This can also be lightly done with dressmaker's carbon.) Do not cut out the toys before stitching. Refold the fabric, right sides together, and pin. Machine stitch along the outline, using tiny stitches and leaving an opening where indicated on the pattern. After stitching, cut out each toy piece adding a ¼″ seam allowance all around it. Then trim the seam allowance to ⅛″ except along the opening. Clip the curved seam allowance at fairly close intervals to ensure smooth edges. Turn the toy right side out. Turn under and baste the ¼″ seam allowance along the opening. Stuff each toy carefully, as indicated in the specific instructions for that toy, retaining some softness and flatness. Push in a small quantity of stuffing at a time, using a blunt tool and pressing by hand to flatten and maintain the toy's shape.

(continued)

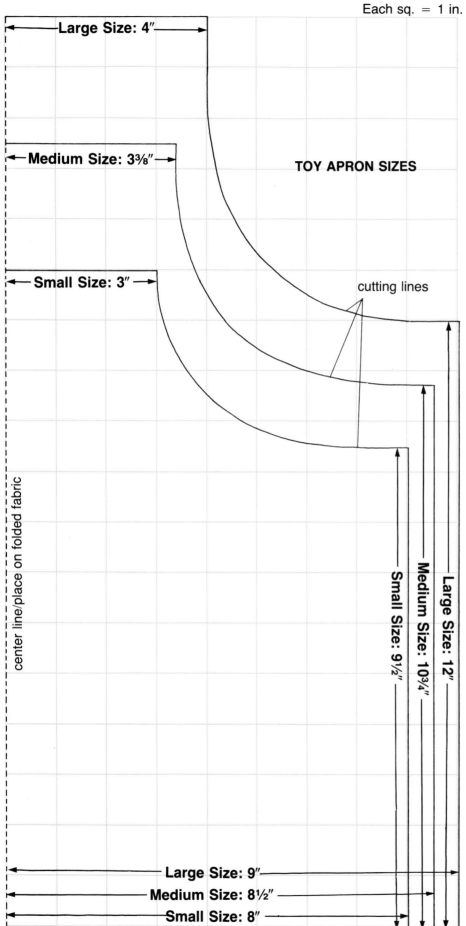

Each sq. = 1 in.

Large Size: 4"

Medium Size: 3⅜"

Small Size: 3"

TOY APRON SIZES

cutting lines

center line/place on folded fabric

Small Size: 9½"

Medium Size: 10¾"

Large Size: 12"

Large Size: 9"

Medium Size: 8½"

Small Size: 8"

BUNNY APRON

Materials

A green quilted or sturdy fabric scrap (see chart for amount)

Brilliant pink, extra-wide double-fold bias tape (see chart for amount)

A 9½" × 13" brilliant pink fabric scrap

Sewing thread: brilliant pink and white

A 34" length of white medium-sized rickrack

An 11½" × 14" white with pink, green, and purple floral fabric scrap

Polyester stuffing

6-ply embroidery thread: 18" black, 24" brilliant pink

5⁄16"-diameter white ball button for nose, optional

5⁄8" diameter white ball fringe for tail, optional

A 15" length of ¼"-wide purple satin ribbon

1. Cutting and trimming the apron—Using the green fabric and pink binding, cut out and trim the apron following Steps 1 and 2 of the General Directions.

2. Making the bunny and basket patterns—Referring to Step 3 of the General Directions, trace the bunny body, ear, basket and handle patterns from the book making sure to copy all dots, facial features and the trim placement lines onto the patterns. Cut out the patterns.

3. Marking and stitching the basket pocket—First read Step 4 of the General Directions. Fold the pink fabric lengthwise, right sides together, place the basket and handle patterns along the fold as indicated on the pattern, and trace the outline and other details onto the fabric. Using small basting stitches, transfer the pattern outlines, pocket top fold line, and the trim placement lines to the front of the fabric, but don't cut out the pieces.

Machine stitch white rickrack along the trim placement line on the handle piece, and then cut out the handle adding a ¼" seam allowance. Clip the seam allowance along the curves, finger press it under and baste. Mark the center top of the handle with a pin, and set the handle aside.

Cut out the basket piece, adding a ¼" seam allowance to all edges. At the basket top, press the ¼" seam

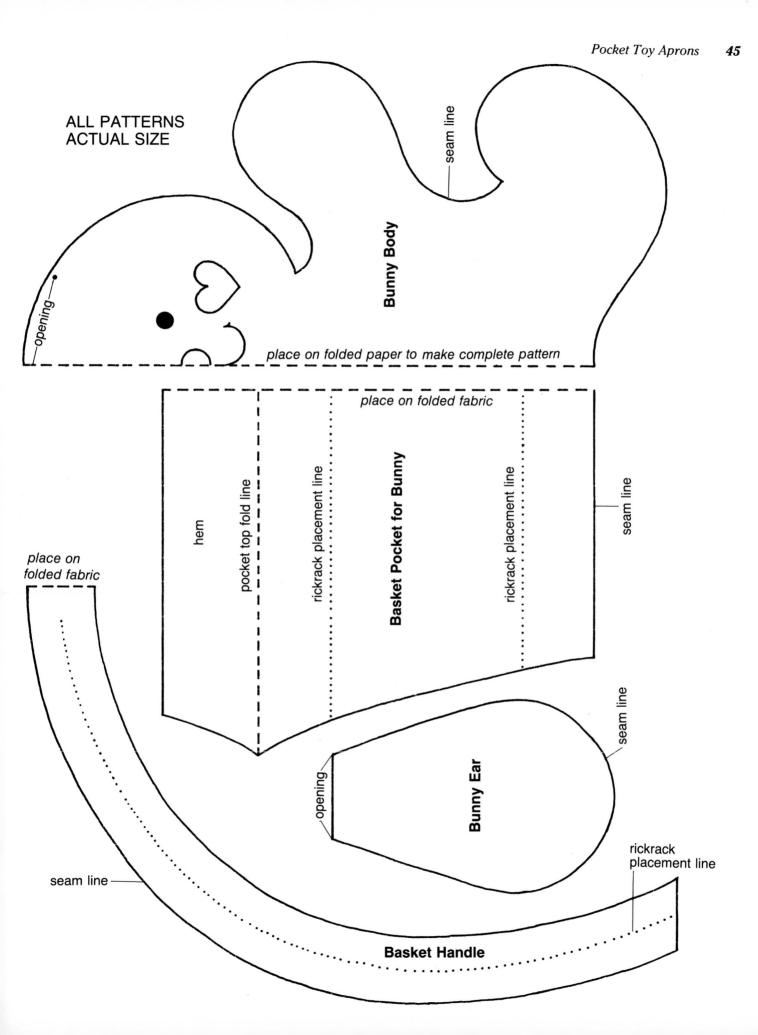

ALL PATTERNS
ACTUAL SIZE

seam line

Bunny Body

opening

place on folded paper to make complete pattern

place on folded fabric

hem

pocket top fold line

rickrack placement line

Basket Pocket for Bunny

rickrack placement line

seam line

place on
folded fabric

opening

seam line

Bunny Ear

seam line

rickrack
placement line

Basket Handle

allowance toward the back and machine stitch close to the edge. Finger press and pin the top of the pocket down along the pocket top fold line bringing it toward the *front* of the basket to make a hem. By machine, stitch down the ends of the hem along the sides of the basket securing the stitches at the start and finish. Clip off the top corners. Grade and clip these seam allowances. Turn the hem to the back of the basket and press along the pocket top fold line.

Clip the seam allowance around the curves of the basket, then finger press, and baste the remaining seam allowance around the basket shape. Machine stitch rickrack along the trim placement line on the basket, and tack the ends on the back of the pocket. Mark the center bottom of the basket with a pin. Pin and invisibly stitch the handle in place at the basket top.

Pin the basket pocket in place on the apron front, matching the center lines. Depending on the size of the apron, the basket bottom should be the following distance from the apron bottom: 1⅛″ (small); 1¾″ (medium); or 2½″ (large). Machine stitch close to the edges along the sides and bottom of the basket, leaving the top open, and stitch the handle close to both edges.

4. Making the bunny—Follow the General Directions, Step 5, using the floral print fabric for the body and the two ears, and leaving the head top open between the dots and the ears open on the bottom. Stuff the body as directed, but do not stuff the ears.

5. Attaching the ears—Press the ears and close the bottom opening with small basting stitches ¼″ from the edge. Pull the bastings to gather the bottom of each ear to a width of ½″. Insert the ears about ⅞″ apart in the head opening and invisibly stitch the opening closed on the front and back, catching the ears. If you wish, you can add a row of decorative running stitches ¼″ inside the edge of the ear, on the front side only, to create an inner ear line.

6. The features—Using a single strand of embroidery thread, satin stitch black eyes and pink cheeks and chain stitch a black mouth. Attach the button nose, if desired.

7. Finishing touches—Securely tack a ball fringe tail on the back, if desired, and tie a purple ribbon around the bunny's neck.

PIGLET APRON
Materials
A blue quilted or sturdy fabric scrap (see chart for amount)

Red extra-wide, double-fold bias tape (see chart for amount)

Sewing thread: white and red

A 9″ × 14″ red fabric scrap

A 60″ length of white extra-wide, double-fold bias tape

A 9″ × 13″ white with red and blue tattersall check fabric scrap

Polyester stuffing

6-ply embroidery thread: 18″ black, 18″ red

A 15″ length of ¼″-wide blue satin ribbon

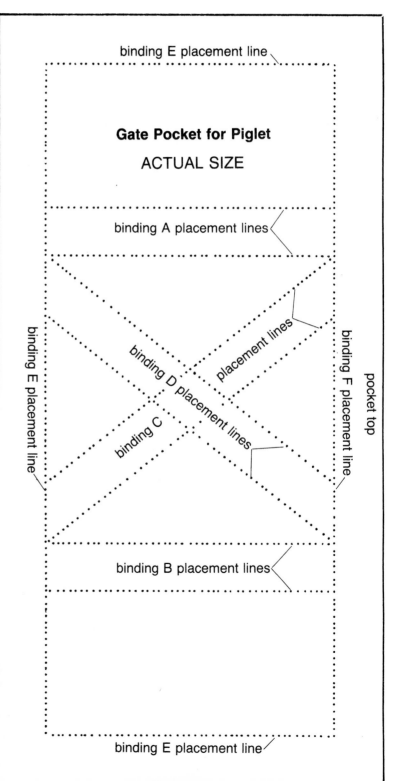

binding E placement line

Gate Pocket for Piglet

ACTUAL SIZE

binding A placement lines

placement lines

binding D placement lines

binding E placement line

binding C

binding F placement line

pocket top

binding B placement lines

binding E placement line

cutting line

FIGURE 1. Making flat tape from double-fold bias binding

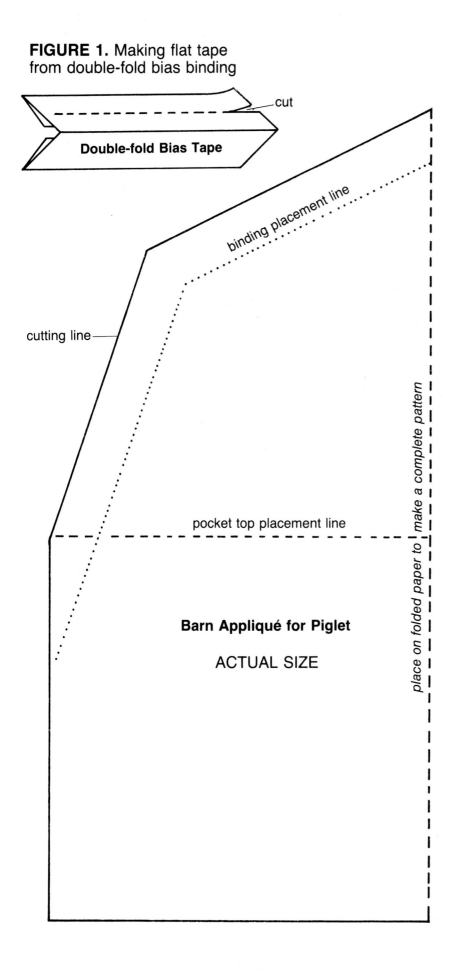

cut

Double-fold Bias Tape

binding placement line

cutting line

pocket top placement line

place on folded paper to make a complete pattern

Barn Appliqué for Piglet

ACTUAL SIZE

1. Cutting and trimming the apron—Using the blue fabric and red binding, cut out and trim the apron following Steps 1 and 2 of the General Directions.

2. Making the piglet barn and gate pocket patterns—Refer to Step 3 of General Directions, and trace the piglet body and ear and the gate pocket patterns from the book, making sure to copy all dots, facial features, and trim placement lines onto the patterns. Trace the pattern for the barn on folded paper copying all the trim placement lines. Cut out the patterns.

3. Marking and trimming the barn appliqué and gate pocket—First read Step 4 of the General Directions. Trace the barn and the gate pocket with details onto the wrong side of the red fabric. Use small basting stitches or light dressmaker's carbon to transfer all the trim placement lines to the front of the fabric as described in the General Directions. Cut out the barn and pocket along the outline.

Cut a 17″ length of the white bias tape. Cut a ¼″-wide strip from the widest side of the fold to make a ½″-wide flat tape (see Figure 1). Cut this tape into the following lengths and mark the back of each with the appropriate letter as follows:

A, 3¾″; B, 3¾″; C, 4⅝″; and D, 4⅝″. One at a time and in order, pin each piece of tape in place on the gate pocket in the position designated on the pattern and machine stitch it along both edges.

From the remaining untrimmed bias tape, cut a 17″ strip (binding E) and machine top stitch it along the inside edge around the sides and bottom of the gate pocket, mitering the tape at the corners (see *Sewing Techniques,* page 162).

Cut a 9″ strip of the remaining untrimmed white bias tape (binding F) and bind the top edge of the gate pocket, letting ½″ of tape extend beyond the pocket at each end.

Stitch the remaining 16″-long strip of bias tape to the roof top of the barn, letting the ends extend about ½″ at the start and finish. It's easiest to apply this tape by first hand basting the edge of the tape along the trim placement line and then machine topstitching through all layers close to the inside edge. Do not trim the ends of the tape.

4. Attaching the pocket and barn—Position and pin the gate pocket to the barn front, matching the bottom and side edges. Fold the roof and pocket top tape ends to the back, pin and securely stitch them. Trim away any red fabric edges of the barn that show beyond the pocket tape on the front. Hand stitch the barn sides and bottom edge to the back of the tape binding on the pocket making sure that the stitches will not show on the tape front. Mark the center bottom of the barn with a pin.

Pin the barn with its pocket in place on the apron front, aligning the center lines. Depending on the size of the apron, the bottom of the pocket should be the following distance from the apron bottom: 1⅛″ (small); 2¼″ (medium); or 3″ (large). Machine stitch close to the edges along the sides and bottom, leaving the pocket top open.

5. Making the piglet—Follow the General Directions, Step 5, using the tattersall fabric for the piglet body and two ears and leaving head and ear openings as marked.

Stuff the body as directed, but don't stuff the ears.

6. Attaching the ears—Baste closed the lower edge of the ears along the seam line, but don't tuck in the seam allowance. Align the ears. Insert their lower edges into the head opening, positioning them at the top dot, and pin in place. Invisibly stitch the ears in place and close the head opening. Softly fold each ear down and slightly forward and tack it invisibly against the head.

7. The features—Using a single strand of embroidery thread, satin stitch black eyes and red cheeks and chain stitch a black mouth.

8. The curly tail—Cut a 1″ × 3″ tattersall fabric strip. Fold under ¼″ at each narrow end to make a hem, leaving a 2½″-long strip. Now, fold both lengthwise edges toward the center and press. Fold the strip in half, press along the center line, and, using small hand stitches, stitch closed the open edges of the strip. Pull the thread to gather the fabric and curl the tail and secure it. Tack one end of the tail to the pig's back.

9. Finishing touches—Tie a blue ribbon bow around the piglet's neck.

MOUSEKIN APRON

Materials

A chartreuse quilted or sturdy fabric scrap (see chart for amount)

Yellow extra-wide, double-fold bias tape (see chart for amount)

Sewing thead: yellow and white

A 7½ × 11″ sturdy yellow fabric scrap that will not fray easily

An 8½″ × 18″ chartreuse, green and orange print fabric scrap

Polyester stuffing

6-ply embroidery thread: 18″ black; 24″ magenta; 3½ yards yellow

A ⁵⁄₁₆″-diameter white ball button for the nose, optional

A 15″ length of ¼″-wide green ribbon

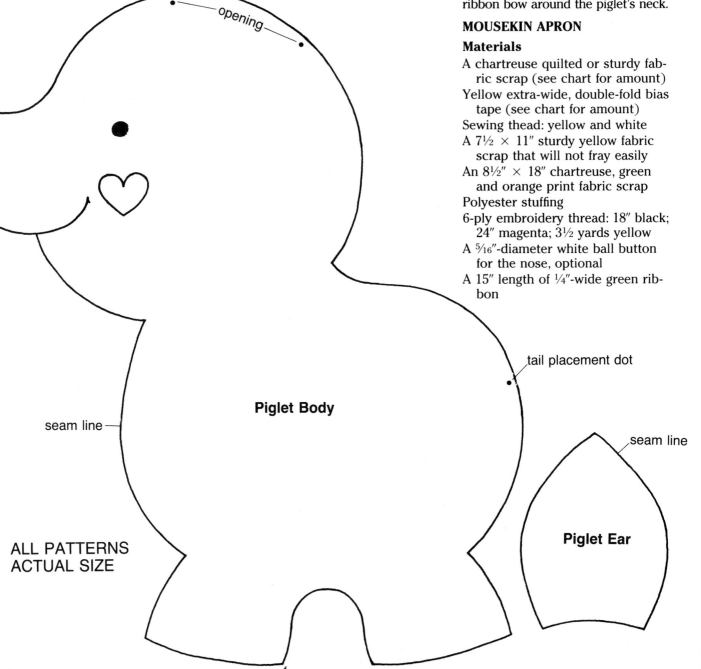

opening

Piglet Body

seam line

tail placement dot

seam line

Piglet Ear

ALL PATTERNS
ACTUAL SIZE

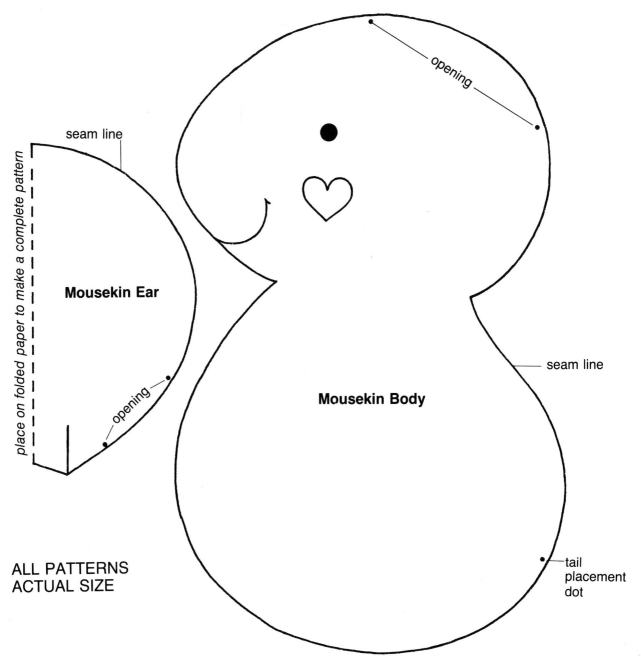

seam line

Mousekin Ear

place on folded paper to make a complete pattern

opening

opening

seam line

Mousekin Body

tail placement dot

ALL PATTERNS
ACTUAL SIZE

1. Cutting and trimming the apron—Using the chartreuse fabric and yellow binding, cut out and trim the apron following Steps 1 and 2 of the General Directions.

2. Making the mousekin and pocket patterns—Refer to Step 3 of the General Directions, and trace the mousekin body and ear and the cheese patterns from the book making sure to copy all dots, facial features, and the trim placement lines onto the patterns. Cut out the patterns.

3. Marking and stitching the cheese pocket—First read Step 4 of the General Directions. Fold the yellow fabric crosswise, right sides together, place the cheese pattern along the fold as indicated and trace around the outside edge. Don't bother to mark the holes yet.

Machine stitch along the outline leaving an opening between the dots. Clip off the corners and turn the pocket right side out. Close the opening with invisible stitches. Press the pocket flat.

Pin the pattern to the pocket and lightly mark the holes with a sharp soft pencil. If you have an intricate and reliable zigzag system on your sewing machine, you may be able to stitch around each hole after basting it and then cut out the center. If not, use the following method.

Stitch 1/16″ outside the holes to hold the layers of fabric together. Make a second row of stitches 1/8″ outside

the holes to provide a guideline for buttonhole stitches. Cut out each hole along the pattern line. Using two strands of yellow embroidery thread, overcast the edges of the holes with buttonhole stitches.

Mark the center bottom and top of the cheese pocket with pins. Pin the pocket to the apron front aligning the center lines and, depending on the size of the apron, placing the bottom of the pocket the following distance from the apron bottom: 1½″ (small); 2½″ (medium); or 3½″ (large). Machine stitch close to the side and bottom edges of the pocket, leaving the top open.

4. Making the mousekin—Follow the General Directions, Step 5, using the print fabric for the mousekin

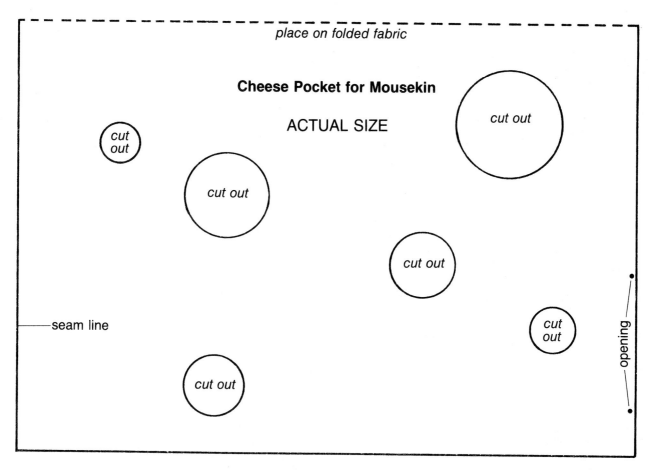

place on folded fabric

Cheese Pocket for Mousekin

ACTUAL SIZE

cut out

cut out

cut out

cut out

cut out

cut out

seam line

opening

body and two ears and leaving head and ear openings as marked. Stuff the body as directed, but don't stuff the ears. Close the opening at the head top and on the ear sides.

5. The features—Using a single strand of embroidery thread, satin stitch black eyes and magenta cheeks and chain stitch a black mouth. Stitch on the ball-button nose, if desired.

6. Attaching the ears—Fold each ear in half along the center fold line at the bottom. Hand stitch a ½"-long line of stitches along the fold to make a tuck. Open the ear and hold it so the tucked or back side faces you. Flatten the tuck and stitch it down on both sides to the back of the ear.

Position and pin an ear to each side of the head, using the uppermost dot as a guide and placing one ear upright and the other tipped toward the back. Stitch the ears invisibly in place. You may also need to tack the back side of the ear to the head to keep it from flopping.

7. The tail—Cut a 1" × 5½" print fabric strip. Fold under and baste a ¼" hem at each narrow end shortening the strip to 5". Fold both lengthwise edges toward the center

and press. Fold the strip in half lengthwise and press again. Using small hand stitches sew the lengthwise edges together and secure the thread. Tack one end of the tail to the mousekin's back and knot the other end.

8. Finishing touches—Tie a green ribbon bow around the mousekin's neck.

DUCKLING APRON

Materials

A yellow quilted or sturdy fabric scrap (see chart for amount)
White extra-wide, double-fold bias tape (see chart for amount)
Sewing thread: white, yellow, yellow-orange, and pink
A 10" × 20" opaque white fabric scrap
Medium-sized rickrack: a 7½" length each of yellow-orange, bright pink, and yellow
A 15" length of ⅜" to ½"-wide flat, crocheted type, white lace
A 7½" × 12" yellow with multicolored floral print scrap
Polyester stuffing

A 3" × 4" orange fabric scrap
6-ply embroidery thread: 18" black, 24" brilliant pink
A 15" length of ¼"-wide orange satin ribbon

1. Cutting and trimming the apron—Using the yellow fabric and white binding, cut out and trim the apron following Steps 1 and 2 of the General Directions.

2. Making the duckling and egg patterns—Refer to Step 3 of the General Directions, and trace the duckling body, wing, and beak, the egg appliqué and the cracked egg pocket from the book, making sure to copy all dots, facial features, and trim placement lines onto the patterns. Cut out the patterns.

3. Making and stitching the egg appliqué—Cut an 8" × 10" piece of the white fabric, fold it in half, right sides together, place the egg appliqué pattern along the fold, as indicated, and trace the outline. Cut out the appliqué, adding a ¼" seam allowance. Transfer the outline and centerline to the front of the fabric with bastings. Clip the seam allowance, press it to the back and baste.

Pin the egg appliqué on the apron

aligning the center lines and depending on the size of the apron, placing the bottom of the egg the following distance from the apron bottom: 1½″ (small); 2½″ (medium); or 3″ (large).

4. Making and attaching the cracked egg pocket—First read Step 4 of the General Directions and fold the remaining piece of white fabric in half to make a 6″ × 10″ piece. Pin the pattern to the wrong side of the fabric, trace around the outside edge, and cut out two pocket pieces, adding ¼″ seam allowances.

Pin the cracked egg pieces right sides together and machine stitch along the edges leaving an opening between the dots. Clip off the points, and clip into the V-shaped areas and around the curves. Turn the pocket right side out, tuck in the seam allowance of the opening, and press it flat.

Stitch the orange row of rickrack along the center trim placement line. Add a row of pink rickrack above it and a row of yellow rickrack below it, so the rickrack is just touching. Stitch a row of lace above and below the rickrack as a border. Tack the ends of the lace and rickrack on the back.

Pin the cracked egg pocket in place on top of the egg appliqué. Machine stitch along the lower curved edge, back-stitching at start and finish.

5. Making the duckling—Follow the General Directions, Step 5, using the floral fabric for the duckling body and two wings and leaving head, tail and wing openings as marked.

Stuff the body, but just stuff the wings very lightly or not at all. Stitch closed the openings on the wings and below the tail, but not on the head. Pin a wing in place on each side of the body and invisibly stitch it along the top to the duckling's body.

6. The features—To make the bill, fold the orange fabric right sides together, and trace two bills. Keeping the fabric folded, machine stitch along the curved edge of each bill using very tiny stitches. Cut out each bill, leaving a ¼″ seam allowance. Trim the curved seam allowances to ⅛″, preferably with pinking shears, or clip the seam allowances after trimming them. Turn each bill right side out. Press both pieces flat and baste the openings closed. Fold the bill pieces in half and tuck one inside the other with the curved edges facing in opposite directions to make the mouth. Baste. Insert the bill in the head opening, pin, and invisibly stitch it in place.

Using a single strand of embroidery thread, satin stitch black eyes and brilliant pink cheeks.

7. Finishing touches—Tie an orange ribbon bow around the duckling's neck.

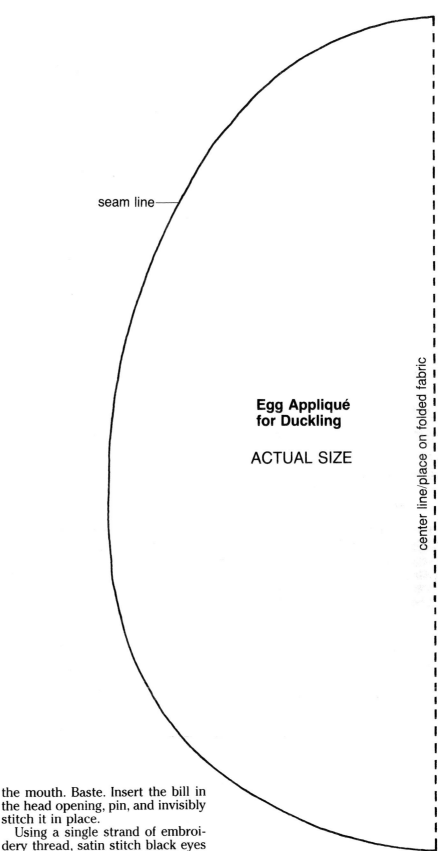

seam line

Egg Appliqué for Duckling

ACTUAL SIZE

center line/place on folded fabric

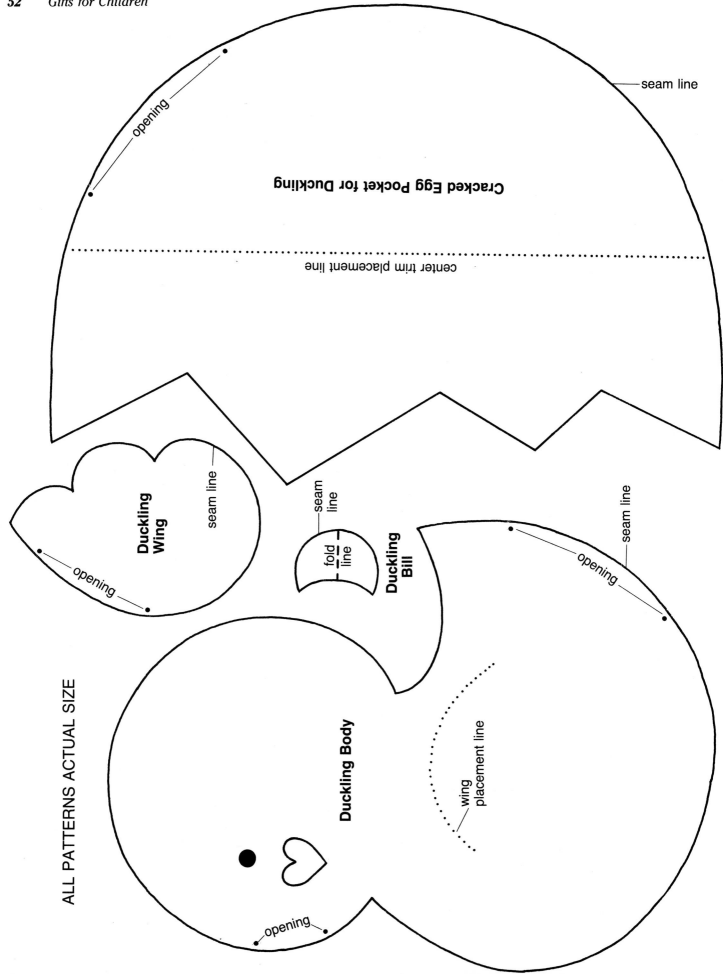

ALL PATTERNS ACTUAL SIZE

From the basic set of patterns that accompany this project, you can create a zebra family or a collection of peppermint-striped Christmas zebras for your tree or table top. The patterns given are for 8"-high, 12"-high, and 15"-high zebras.

The smallest patterns are for ornaments, or you can make them in sweet pastel-striped fabrics for an extra-special baby. The legs are just the right size for tiny hands to grasp. For an infant, stitch the ears and ribbon on very securely and omit the bell, or bury it inside the stuffing and carefully double stitch and knot the opening. Also consider using the largest patterns to make an "autograph" zebra. Tuck a ballpoint pen or laundry marker into the neck ribbon and ask friends to just "sign on a line."

This design, as with all

Zebra Toys and Ornaments

striped projects, requires very careful laying out, cutting, and stitching of all the pieces. When the stripes run parallel to a seam, center the pattern so that the seam line always falls within a white stripe. The zebras don't look

as nice if the dark stripes are next to the seams.

The zebra legs can remain floppy or you can tack them together so they can be balanced to stand. Keep in mind, however, that the largest 15"-high zebra will be difficult for a very small child to balance even when stitched to stand, so it might be less frustrating for the child, if you omit the tacking altogether.

Locating black-and-white striped fabric was not quite as easy as I had expected, so I used navy and white stripes instead. But even they were somewhat hard to find, so if stripes are unavailable, combine patches of two friendly prints that you have on hand to turn the zebra into a horse. If you are not using stripes, disregard the bias direction lines and cut all the pieces on the straight of the grain.

GENERAL DIRECTIONS FOR MAKING ALL SIZES OF ZEBRAS

1. Making the patterns and cutting out the fabric—Trace the patterns from the book, label each, and copy all the arrows as well as the dots, seam, fold, and gathering lines. All the pattern lines are cutting lines for fabric and include ¼" seam allowances.

Using the directional arrows to aid in the placement of the patterns on the stripes, cut from the striped fabric six striped A patches on the straight of the grain and two diagonally striped A patches on the bias. Also cut eight diagonally striped B patches on the bias, marking the dot on the wrong side of the fabric. Cut four striped C legs with the stripes

horizontal or parallel to the short edges of the patches, two striped D patches and one striped G ear, with the stripes vertical, or parallel to the long edges. Handle the bias patches gently so they won't stretch.

From the solid fabric cut two E and four F patches and one G ear.

Referring to Figure 1, arrange the patches on a flat surface to form the zebra body front and back (the reverse of the front). Refer to the photograph on page 54 to note the direction of the stripes on each patch.

2. Joining the patches—Pin and stitch the A and B body patches, right sides together, into three vertical rows by stitching the horizontal seams between them (Figure 1, page 55). Press open the seam allow-

ances of all the patches in the zebra as you work.

Pin and stitch the vertical rows together. Join a D and E patch together, along the sides then attach them to the free straight edge of the B patch. Repeat for the back. In order to press the seam allowances flat, clip them to the seamline under the chin and at the neck back (see Figure 2, page 55).

3. Joining the front and the back and stuffing the zebra—Pin the front and back, right sides together. Lightly mark a ¼" seam line to provide an accurate guideline for stitching.

Machine stitch along the seam line, leaving an area open between the dots along the bottom edge only.

Zebra Ornaments, an Adult Zebra, and a Baby Zebra gambol across a field of straw.

Trim all seam allowances above the dots to ⅛″ and clip them along the curves. Clip diagonally into the corners at the chin and neck back.

Separately hand baste the seam allowance on the front and back between the dots ¼″ from the edge to provide a guideline. Turn the zebra right side out. Tuck under and baste the seam allowance along each side of the opening.

Stuff the animal firmly but keep it flat; after stuffing, the width of the neck A patch should be about 1″ across for the ornaments, 1⅜″ across for the baby, and 1⅞″ across for the largest zebra.

4. Making and attaching the legs—Stitch a solid F hoof to the lower edge of each striped C leg. Fold the leg and hoof lengthwise, right sides together, and stitch across the bottom of the hoof and up the side of the leg. Clip off the hoof corners, turn the leg right side out and stuff it, keeping it flat. Baste the seam allowances together ¼″ from the top. Pin two legs together, stacking one on top of the other and matching the seams, and join them by securely hand stitching ¼″ from the top edges. Repeat for the second pair of legs.

Insert a pair of legs into each end of the lower body opening, lining up the leg seams with the seams on each end of the lower center body A patch. Pin and invisibly stitch the legs in place, closing the opening. Remove all visible bastings that remain on the body and legs.

If you want the zebra to stand, tack the legs together on the front and back of each set about ¼″ down from the small bodies and ½″ down from the large bodies. If they're still too wobbly, take small stitches between the leg tops and the B patches of the body pulling the front legs toward the body front and the rear legs toward the back. The largest zebra will be wobbly and difficult to balance even when stitched to stand.

5. The ears—Pin each solid ear to a striped ear, right sides together. Machine stitch leaving an opening between the dots. Trim the seam allowance, except between the dots, to ⅛″. Clip the seam allowances along the curves, turn the ear piece right side out and press flat with your hand. Close the opening with invisible stitches. Using tiny hand stitches, gather the ear piece along the cen-

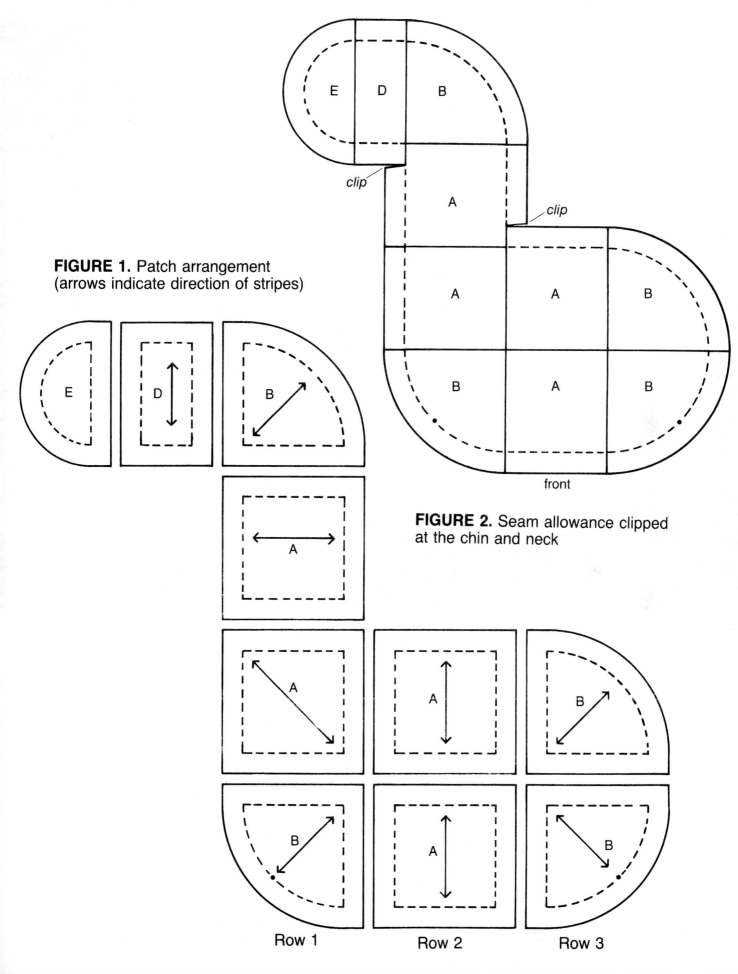

FIGURE 1. Patch arrangement (arrows indicate direction of stripes)

FIGURE 2. Seam allowance clipped at the chin and neck

Row 1　　Row 2　　Row 3

ter line. Pull the thread to gather the fabric tightly and then wrap the thread around the gathering to pinch the ears tightly. Tack the ear piece in place at the head top between the fringes (you may want to remove one fringe to do this).

ZEBRA ORNAMENT

Materials (for one zebra)

An 11″ × 15″ red or green narrow-striped fabric scrap (3 stripes together should measure approximately ¼″ across)

A 5″ × 8″ red or green solid fabric scrap that matches the stripe color

A white marking pencil

Polyester stuffing

6-ply embroidery thread: 5 yards red or green to match the stripes, 18″ black

A 15″ length of invisible nylon thread for a hanging loop

A 12″ length of ¼″-wide red or green satin ribbon

A small silver jingle bell

1. Making the pattern, cutting, and assembling the zebra—Follow all of the General Directions except for making the ears (Step 5).

2. The tail—To make the tail, cut red or green embroidery thread into two 40″ lengths. Thread one length through a needle, and pass the needle through the fabric at the tail area (center back). Pull the thread through the fabric to within 4″ of the end. Trim the thread ends to within 3½″ of the fabric. Repeat nine times. Divide the 18 tail threads into three sections of six threads each. Braid the sections to a length of 1¼″ and knot the ends together. Trim the ends to 1″.

3. The mane—To make the mane, thread the needle with a 36″ length of 6-ply red or green embroidery thread, and, following the steps outlined in Figure 3, stitch and knot a loop starting ¼″ above the body on

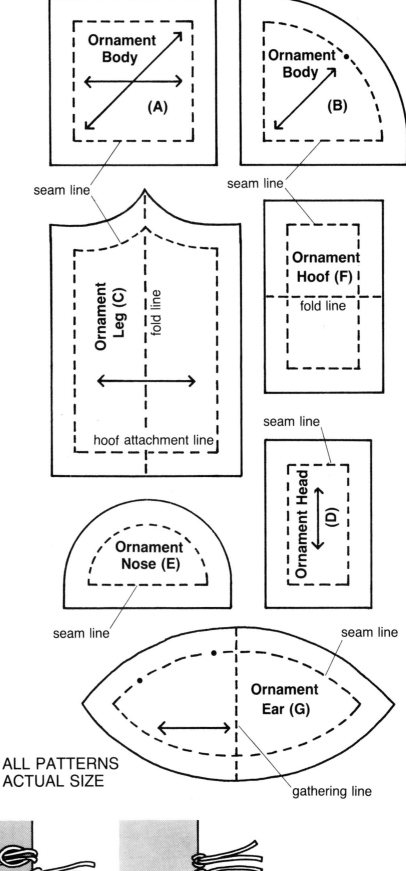

ZEBRA OR HORSE ORNAMENT

ALL PATTERNS ACTUAL SIZE

FIGURE 3. Making fringe

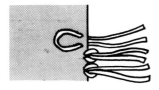

1. Stitched loop

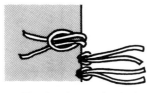

2. Ends threaded through loop

3. Ends pulled tightly

the seam along the back of the neck. Repeat the procedure, clipping the thread after each loop is made, and placing the fringes very close together all the way along the back of the neck to the head seam. Trim the fringe ends to ½".

4. The ears—Make and attach the ears following the General Directions, Step 5.

5. The eye—Draw an ⅛"-diameter circle for the eye centered exactly on the head seam between B and D. Using one strand of black embroidery thread, satin stitch the eye (see *Embroidery Stitches*).

6. Finishing touches—Attach a hanging loop to the top back of the neck, if desired. Tie a ribbon bow around the neck and decorate it with a bell.

HORSE ORNAMENT

Materials (for 1 horse)
An 8" × 12" red with green-and-white print fabric scrap
A 5" × 10" red-with-white dot fabric scrap
A 5" × 8" solid green fabric scrap
Polyester stuffing
6-ply embroidery thread: 5 yards green, 18" black
A white marking pencil
A 12" length of ¼"-wide white satin ribbon
A small, silver jingle bell

1. Making the patterns—Trace the patterns as described in the General Directions, Step 1.

2. Cutting out the fabric—Disregard the bias direction lines given for stripes and cut all pieces on the straight of the grain. From the red and green print fabric cut four A and four B patches, and four C pieces. From the red dot fabric cut four A, four B, and two D patches, and one G ear. From the green fabric cut two E and four F patches and one G ear.

3. Assembling the horse—Follow the General Directions through attaching the legs, Step 4, arranging the patches alternately, as shown in the photograph on page 54.

4. The tail—To make the tail, cut six 12" lengths of green embroidery thread. Thread each length through a needle, double the thread, and stitch through the fabric at the tail area in the center back, pulling the thread halfway through the horse. Cut the needle free, leaving four 3"-long ends. Tie the threads together once close to the body. Repeat with

the remaining strands at the same spot to make 24 thread ends. Trim the tail to about 2½".

5. The mane—To make the mane, follow Step 3 of the Zebra Ornament directions.

6. The ears—Make the ears following Step 5 of the General Directions.

7. The eyes—Draw a ⅛"-diameter circle for each eye exactly centered on each side head seam between patches B and D. Using one strand of black embroidery thread, satin stitch the eyes (see *Embroidery Stitches*).

8. Finishing touches—Attach a hanging loop and decorate with a ribbon as for the Zebra Ornament, Step 6.

BABY ZEBRA

Materials
An 8" × 35" black- or navy-and-white-stripe fabric scrap with dark stripes about ¼" wide and cut so the stripes are parallel to the 8"-edge.
A 5½" × 12" black or navy fabric scrap
Polyester stuffing
6-ply embroidery thread: 12 yards navy or black, ½ yard black
A white marking pencil
⅝ yard ⅜"-wide green satin ribbon

1. Making the pattern, cutting, and assembling the zebra—Follow all of the General Directions, except for making the ears, Step 5.

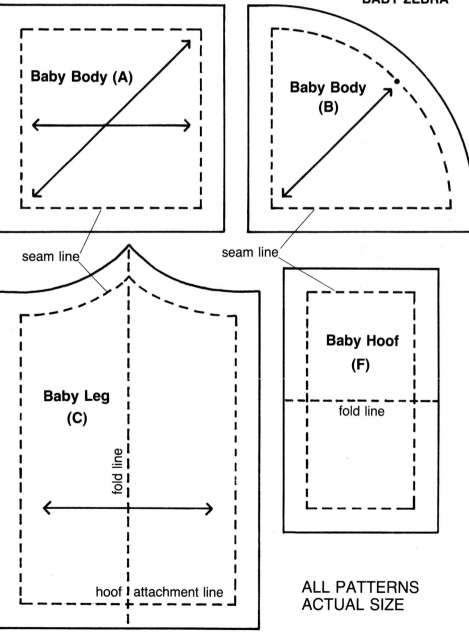

BABY ZEBRA

Baby Body (A)

seam line

Baby Body (B)

seam line

Baby Leg (C)

fold line

hoof attachment line

Baby Hoof (F)

fold line

ALL PATTERNS ACTUAL SIZE

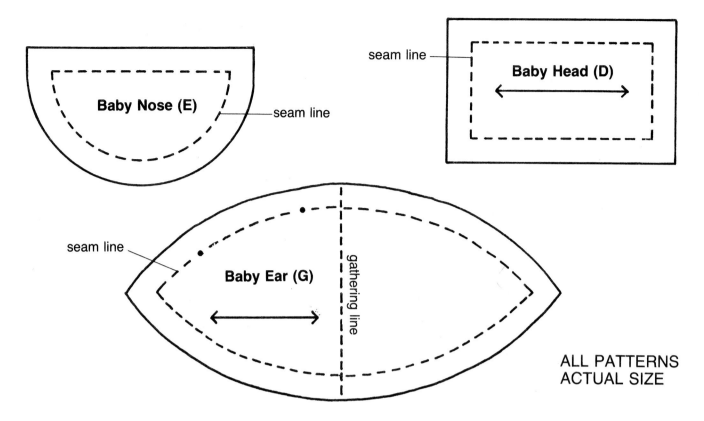

ALL PATTERNS
ACTUAL SIZE

2. The tail—To make the tail, cut nine 20″ lengths of navy or black embroidery thread. Thread each length through a needle, double the thread, and stitch through the fabric at the tail area in the center back, pulling the thread halfway through the zebra. Cut the needle free, leaving four 5″-long ends. Repeat with the remaining strands at the same spot to make 36 thread ends. Divide the tail threads into three sections of 12 strands each. Braid the sections together to a length of 2″ and knot. Trim the thread ends to 1″.

3. The mane—To make the mane, cut the remaining thread into one-yard lengths. One at a time and following the steps outlined in Figure 3, stitch fringes very close together along the seam at the back of the neck, starting 3/8″ above the body and ending at the head top seam. Trim the ends to 3/4″ after you pull them through the loop.

4. The ears—Make and attach the ears following Step 5 of the General Directions.

5. The eyes—Draw a 1/4″-diameter circle for each eye exactly on each side head seam between patches B and D. Using one strand of black embroidery thread, satin stitch the eyes (see *Embroidery Stitches*).

6. Finishing touches—Tie a green satin ribbon around the neck.

LARGE ZEBRA

Materials

A 12″ × 38″ black- or navy-and-white-stripe fabric scrap, with dark stripes about 3/8″ wide and cut so the stripes are parallel to the 12″ edge

A 7″ × 13″ black or navy fabric scrap

Polyester stuffing

6-ply embroidery thread: 18 yards navy or black, 1/2 yard black

A white marking pencil

3/4 yard 5/8″-wide green satin ribbon

1. Making the pattern, cutting, and assembling the zebra—Follow all of the General Directions, except for making the ears, Step 5.

2. The tail—To make the tail, cut twelve 28″ lengths of navy or black embroidery thread. Thread each length through a needle, double the thread, and stitch through the fabric at the tail area in the center back, pulling the thread halfway through the zebra. Cut the needle free, leaving four 7″-long ends. Repeat with remaining strands at the same spot to make 48 thread ends. Divide the tail threads into three sections of 16 strands each. Braid the sections together to a length of 3″ and knot. Trim the thread ends to 1 1/2″.

3. The mane—To make the mane, cut the remaining thread into one-yard lengths. Thread the needle with one length of thread at a time and, following the steps in Figure 3, stitch fringes very close together along the seam at the back of the neck, starting 5/8″ above the body and ending at the head top seam. Trim the ends to 1″ after pulling them through the loop.

4. The ears—Make the ears following Step 5 of the General Directions.

5. The eyes—Draw a 1/4″-diameter circle for each eye exactly on each side head seam between patches B and D. Using one strand of black embroidery thread, satin stitch the eyes (see *Embroidery Stitches*).

6. Finishing touches—Tie a green satin ribbon around the neck.

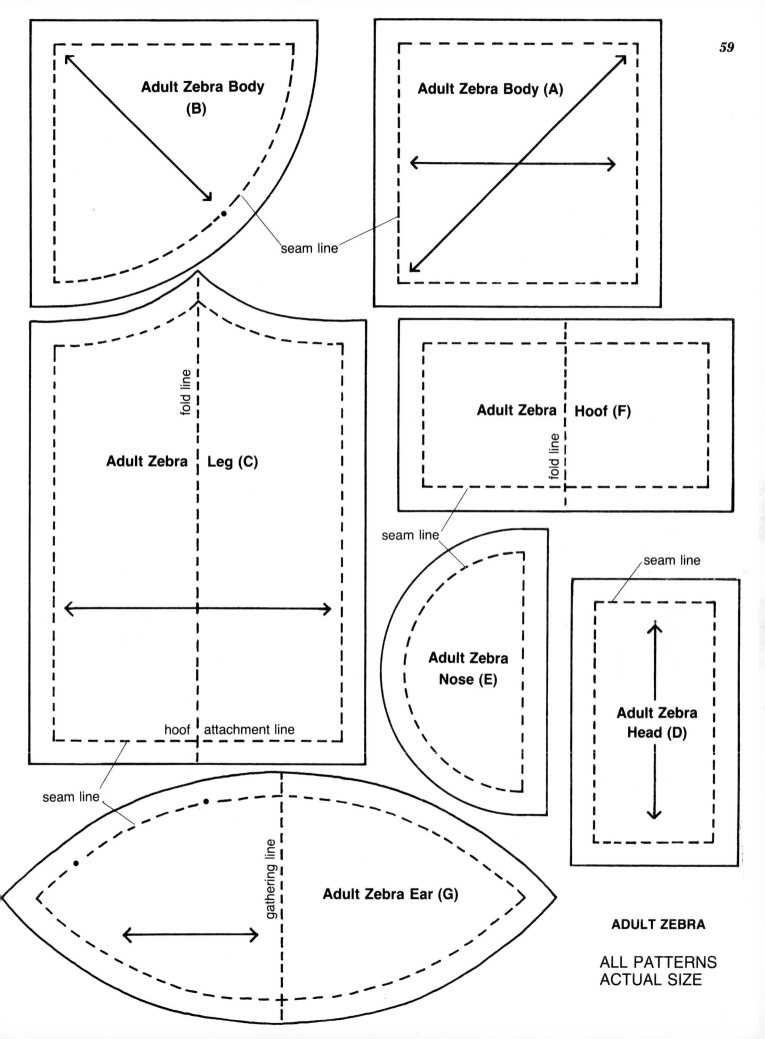

Adult Zebra Body (B)

seam line

Adult Zebra Body (A)

59

fold line

Adult Zebra   Leg (C)

Adult Zebra   Hoof (F)

fold line

seam line

hoof   attachment line

Adult Zebra
Nose (E)

seam line

Adult Zebra
Head (D)

seam line

gathering line

Adult Zebra Ear (G)

ADULT ZEBRA

ALL PATTERNS
ACTUAL SIZE

The bear family, Papa and Mama bear and their tiny baby "Cubcake" are happily at home in their portable Cupcake Bake Shop. The bakeshop can be toted by means of the loop handle stitched to the top of the frosting area, and the bears can easily enter and leave the shop through the velcro-fastened door. The time-consuming embroidery on the door sign is optional. Interfacing added to the lining of the cupcake side section gives the shop support, but if you wish to make it even stronger, purchase an 18" by 35" piece of

Cupcake Bake Shop

sturdy regular or fusible interfacing and back all the lining pieces. I used the same fabric for both the cupcake side and the lining.

The frosting rose that tops the cupcake also looks pretty in a little girl's hair when it is stitched together with a few ribbon leaves to a barrett or a clip. It is easily made by gathering satin ribbons of various widths as explained in the following instructions.

The bears make perfect little pocket pals or Christmas tree ornaments, too. If you don't want to take the time to dress them, stitch them up in bright Christmas prints with narrow ribbon bows and tiny bells at their necks, but make very sure the fabric does not fray easily.

Cupcake Materials

⅝ yard ginger-colored fabric, preferably with tiny white print or dot

An 11" × 24" piece of medium-weight interfacing

An 8" × 30" piece of pink-and-white-stripe fabric

A 3" × 3" white fabric scrap

A 7" × 7" pink fabric scrap (enough to fit your embroidery hoop)

An 18" × 35" piece of thin polyester quilt batting

Sewing thread: ginger brown, white, light pink, pale green

1 yard ¼-wide white double-fold bias tape

2 yards white corded piping

⅞ yard 1"-wide eyelet ruffle, including ¼" binding

6-ply embroidery thread: 18" white and 1 yard medium green

Satin ribbon: ¼ yard each of ⅜"-, ⅝"-, and 1"-wide pink; ½ yard ⅝"-wide pale green; ¼ yard ⅛"-wide pale yellow

1 light duty ½"-diameter circular Velcro fastener

Bear Bodies

¼ yard ginger-colored fabric, preferably with tiny white print or dot

Ginger-colored thread

Polyester stuffing

6-ply embroidery thread: 2 yards each of black and medium pink

Papa Bear's Clothes

A 5½" × 13" white fabric scrap

White thread

A 3½" length of white ⅝"-wide bias tape or ½"-wide grosgrain ribbon

6-ply embroidery thread: an 18" length each of pink and medium green

A 12½" length of white ¼"-wide double-fold bias tape or ¼"-wide grosgrain ribbon

Mama Bear's Dress

A 3" × 10¼" pink floral fabric scrap

Pink thread

A 19" length of ½"-wide white lace ruffle, including a ¼"-wide binding

Satin ribbon: a 4½" length of ¼"-wide pale green, a 3½" length of ¼"-wide pale pink, and a 2" length of ⅛"-wide yellow

Baby Bear's Bib and Ribbon

A 3" × 4" pale green fabric scrap

An 18" length of 6-ply medium green embroidery thread

A 3¼" length of ½"-wide white lace ruffle, including a ¼"-wide binding

A 3¼" length of pink baby rickrack

A 12" length of ⅛"-wide pale pink satin ribbon or an equal amount of pink yarn or embroidery thread

Equipment

Small, sharp scissors

Presser foot sewing machine attachment

Crochet hook

Small embroidery hoop

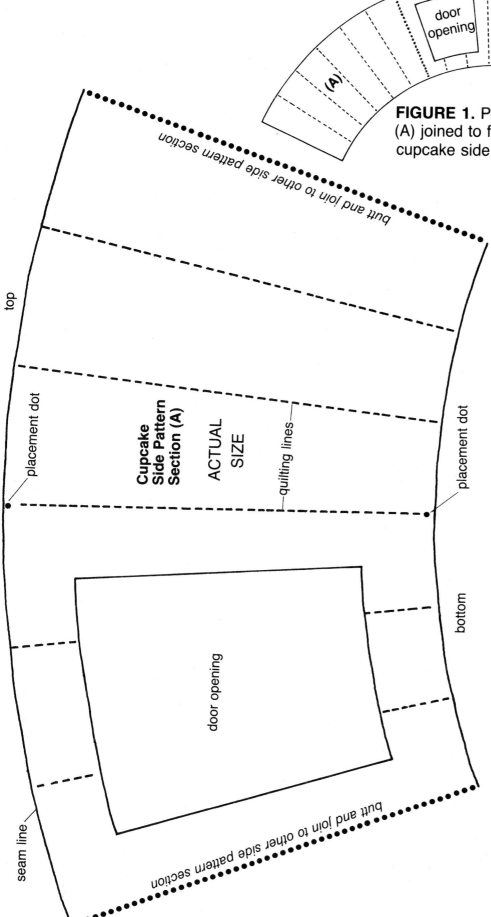

FIGURE 1. Pattern sections (A) joined to form complete cupcake side

Cupcake Side Pattern Section (A)

ACTUAL SIZE

quilting lines

top

placement dot

placement dot

seam line

bottom

door opening

butt and join to other side pattern section

butt and join to other side pattern section

THE CUPCAKE

1. Making the patterns—Trace three cupcake sides (pattern section A) on tracing paper, copying all the lines and dots, but omitting the door opening on two of the sections. Cut out the sections and tape them together along the heavy dotted lines, placing the section with the door in the middle, as shown in Figure 1. Cut out the door opening.

Trace and cut out pattern pieces for the following: cupcake base (B), door (C), frosting (D), frosting top (E), and the door sign with lettering (F), copying all the placement dots and other markings.

2. Cutting the side and lining pieces—Working on the wrong side of the ginger-colored fabric and adding ¼" seam allowances, trace and cut out the following: one side (A) with the door marked to the left of center (the lining) and one side (A) with the door marked to the right of center (the outside), two cupcake bases (B), one frosting top (E), and six frosting sections (D, page 64). Also cut two door pieces (C), but do not add seam allowances because the edges of the door will be bound with tape. Draw the placement dots on the wrong side of the side piece on which the door is marked to the left of center. Do not cut out the door opening. Transfer the placement dots and quilting lines to the right side of the exterior cupcake side section (the one with the door to the right of center), marking the placement dots in the seam allowances. Then, using a pencil and ruler, draw each quilting line directly onto the right side of the fabric. Transfer the placement dots for the base (B) to the right side of one of the base pieces, marking the dots in the seam allowance. Mark the circle for the door knob on the front side of one of the door pieces; this will be the door front. Do not transfer the placement dots for the sign. Set the lining pieces aside.

ALL PATTERNS
ACTUAL SIZE

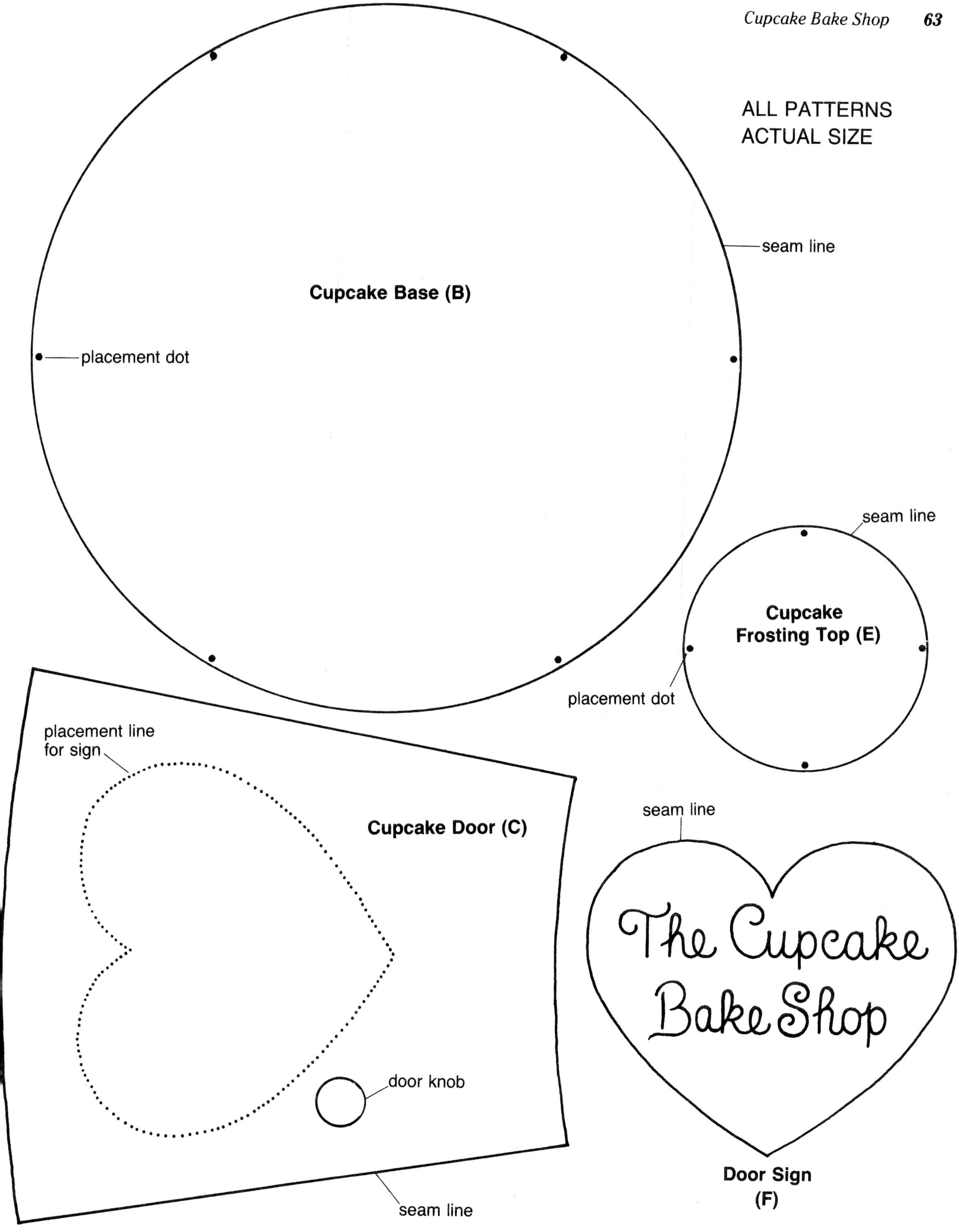

Cupcake Base (B)

seam line

placement dot

**Cupcake
Frosting Top (E)**

seam line

placement dot

placement line
for sign

Cupcake Door (C)

seam line

door knob

seam line

*The Cupcake
Bake Shop*

**Door Sign
(F)**

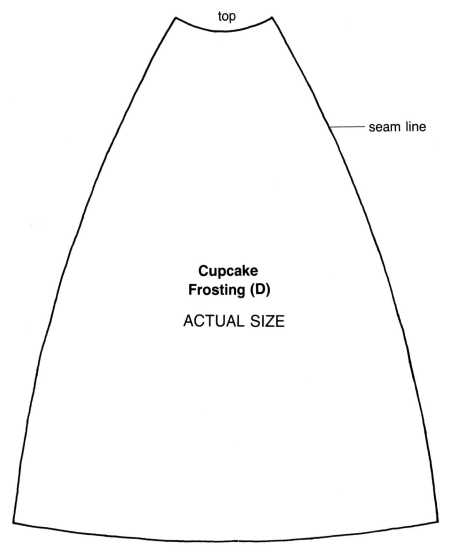

top

—— seam line

**Cupcake
Frosting (D)**

ACTUAL SIZE

bottom

3. Interfacing the side section— Cut a side (A) from the interfacing, adding a ¼″ seam allowance. Copy all placement dots and the door outline to the left of center. Baste the interfacing to the lining piece marked with the door to the left of center on the wrong side of the fabric aligning the door lines.

4. Cutting out the handle and frosting—To make the handle, cut a 2½″ × 8″ strip from one edge of the pink-and-white striped fabric and set it aside. Working on the wrong side of the same fabric, pin, trace, and cut out six frosting pieces (D), adding ¼″ seam allowances. On the wrong side of the white fabric, pin, trace, and cut out a frosting top (E), adding a ¼″ seam allowance.

5. Marking the door sign—Using a sharp soft pencil, go over the writing line on the back of the door sign pattern (F). Lay the pattern on the right side of the pink fabric, pen-cilled side down, and rub off the design with your fingernail. Trace the heart shape very lightly on the fabric. Remove the pattern, and, using a very sharp pencil on the fabric, go over the letters again. Set aside.

6. Assembling the cupcake lining—First machine staystitch ⅛″ outside the door opening on the side lining piece (A), the one on which the door is marked to the left of center on the interfacing side. Cut out the opening. Machine staystitch across the bottom of the side lining section, ¼″ from the edge.

Pin the ends of the side lining piece (A) right sides together and stitch. Press open the seam allowances. Clip at intervals along the bottom edge of the lining almost to the staystitching.

Pin the side lining (A) to the base lining (B), matching placement dots. Machine stitch. Trim the seam allowance to ⅛″, preferably with pink-

ing shears, and set aside.

Pin the six ginger-colored frosting sections (D), right sides together, along their sides, and stitch. Clip the seam allowances along the curves. Hand baste along the seam line around the top edge.

Hand or machine baste along the seam line of the ginger-colored frosting top (E). Clip the seam allowance in several places, almost to the seam line, turn under the seam allowance, and baste. Pin the ginger-colored frosting top to the top of the frosting side lining and join them with invisible hand stitches.

Pin the bottom edge of the frosting lining to the top edge of the cupcake side lining, right sides together, and machine stitch. Clip the seam allowance and press it as far open as possible. (Try steaming then finger pressing.)

8. Trimming the cupcake exterior side section—Pin the exterior cupcake side piece to a piece of quilt batting and baste around the edges. Cut off the excess batting. To keep the fabric from shifting during quilting, place several pins perpendicular to each quilting line. Quilt along the lines by hand or machine.

Machine stitch ¼″ outside the door opening line. Cut out the door opening along the pattern line and overcast the cut edges.

Cut a 14″ length of white bias tape and hand stitch one side of the tape along the door opening on the right side of the fabric, folding and mitering the tape at the corners.

Pin the ends of the side piece right sides together and stitch.

Cut a 29″ length of the eyelet ruffle and stitch the ends, right sides together. Pin and baste the ruffle to the top edge of the cupcake side, right sides together, aligning the ruffle seam with the back side seam, and machine stitch. Set aside.

Trim the seam allowance of the piping to ¼″. Baste a 20″ length of piping along the bottom right side of the cupcake side piece, aligning the cut edges. Machine stitch, using a presser foot attachment, along the edge of the piping. Clip the seam allowance at 1″ intervals almost to the stitching line.

9. Joining the cupcake exterior base and side pieces.—With the right side facing up, pin the base (B) to a piece of batting, and trim off the excess batting. Mark the placement dots on the batting by pushing a pin through the dots on the fabric and marking the pinholes on the batting with a pencil.

Pin the base to the lower edge of the cupcake side (A), right sides together and matching the dots, and machine stitch. Trim the seam allowance to ⅛". Set aside.

10. The frosting—Pin and baste each of the six striped frosting pieces (D), right side out, to quilt batting, and cut off the excess batting.

Cut six 6½" lengths of piping. Baste a strip of piping along both long curved edges of three of the frosting pieces. Machine stitch over the piping stitching line to provide a stitching guideline on the batting. Pin the frosting pieces, right sides together, along the sides, alternating the piped and unpiped pieces, and machine stitch. Clip the seam allowances along the curves and then turn the frosting right side out. Machine stitch ¼" from the lower edge.

11. Making the handle loop—Fold the 2½" × 8" piece of striped fabric lengthwise and right sides together to make a 1¼" × 8" strip. Machine stitch lengthwise along the open edges, leaving a ¼" seam allowance. Turn right side out and press flat. Machine topstitch lengthwise along both edges. Fold the handle softly into a loop so the cut edges meet, and then pin and baste the butted ends of the loop in place on top of one section of the frosting dome.

12. The frosting top—Hand baste the seam line on the frosting top (E). Clip the seam allowance at several intervals, turn it under to the wrong side, and baste in place. Remove the basting along the seam line. On the wrong side of the fabric, mark quarter sections of the frosting top with dots.

Cut a 12" length of the eyelet ruffle and take out stitches to undo the binding. Join the ends of the eyelet, right sides together, with a ¼" seam allowance. Mark dots close to the unfinished edge to indicate quarter sections. Hand baste along the former stitching line of the eyelet, then pull the thread to gather it into a ruffle. Pin the ruffle to the underside of the frosting top (E), matching the dots, and invisibly stitch them together.

Pin the ruffled top in place on top of the striped frosting piece, overlapping the handle, and invisibly stitch them together.

13. Joining the cupcake top and bottom—Turn the base/side unit inside out and place the top inside it, right sides together, making sure the handle is at the center back. Pin,

baste, and stitch, matching the lines of piping on the frosting to the back seam and quilting lines of the side. Clip the seam allowance. Carefully turn the cupcake right side out through the door opening. Gently poke and pull it into shape.

14. Attaching the lining—Turn the lining wrong side out, fold it to fit through the door opening, and push it through. Arrange the lining inside the cupcake by touch, aligning the seams. The lining will be lumpy. Match up the doorways, then pin and baste them together. Fold the tape that is along the door front around the edges to the inside lining and pin it in place through the front of the cupcake. Fold back the edges of the door to hand stitch the tape to the lining.

Tack the lining to the cupcake under the lace where each seam of the frosting meets the top of the side.

15. Finishing the door sign—Using a single strand of medium-green embroidery thread and an embroidery hoop, chainstitch the letters marked on the pink fabric. Cut the heart out of the fabric adding a ¼" seam allowance. If the fabric is sheer, cut out a second heart shape without a seam allowance and baste it to the back of the embroidered heart. Clip the seam allowance around the curves and clip into the V-shaped area at the top of the heart. Finger press the seam allowance toward the back and baste.

Cut a 10" length of piping and invisibly appliqué the edge of the heart to it, clipping the piping seam allowance along the curves and at the heart tip. Set aside.

16. Finishing the door—Using two strands of white embroidery thread, satin stitch the door knob marked on the door front.

Pin the door front right side out to a piece of quilt batting and baste them together ¼" from the edge. Trim the batting to fit the door front.

Pin the heart sign in place on the door front and invisibly appliqué it to the door, placing the stitches along the line where the heart and piping meet. Push a little quilt batting under the heart, if you want it to be extra puffy.

Pin and baste the door front to the door lining, wrong sides together.

Cut an 18" length of bias tape and hand stitch it around the door edges, front and back, mitering the corners.

Pin the door in place on the right

side of the door opening and stitch invisibly along the folded edge of bias tape. Attach a velcro fastener on the back side of the door knob area following the manufacturer's directions.

17. Making the rose—To make the stamens, cut two 3½" lengths of ⅛"-wide yellow satin ribbon and tightly knot both ends of each strip. Trim off any frayed ends of ribbon. Fold each ribbon in half across the middle, and finger press the folds. Set aside.

From the ⅜"-wide pink ribbon cut a 4½" length. From the ⅝"-wide pink ribbon cut a 6" length. From the 1"-wide ribbon cut a 7½" length.

One by one, softly fold each strip in half, end to end, and right sides together, and stitch across the ends leaving a ⅛" seam allowance. Turn each loop right side out, sew gathering stitches along one edge, pull the thread tightly to gather the ribbon into a rosette, and knot the thread.

Push the folded end of each stamen strip first through the center hole of the smallest rosette, then through the medium-sized rosette and the largest rosette setting one rosette inside the next. Pull all the stamens through the rosettes so that only the knots remain in sight on the front and tack the stamens to the back of the rosettes.

18. The leaves—Cut six 3" lengths of ⅝"-wide green ribbon. Lightly mark a line across the center on the wrong side of each strip. One at a time, lay each strip wrong or dull side up and then fold both ends down along the center line as shown in Figure 2, Drawing 1. Turn the ribbon over and tack the ends down at the center to the edge of ribbon behind them, as shown in Drawing 2. Turn the ribbon over again and join the inner edges with tiny stitches that won't show on the front, Drawing 3. Turn to the right side again and fold the side edges softly to the center back as in Drawing 4. Pinch the folds together toward the front and stitch across the bottom of the leaf ¼" inch from the edge, Drawing 5.

19. Attaching the rose—Using a stitch or two, tack a leaf, right side up, over the lace at each piping line on the frosting top so that the point of the leaf turns down and is aligned with the edge of the lace.

Set the rose in place on top of the leaves and pin securely with several pins set perpendicular to one another. Using pink thread, tack the

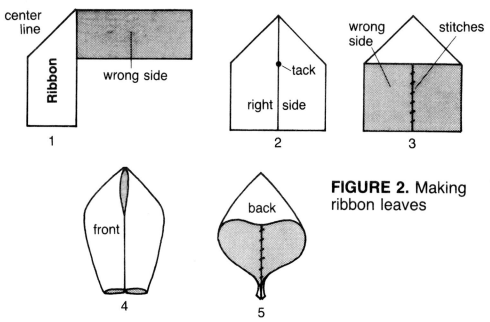

FIGURE 2. Making ribbon leaves

rose in place with one stitch at the center of each frosting section, placing the stitches at the edge of the white frosting topping next to the lace and knotting each tack securely on the front. Hold one hand inside the door opening to make this easier.

Cup each leaf a little to make it curl up slightly.

THE BEAR FAMILY

1. Making the bodies—Copy the patterns for the bodies and ears on tracing paper. Label the figures and cut them out. Using a sharp soft pencil, mark the facial features, dots, and neck, arm, and leg stitching lines on the patterns.

To make the bears, cut two 5½″ × 7″ ginger-colored fabric pieces. To make a bear front, pin the body pattern, face down, to the wrong side of one piece of fabric. Trace around the pattern, but don't cut the fabric. Transfer the two placement dots on the head. Transfer the features, neck, arm, and leg lines to the right side of the fabric by turning the pattern and fabric over and taping them, pattern down, to a bright window. Using a soft pencil, trace the details onto the right side of the fabric. Trace another body section for the back and transfer the dots on the head. Cut out the front and back pieces, adding carefully marked ⅝″ seam allowances.

Baste along the seam line between the dots on the head on both pieces of fabric for each bear to provide a guideline for turning under and stitching the head seam after stuffing the bear. Set the pieces aside.

2. The ears—To make the bears' ears, cut a 3″ × 5″ piece of ginger-colored fabric. Fold the fabric in half lengthwise, right sides together, and trace two ears for each bear. Keeping the fabric folded, machine stitch along the curved edge of each ear, using very tiny stitches. Cut out the ear, leaving a ¼″ seam allowance. Trim the curved seam allowance to ⅛″, preferably with pinking shears, or clip the seam allowance after trimming it. Using a crochet hook, turn each ear right side out. Finger press the ear flat. Hand baste along the open edge of the ear on the seam line and slightly pull the thread until the opening is about ⅞″ across for Mama and Papa Bear, or ½″ across for Baby Bear. Knot the thread and set the ears aside.

3. Joining and finishing the body sections—Pin the front and back for each bear right sides together. Using very tiny stitches and leaving open the space between the dots on the head, machine stitch along the seam line of each bear. Trim the seam allowances to ¼″ between the dots on the head and to ⅛″ elsewhere. Clip around the curves and into the V-shaped areas.

Gently turn the bear right side out through the head opening, using a crochet hook to push in the legs and arms. Pull gently to shape and flatten the puckers. Clip the seam allowance along the opening. Using a crochet hook, push stuffing into the bear, but keep its figure flat. Turn under the seam allowance above the front and back head opening and baste each one in place. Remove the bastings along the seam line.

Pin each ear in place on the head front and invisibly stitch to the front section only. Push extra stuffing into the head, if necessary.

Pin the head opening closed and stitch invisibly.

Topstitch by hand along the leg, neck, and arm lines using tiny stitches of ginger-colored thread. To make even lines, turn the bear over each time you pass the needle through it.

4. The face—Using one strand of embroidery thread, satin stitch the cheeks with pink thread and the eyes and nose with black thread. Backstitch the mouth and eyebrows with black thread.

PAPA BEAR'S CLOTHES

1. The patterns—Trace the apron and hat crown patterns from the book onto tracing paper, copying all the lines and placement dots.

2. The hat—Trace the hat crown and its placement dots onto the wrong side of the white fabric. Cut out the crown, adding a ¼″ seam allowance. Machine baste along the seam line and pull the thread to gather the hat tightly. Secure the thread.

Softly fold the 3½″ length of bias tape or ribbon in half crosswise, right sides together and stitch across the ends leaving a ¼″ seam allowance. Mark the edge of the tape or ribbon into quarters with dots on the wrong side. Pin the tape or ribbon to the gathered edge of the crown, overlapping the seam allowance and matching the placement dots, and stitch invisibly.

Topstitch along both edges of the tape or ribbon with tiny green running stitches. Push a small amount of batting into the hat and stitch the hat invisibly to the bear's head.

3. The apron—Fold the remaining white fabric in half lengthwise and place the bottom of the apron pattern along the fold. Pin, trace, and cut out the apron, adding a ¼″ seam allowance. Open the fabric out; the shape above the fold is the apron front and the shape below the fold is the apron back. Center the pattern on the right side of the apron front and transfer the heart motif. Center the pattern on the right side of the apron back and mark the pocket lines. (When completed, the pockets will fold to the apron front.)

Fold the apron right sides together and machine stitch along the seam line, leaving it open below the dot on one side. Trim the seam allowances to ⅛″ above the dot, clip

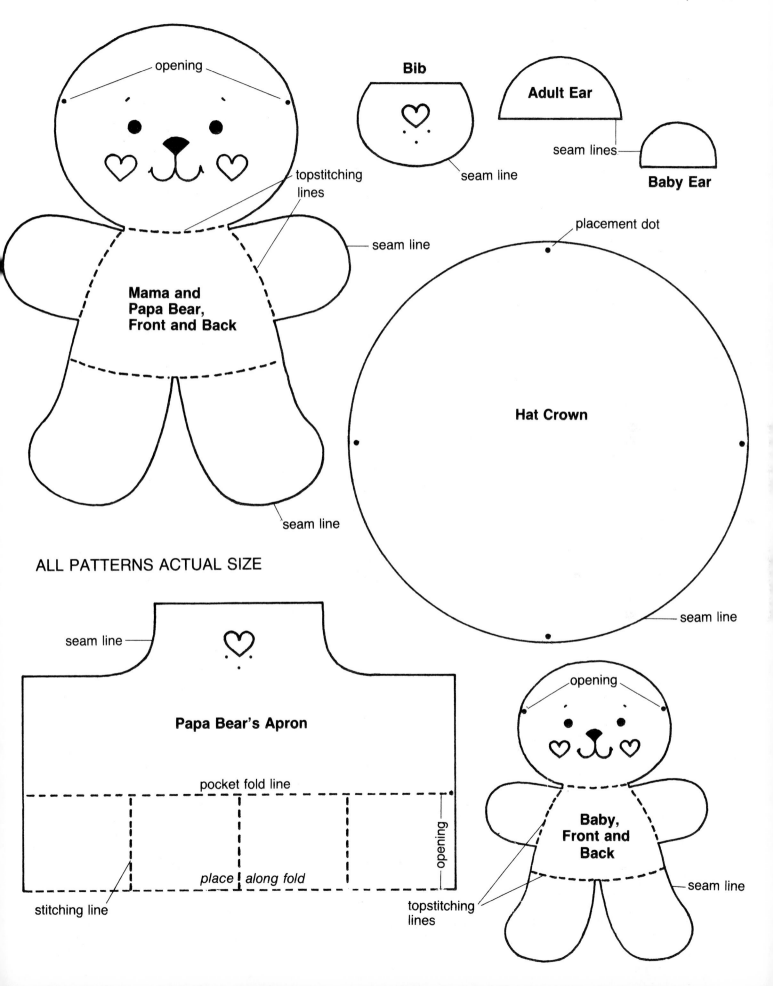

opening

Bib

Adult Ear

seam lines

Baby Ear

seam line

topstitching lines

seam line

Mama and Papa Bear, Front and Back

placement dot

Hat Crown

seam line

seam line

ALL PATTERNS ACTUAL SIZE

seam line

Papa Bear's Apron

pocket fold line

place | along fold

opening

stitching line

opening

Baby, Front and Back

seam line

topstitching lines

them along the curves, and clip off the corners. Turn the apron right side out through the opening. Press. Using tiny green running stitches topstitch along the bottom of the apron. Fold the bottom up toward the front along the dotted line to make a pocket and pin in place.

Using tiny green running stitches, topstitch along the edges of the pocket and apron, but not the lower edge.

Using one strand of pink embroidery thread, satin stitch the heart on the apron top. Using green embroidery thread, make lazy daisy stitches for leaves below the heart.

Stitch together the lengthwise open edges of the ¼"-wide bias tape or use grosgrain ribbon as is. Cut two 5" lengths for waist ties and a 2½" length for the neck strap. Knot one end of each 5" strip and tack the cut end to the underside of the back of the apron, one strip on each side. Pin the apron in place on the bear. Pin the ends of the neck strap to the underside of the front top, one on each corner, overlapping the strap by about ¼". Tack the strap in place. Tie a bow at the waist back.

MAMA BEAR'S DRESS

1. The dress bodice—Cut a 1½" × 2½" strip from the pink floral fabric. Fold it in half crosswise, wrong sides together, and press it flat. Baste the cut edges together and set aside.

To make the shoulder straps, cut two 2⅝" lengths of the ¼"-wide green ribbon and position one on each side of the bodice, right side up, so the ribbon overlaps the edge by about ⅛" and extends above the folded edge of the bodice (see Figure 3). Attach them with tiny hand stitches. Cut two 2⅝" lengths of lace ruffle and attach one under the outer edge of each ribbon with tiny stitches.

2. The skirt—Cut a 2" × 8¾" strip from the remaining floral fabric, fold it in half lengthwise, right sides together. Stitch the ends closed leaving a ¼" seam allowance. Clip off the corners of the seam allowance, turn the skirt right side out, and press flat. Mark the center of the long open edges with a dot, then machine baste them together leaving a ⅛" seam allowance. Pull the threads to gather the fabric to a length of about 4¼"; tie the threads securely.

Cut a 9"-long strip of the lace ruffle and invisibly stitch it to the underside of the lower edge of the skirt, turning under both ends.

To make the waistband, cut a 12"

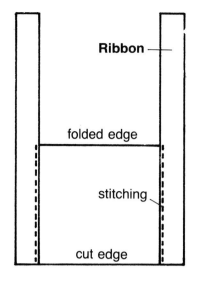

FIGURE 3. Mama Bear's dress bodice

length of the green ribbon and mark the center point. Center the ribbon right side up, on the right side of the gathered skirt top, overlapping the edge of the skirt by about ⅛", and hand stitch the ribbon in place along its edge.

3. Finishing the dress—Center the skirt top on the bodice, overlapping the bodice by about ¼", and join them with tiny stitches. Position the free end of each strap about ½" from the corresponding back edge of the skirt so the waistband overlaps it by about ¼" and sew in place. (It's actually best to pin-fit the dress on the bear and then remove it for sewing.)

Cut a 4½" length of the ½"-wide lace and invisibly stitch it along the inside edge of the straps and neckline. Ease in any extra fullness at the shoulder/neck point.

4. The flower—Using a 3½" length of ¼"-wide pink satin ribbon, make a single-layer rosette following Step 17 of the cupcake instructions.

Make the stamen by knotting one end of a 2" length of yellow ribbon. Trim the ribbon to ½", thread the cut end through the center of the rosette, and tack it to the back.

Make the leaves by cutting the remaining ¼"-wide green ribbon into three 1½" lengths and following Step 18 of the cupcake directions.

Attach the leaves to the back of the flower, and then tack the flower to the bear's ear. If necessary, tack the edge of the flower to the ear to conceal the leaf ends.

BABY BEAR'S CLOTHES

1. The bib—To make the bib, trace the pattern and its details from the book onto tracing paper. Cut the green scrap into two 2" × 3" pieces. On the wrong side of one piece, trace the outline of the bib. Hand baste along the outline. Darken the heart on the pattern with a sharp soft pencil. Hold the pattern in position on the right side of the bib front and rub the heart to transfer its shape to the fabric. Remove the bastings, but don't cut out the bib.

Pin the two green fabric pieces right sides together. Machine stitch along the curved line on the marked piece using tiny stitches. Trim the curved seam allowance to ⅛" and clip. Trim the seam allowance along the straight edge to ¼". Turn the bib right side out. Tuck in the top seam allowance and invisibly stitch the seam closed. Press flat. Using a single strand of green embroidery thread, embroider the leaves with lazy daisy stitches. Satin stitch the heart with pink embroidery thread.

Stitch ½"-wide white lace along the curved edge of the bib, and cover the seam with a strip of pink rickrack.

Cut two 4" lengths of ⅛"-wide pink satin ribbon, and tack one on each side of the bib top. Pin the bib on the bear and invisibly stitch it in place. Tie the bib at the back and trim the ribbon ends.

2. The bow—Tie the remaining pink ribbon into a very small bow. Stitch the bow at the center, pull tightly, then wrap thread around the center to pinch the bow, and secure the thread. Trim the ribbon ends and tack the bow to the bear's ear.

Rainbow Quilt

When our daughter was four years old she had some especially endearing ways to tell us how much she loved us. One of my favorites was a bedtime ritual that always followed the final tuck-in and goodnight kiss. "Mommy", she would call as I left the room. "I love you! You're a heart and a rainbow and a sun!" Tracy inspired this quilt, and it's my lasting response to her for the many times she called out that lovely affirmation! It symbolizes my wish that I might always be a continuous source of love (the hearts), hope (the rainbow) and warmth (the sun) in her life in the years to come.

If you would like to make the quilt, keep in mind that it doesn't need to "say" anything at all. The directions have been written for the quilt just as it appears in the

photograph, but it looks fine without any words and without the blanket stitches. You can machine or hand appliqué it, and you can machine or hand quilt it. Since I have provided an entire alphabet with the directions, you can stitch any message at all. If you change the number of lines, however, experiment with the spacing between them.

The blanket stitching is a lovely finishing touch, but it will take a very, very long time and while you're working you'll probably wonder more than once, as I did, why you ever started it in the first place! If you're still convinced that you want to do it, be sure to use a very light-weight (about ¼″ thick) batting or you'll have a real problem when you try to blanket stitch together the edges of the quilt.

Use only permanent press fabrics that don't fray easily and wash every piece before you cut it. I used batiste to back the appliqués, because the strong turquoise background showed through the lighter colors and made them look murky. The finished size of this quilt is an unorthodox 52½″ × 63″. It's not really a baby quilt, and it's not really a twin quilt. It's a kid quilt!

Materials

A 15″ × 15″ piece, or ½ yard, yellow fabric
A 9″ × 18″ piece, or ⅛ yard, yellow-orange fabric
A 13½″ × 27″ piece, or ⅜ yard, orange fabric
A 13½″ × 31″ piece, or ⅜ yard, brilliant pink fabric
A 13½″ × 36″ piece, or ⅜ yard, magenta fabric
A 13½″ × 40″ piece, or ⅜ yard, purple fabric
1⅝ yards 44″-wide turquoise fabric
3⅛ yards 44″-wide green fabric
1⅜ yards 44″-wide white batiste, optional

A 54″ × 64″ piece of polyester quilt batting
6-ply embroidery thread: 20 skeins white, optional; 6 yards black; 1 yard brilliant pink
Sewing thread: spools to match all fabrics and white

Equipment

3 pieces (five, if you are using lettering) of 15″ × 20″ tracing paper
A box of quilter's pins
A white marking pencil
A large-eyed needle

1. Making the patterns—Fold a 15″ × 15″ piece of tracing paper into

quarters, trace a quarter section of the sun pattern with the dots and features. Complete the pattern, making a full circle and tracing the dots on all the sections; cut out the pattern. To make a template, cut out the eyes and cheeks on the sun face pattern. Also cut along the mouth line. All pattern lines are stitching lines, so add ¼″ seam allowances when cutting fabric.

Trace each rainbow band pattern onto folded tracing paper, label the pattern with the band number and color, and cut out the pattern.

Trace patterns for the cheek and sun ray, label each, and cut them out. Trace four border heart patterns with number placement

A Rainbow Quilt with a personal message of love.

guidelines spaced 2¼″ apart. Center and trace one digit of the date on each heart.

Draw letter guidelines spaced 2¼″ apart on 4″ × 20″ strips of tracing paper. Then trace the letters of your choice onto the strips. Tape the strips together so the words end flush right with a ¾″-wide right hand margin and a 1⅜″ space between each line. Using a soft pencil, darken the back of each letter. Set aside.

2. Cutting the background fabric—Measure and trim away ¼″ from each selvage edge of the turquoise background fabric. Cut a 42½″ × 53″ piece for the quilt background; these dimensions include a ¼″ seam allowance. Set aside.

Measure and trim away ¼″ from each selvage edge of the green backing/border fabric. Referring to Figure 1, cut two 32″ × 53″ green backing sections and four 5¾″ × 53″ border pieces. All dimensions include a ¼″ seam allowance. Pin and stitch the lengthwise edges of the backing sections right sides together to make a 53″ × 63½″ piece. Set aside.

(continued)

ALL PATTERNS
ACTUAL SIZE

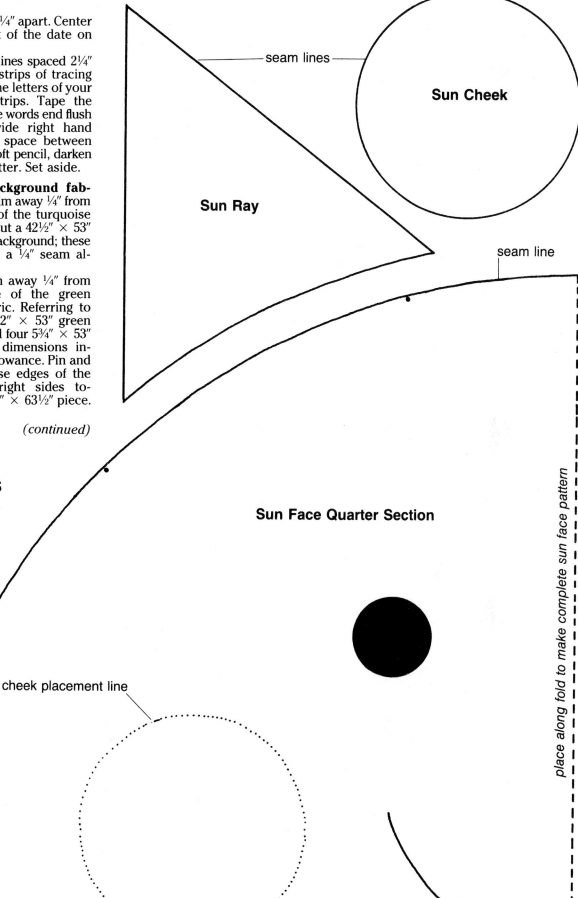

seam lines

Sun Cheek

Sun Ray

seam line

Sun Face Quarter Section

place along fold to make complete sun face pattern

cheek placement line

place along fold to make complete sun face pattern

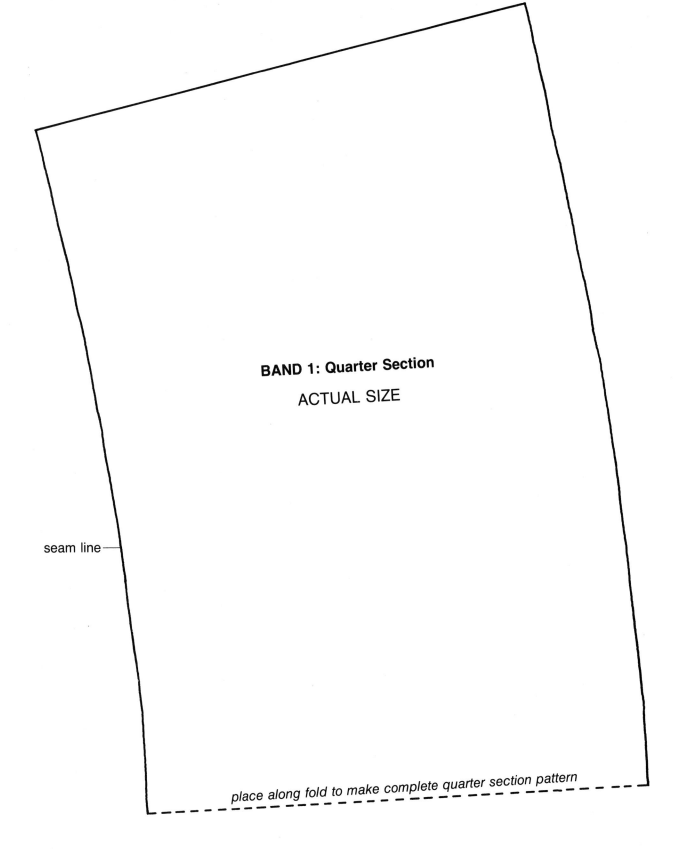

BAND 1: Quarter Section

ACTUAL SIZE

seam line

place along fold to make complete quarter section pattern

3. Making the sun face—Pin the sun face pattern to the wrong side of the yellow fabric and lightly trace the outline, dots, and features. Cut out the sun face adding a ¼″ seam allowance. Using tiny basting stitches, transfer the outline and features to the front of the fabric. Mark the dots on the front with pins or small bastings. Clip the seam allowance almost to the seam line, finger press it to the back to make a hem and baste.

From the brilliant pink fabric, trace and cut out two cheeks. Transfer the seam line to the front of the fabric with bastings. Clip, finger press, and baste the seam allowances. Pin the cheeks in place on the sun face, invisibly appliqué them, and edge them with white blanket stitches, if desired. Using a full 6-ply strand of embroidery thread, satin stitch black eyes and chain stitch a pink mouth. Make twelve tracings of the sun ray pattern on the back of the yellow-orange fabric, spacing them ½″ apart, and cut them out, adding a ¼″ seam allowance to each. Finger press the seam allowances to the back along the straight edges by first folding the tip down to the seam allowance line and then folding in the sides. This will make neat points. Pin the sun rays in position around the sun face. Invisibly stitch the rays to the sun and, if desired, edge the face with white blanket stitches. Set aside.

4. Making the rainbow—On the back of each rainbow fabric, trace four times around each rainbow band section as follows, saving the scraps for the border hearts and adding a ¼″ seam allowance to each piece: four each, purple band 1 sections, magenta band 2 sections, pink band 3 sections, and orange band 4 sections.

Pin and stitch the four pieces of each color end to end and right sides together to make four long rainbow bands. Press open the seam allowances. Using basting stitches, transfer the seam lines to the front of each band. Finger press and baste under both curved seam allowances on the orange band. On the remaining bands, baste only the seam allowance along the top curved edge.

To join the bands, lay the purple band on a flat surface. Overlap the bottom cut edge of the purple band with the top hemmed edge of the magenta band. Match the seams, pin, and invisibly stitch them together.

(continued)

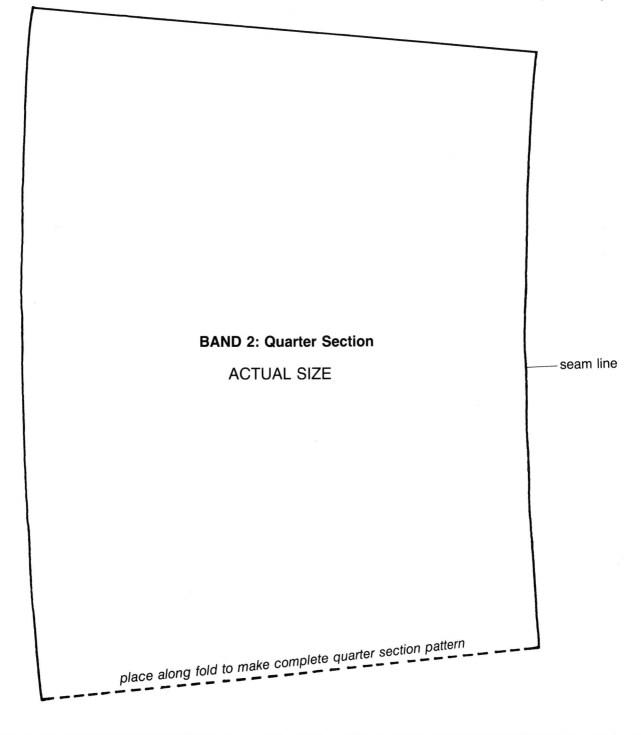

BAND 2: Quarter Section

ACTUAL SIZE

— seam line

place along fold to make complete quarter section pattern

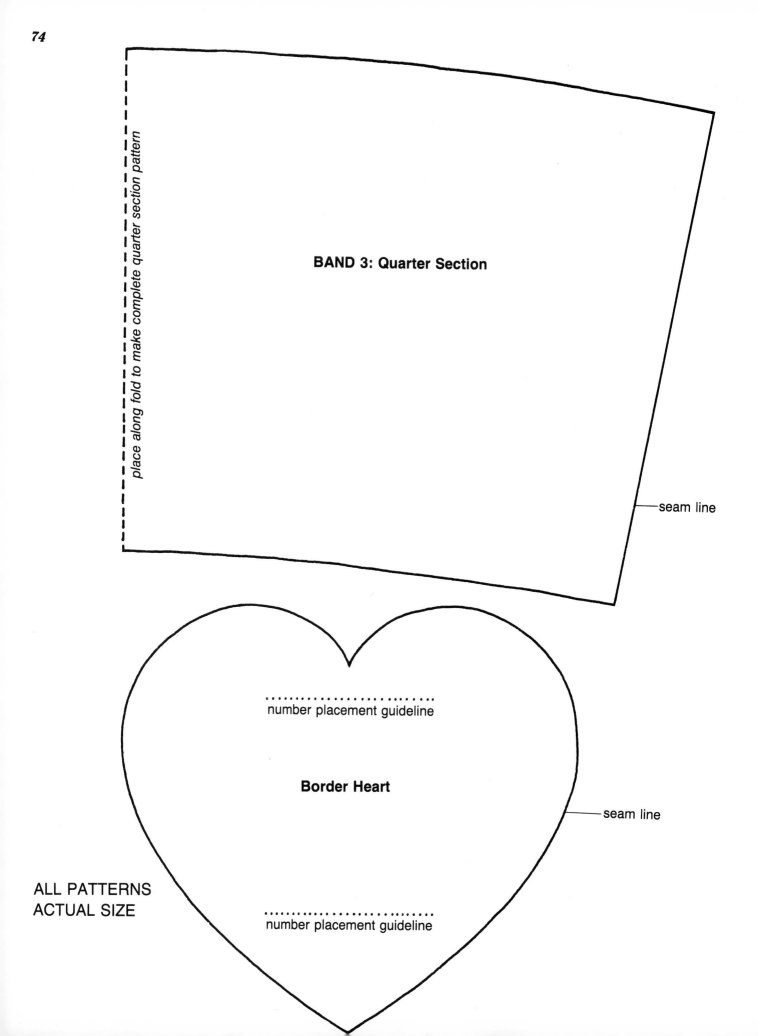

place along fold to make complete quarter section pattern

BAND 3: Quarter Section

seam line

number placement guideline

Border Heart

ALL PATTERNS
ACTUAL SIZE

seam line

number placement guideline

Similarly attach the pink and then the orange band. If desired, add white blanket stitches between the rows.

5. The border hearts—On the back of a scrap of each rainbow fabric, trace one border heart with a number in reverse centered in it, but don't cut out the heart. Transfer the seam line and number to the front of the fabric with bastings. Using a full 6-ply strand of white embroidery thread, chain stitch each number (see *Embroidery Stitches*). Cut out each heart, adding a ¼″ seam allowance. Clip the seam allowance almost to the seam line, finger press to the back, and baste. Set the hearts aside.

6. Adding the backing—Back the rainbow, sun, and hearts with ba-tiste or, if desired, very, very thin batting scraps. Baste the layers together and trim away any excess, if necessary. Cut the batiste without a seam allowance and tack it on the back of the fabric pieces at a few strategic but inconspicuous spots so the layers will be permanently attached together.

(continued)

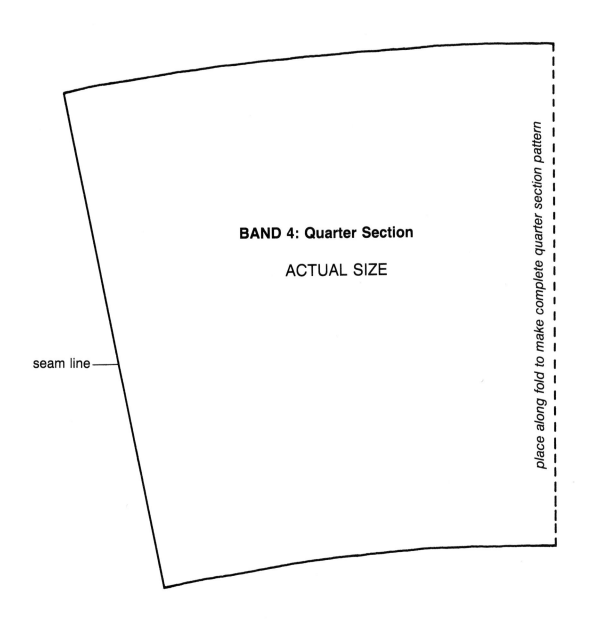

seam line

BAND 4: Quarter Section

ACTUAL SIZE

place along fold to make complete quarter section pattern

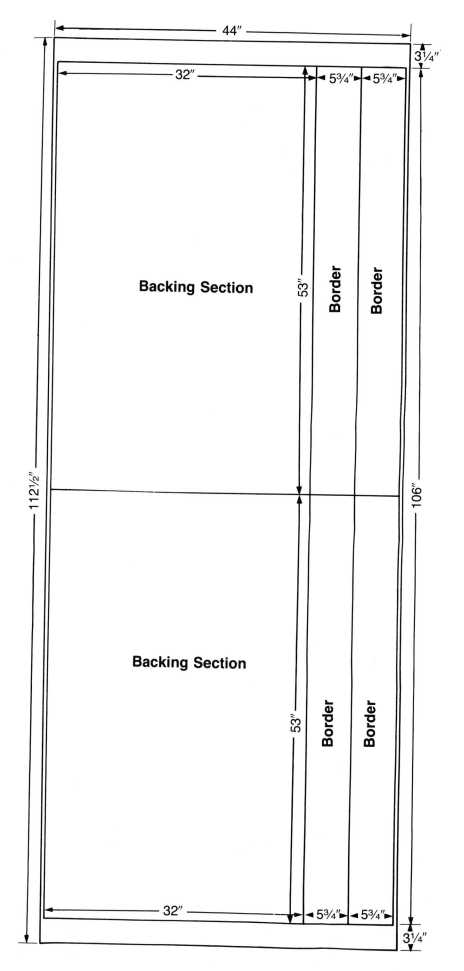

FIGURE 1. Layout for backing sections and border pieces

7. Assembling the quilt top—Lay the turquoise background fabric right side up on a flat surface. Referring to Figure 2, mark the rainbow placement points with pins as follows. Starting at the lower left corner, place a pin ¼″ and 21¼″ in from the left side on the bottom edge. On the right edge, place a pin 21¼″ up from the bottom and 10¾″ down from the top. Pin the completed rainbow in position within these markings and appliqué it invisibly to the background fabric. If you wish, edge the rainbow with white blanket stitches.

Pin a green border piece, right sides together, to each long side edge of the turquoise background section. Machine stitch and press open the seam allowances. Similarly, pin, stitch, and press the remaining border pieces to the top and bottom.

Lay the quilt top, right side up, on a flat surface. Referring to Figure 3, mark the sun placement points with two pins: one 10½″ from the upper left corner of the turquoise backing along the top edge and the other 10½″ down from the same corner along the left edge of the turquoise fabric. Pin the sun to the turquoise fabric backing so that a ray tip touches each of the pins and a ray touches the rainbow. Invisibly appliqué the sun in place. If desired, edge the sun with white blanket stitches.

8. Lettering the quilt—Pin the top lettering pattern to the area above the rainbow, placing the highest line 3″ below the top border seam and ¾″ to the left of the right border seam. Pin the bottom lettering pattern to the area below the rainbow, placing the lowest line 2½″ above the bottom border seam and ¾″ to the left of the right border seam. Adjust these measurements if you use a different number of lines. Rub off the lettering onto the fabric. Remove the patterns and redraw any incomplete areas. Using 6-ply white embroidery thread, chain stitch the letters.

9. Quilting—Place the quilt top and quilt backing fabric right sides together over a piece of batting. Pin around all the edges and machine stitch ¼″ in from the edge, leaving a 15″-long opening along one edge for turning. Clip off the corners and turn the quilt right side out. Spread the quilt out on a flat surface. Using lots of pins, pin around the quilt sides to flatten and place the seam exactly on the edge. Baste around the edge. Insert pins within the quilt design area to keep the layers together. Baste horizontally, vertically, and diagonally to prevent shifting of the layers when you quilt. Quilt on or close to the design lines and border. If you wish, finish both edges of the border with white blanket stitches.

10. Finishing touches—Pin the border hearts in place and invisibly appliqué them. If desired, add white blanket stitches around the edges.

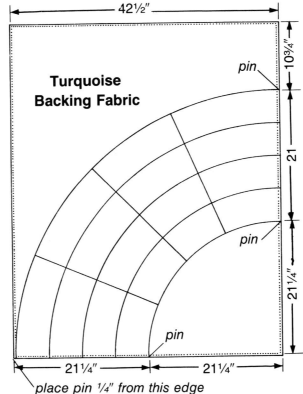

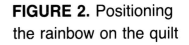

FIGURE 2. Positioning the rainbow on the quilt

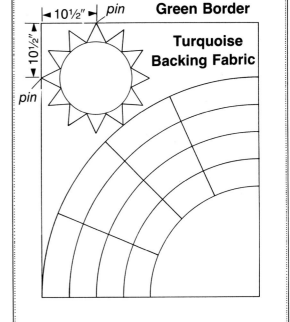

FIGURE 3. Positioning the sun on the quilt top

ACTUAL SIZE

ACTUAL SIZE

ACTUAL SIZE

Stitchery
for
the
Home

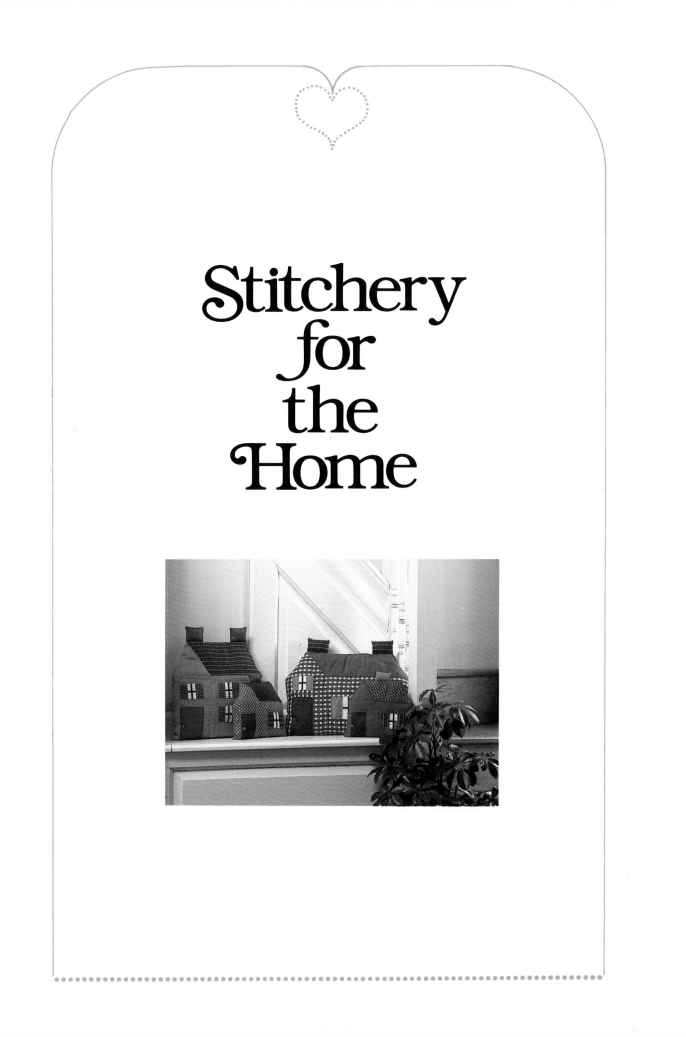

Proud Lion is a creature of many talents, who will become a faithful sewing companion. His generous 7"-diameter size holds a lion's share of needles and pins, and there's a pocket on the back that is just right for holding your embroidery thread, instruction sheets, and such. The ribbon-backed tape measure that joins the pincushion and scissors can be draped around your neck so that when you sit down, all your sewing needs will rest on your lap and be right at hand.

The inexpensive plastic craft scissors I used are specially designed for safe use by children, but they do have a metal cutting edge that's suitable for trimming threads. I stitched the loop in place that holds the scissors,

Proud Lion Pincushion

but you may wish to use a snap or velcro fastener so you can attach whatever type of scissors you'll need.

The tape measure is cut at 55", but if you're of more or less than average size, adjust the tape and ribbon lengths accordingly. For the best look, match the colors of the

tape and ribbon you choose.

Without the pins, tape measure, and scissors, this design lends itself to several other uses. Because of the small size and the pocket on the back, you can use the pattern to make a perfectly beastly tooth fairy pillow. To stitch a cuddly crib toy or a bib appliqué, use a collection of soft or bright prints to piece the mane. If making a crib toy, consider using different colors and different faces on each side—happy and sad, or awake and asleep—and add a small ribbon loop so the lion can be carried or dragged around easily. You can also pad the completed lion with quilt batting, back it, and make a potholder, or add a lining and bias tape shoulder straps to make a pet purse.

Materials
A 9" × 15" red or yellow with white floral fabric scrap
A 9" × 15" red or yellow with white dot fabric scrap
A 5" × 7" red or yellow fabric scrap
A 5" × 7" white fabric scrap
Sewing thread: red or yellow and white
35" white medium-sized rickrack
2 yards 6-ply black embroidery thread
Polyester stuffing
Red or yellow tape measure
1¾ yards of ⅝"-wide red or yellow grosgrain ribbon
18 white or black ball-headed straight pins
Safety scissors

Equipment
A 4" or 5" embroidery hoop

1. Making the patterns and cutting the fabric—Trace and label all the patterns on page 85, copying all the features and matching dots. The pattern lines include ¼" seam allowances.

From each red or yellow print cut nine lion mane sections, then fold the remaining piece of each print and cut one back pocket piece from each.

From the solid red or yellow scrap cut one face section, then flip the pattern so it faces in the opposite direction and cut a second face section. Transfer an eye onto the front of each piece. Also draw, but don't cut out, two red or yellow ear pieces.

From the white fabric, cut one

nose and one jaw piece, and transfer the facial details to the fabric front. Reserve the remaining white fabric for finishing the ears.

2. The ears—To make the ears, lightly draw stitching guide lines on the wrong side of the red or yellow fabric ¼" inside each ear shape. Pin both ear sections to the remaining white fabric, right sides together, and, using small machine stitches, join the two layers, leaving the bottom open. Trim the seam allowances ⅛" from the stitching line along the curved edges. Trim the fabric along the bottom edge to leave a ¼" seam allowance. Clip the seam allowances along the curves or trim them with pinking shears. Turn the ears right side out and finger press them flat. Baste the bottom edges of the

ears closed along the seam line, without tucking in the seam allowances. Set aside.

3. The mane—To make the mane, stitch the mane pieces, right sides together, along the side edges, alternating the prints, to make a ring of eighteen pieces. (It is not necessary to pin the pieces before stitching them.) Press open the seam allowances. Baste ¼″ from the inner edge of the mane. Baste rickrack along the outer right side edge of the mane along the seamline and then secure it by machine stitching ¼″ from the edge. Set aside.

4. Making and attaching the face—To make the face, stitch one side of the face along the center line to the side of the nose, right sides together. Similarly, stitch the other side of the face to the nose. Press open the seam allowances. Stitch the jaw to the bottom of the upper face, right sides together, and press open the seam allowances. Baste around the face on the seam line and clip the seam allowance nearly to the bastings. Finger press the seam allowance to the back of the face and baste. Pin and baste the head in place on the mane section, matching the seams of both. Insert the ears between the mane and face, centered behind the face sections, and pin. Invisibly appliqué the face to the mane using matching thread and making the stitches very close together.

Using two strands of black embroidery thread, embroider the eyes and nose with padded satin stitches and the eyelashes and eyebrows with straight stitches. Using one strand of black embroidery thread, chain stitch the mouth and make French knot whiskers.

5. The pocket—Choose one back/pocket piece for the pocket and reserve the other for use as the pincushion back. Crease the pocket fabric along the center fold line, open the fabric, and mark the line with bastings. On the right side of the fabric, machine stitch rickrack on top of the bastings. Refold and press the pocket section so that only one edge of rickrack and no stitches show. Baste the pocket to the right side of the pincushion back along the curved edge.

6. Joining the front and back of the pincushion—Pin and baste the front and back of the pincushion, right sides together, matching the pocket top fold to the seams on the mane. Machine stitch on the front side, using the rickrack stitching line as a guide and leaving open the space between two adjoining mane sections for turning. Trim the seam allowances, except along the opening, to ⅛″ with pinking shears or clip along the curves after trimming.

Turn the pincushion right side out. Turn under the seam allowances, separately, along the opening. Pack stuffing very firmly into the pincushion and stitch the opening closed invisibly.

7. Attaching the tape measure and scissors and adding the pins—Remove the metal piece from the end of the measuring tape and cut the tape at the 55″ mark. Cut the red or yellow ribbon to a length of 57¾″. Place the tape over the ribbon, extending the ribbon 2⅜″ beyond the tape at the 1″ end and ⅜″ beyond the tape at the 55″ end. Machine stitch the tape to the ribbon along both lengthwise edges, and, for best results, stitch the edges in same direction. Fold the ⅜″-long ribbon end toward the tape front and securely stitch the ribbon edges to the back center top of the pincushion so the tape is facing toward the lion's front. Insert the 2⅜″-long ribbon end, front to back, through one of the scissor handles, turn under ⅝″ of ribbon at the cut end, and then secure the end invisibly to the ribbon back.

Place a white or black ball-headed straight pin where each mane seam joins the face in the pincushion.

A Proud Lion Pincushion being put to use by the author.

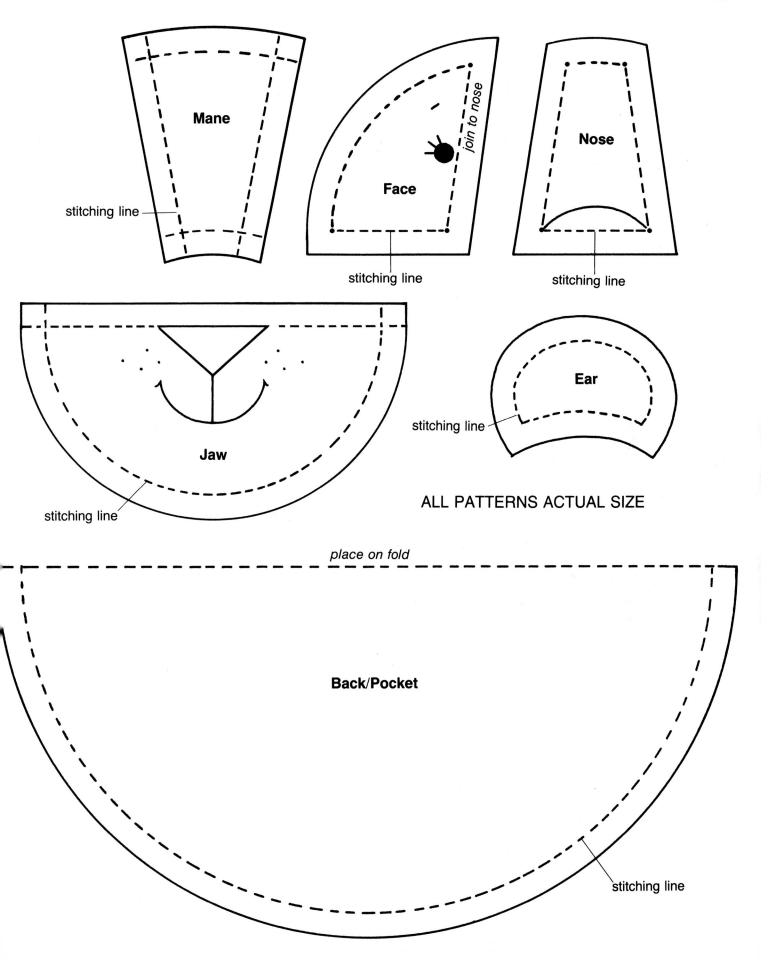

Mane

stitching line

Face

join to nose

Nose

stitching line

stitching line

Jaw

Ear

stitching line

stitching line

ALL PATTERNS ACTUAL SIZE

place on fold

Back/Pocket

stitching line

Old Homestead Accessories

Each of these easy-to-make patchwork designs is based on the traditional Old Homestead quilt block. All of the patterns do double duty, so in addition to constructing a pillow village, you can use them to make other gifts as well. For example, the small square house pattern also makes a perfect potholder, and the rectangular house pattern made in Christmas fabrics can be turned into holiday place mats.

Using different colors and trims, you can even design a set of house portrait place mats for an extra-special personalized gift. The large square house pattern can be used for a needlework bag. Whatever their end use, it's always advisable to pre-shrink all washable fabrics for any sewing project, and it's especially important for this place mat design.

As to sizes, the square pot-holder is about 8¼" × 9¼",

and the finished size of the square house pillow is about 7" × 8". The rectangular house pillow is about 11½" × 17", and the place mat is 12½" × 17". The large square house pillow is about 13" × 13", and the tote is approximately 14¼" × 14¼", excluding the handles.

The houses can be made quite simply, or they can be embellished with quilting, grosgrain ribbon window mullions and lace trim.

GENERAL DIRECTIONS FOR THE SMALL SQUARE HOUSE PATCHWORK

(to be used with specific directions for potholder or pillow)

1. Making the patterns and cutting the fabric—Trace the patterns, copying all the dots and window mullion placement lines. Label each pattern, and cut it out; the pattern lines include ¼″ seam allowances. Trace around the patterns on the wrong side of the specified fabrics, but make sure to flip the roof pattern so it faces in the opposite direction from that in the book before tracing its outline.

2. Trimming the window—Cut the ribbon into a 1½″-long and a 2½″-long strip and hand stitch them along the appropriate trim placement lines on the window section (G) to make mullions.

3. Assembling the house—Referring to Figure 1, arrange the pieces in order on a flat surface. Working from left to right and top to bottom, join the pieces right sides together as follows, pressing open the seam allowances as you work:

a) Join the roof peak (A) to the roof (B), matching the dots.

b) Join the top end (C) piece to one of the side (D) pieces, end to end.

c) Make the door unit by joining one of the bottom end (E) pieces to each side of the door (F).

d) Make the window unit by joining the window (G) pieces along their sides.

e) Join the remaining side (D) piece to the lower edge of the window strip.

f) Join the window/side unit to the door unit.

g) Join the roof unit to the top end/side (C/D) strip.

h) Join the lower house to the upper house.

4. Quilting the house—If you are quilting the house, place it right side up on top of a piece of batting. Pin and baste them together ¼″ from the edge. Hand or machine quilt on or next to the seam lines illustrated in Figure 2. If you wish, add other decorative lines of stitching such as door panels. Cut out the house. Reserve the batting scraps for the chimney.

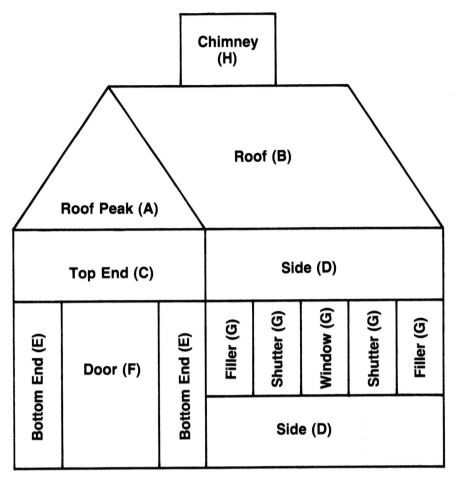

FIGURE 1: Small Square House pattern piece layout

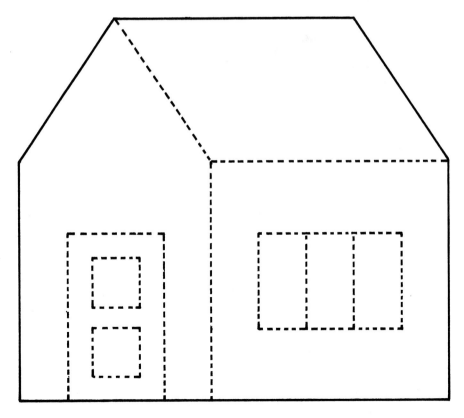

FIGURE 2. Small Square House quilting guide

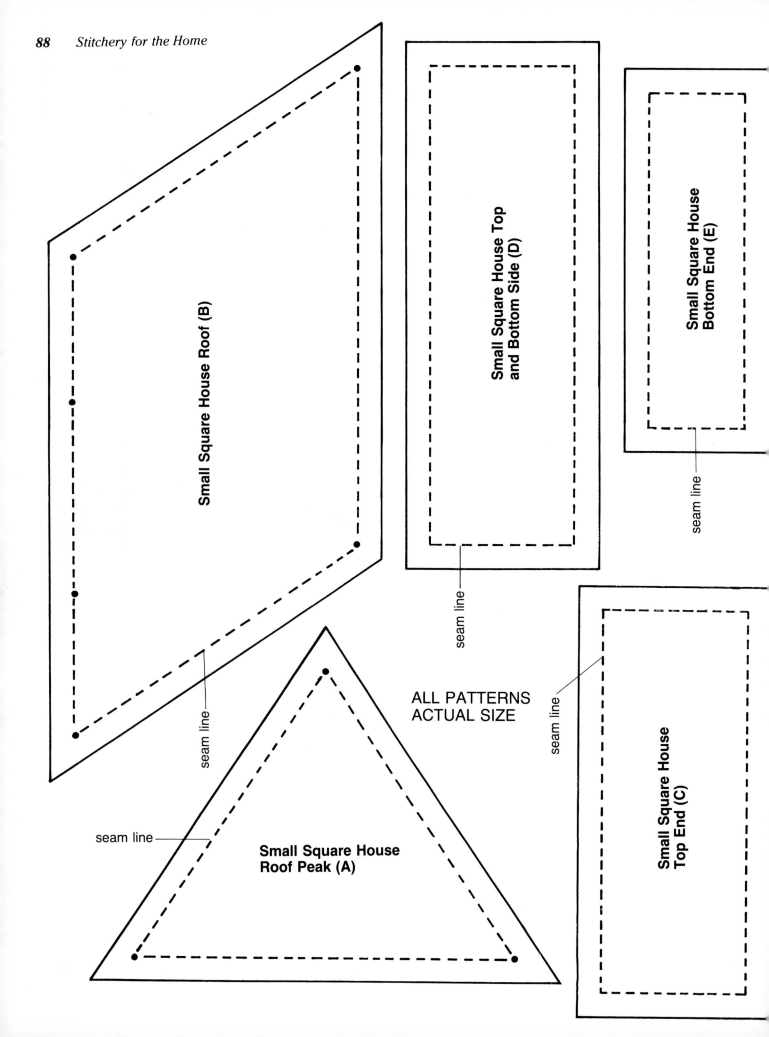

Small Square House Roof (B)

seam line

Small Square House Top and Bottom Side (D)

seam line

Small Square House Bottom End (E)

seam line

ALL PATTERNS ACTUAL SIZE

seam line

seam line

Small Square House Roof Peak (A)

Small Square House Top End (C)

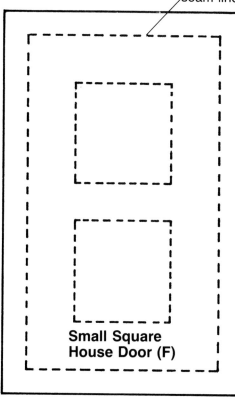

seam line

**Small Square
House Door (F)**

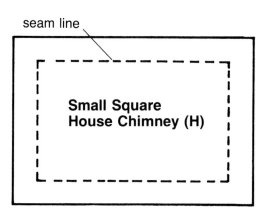

seam line

**Small Square
House Chimney (H)**

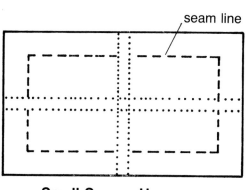

seam line

**Small Square House
Window/Shutter/Filler (G)**

A Small Square House Potholder is a pretty aid for carrying a hot tea kettle.

On a cozy stairwell seat, two Small Square House Pillows nestle against a Large Square House Pillow (left) and a Rectangular Pillow (right).

SMALL SQUARE HOUSE POTHOLDER

Materials

A 4½" × 21" blue floral print fabric scrap

A 3½" × 3½" blue-and-white stripe fabric scrap

A 2" × 3" golden yellow fabric scrap

A 4½" × 8½" white-with-blue-dot fabric scrap

A 2" × 3" golden-yellow-with-red dot or print fabric scrap

A 3" × 4½" solid blue fabric scrap

A 4" length of ⅛"-wide white grosgrain ribbon, optional

Sewing thread: white; blue and yellow thread for quilting, optional

An 11" × 11" piece of thick polyester quilt batting, or two layers of thin batting

An 11" × 11" teflon-coated ironing board cover scrap, or an equal amount of fabric

1¼" yards of ¼"-wide white double-fold bias tape

A 17" length of ⅜"- to ½"-wide white, flat, crocheted-type lace trim, optional

A ¼"- to ⅜"-diameter yellow button

A ½"-diameter, white all-purpose plastic ring, or an extra 3" of the ¼"-wide white double-fold bias tape (above)

1. Making the patterns and cutting the fabric—Follow the General Directions for the Small Square House Patchwork, Steps 1 and 2, to make the patterns and cut the fabrics, for the potholder, using the fabrics as follows:

a) From the blue floral print, cut one roof peak (A), one top end piece (C), two side pieces (D), two bottom end pieces (E), and two windows (G) for fillers. Copy the matching dots.

b) From the blue-and-white stripe fabric cut two window (G) pieces, for shutters with the stripes horizontal to the short edge.

c) From the golden yellow fabric cut one window (G) piece and transfer the mullion lines, if desired.

d) From the white-with-blue-dot fabric, cut one roof (B) and transfer the matching dots to the fabric.

e) From the yellow-with-red-dot fabric, cut one chimney piece (H).

f) From the blue fabric, cut one door (F), lightly marking the position of the door panels on the front, if desired.

2. Assembling and quilting the house—Stitch the house together and quilt it, following the remaining General Directions for the Small Square House.

3. Backing and trimming the potholder—Pin the teflon-coated fabric, right side out, to the batting side of the potholder, and trim it to match, reserving the scraps for backing the chimney.

Baste ¼″ from the edge of the house to provide a guideline for placing the bias tape. Machine stitch ⅛″ from the edge. Hand stitch the bias tape invisibly to the front and then to the back of the potholder.

4. The chimney—To make the chimney, place the teflon-coated scrap on a flat surface, teflon side down, place the batting scrap on top, and center the red-dotted chimney piece (H), right side up, over both. Pin and baste the layers together ¼″ from the edge. Machine stitch ⅛″ from the edge. Trim the layers to match the dotted fabric. Hand stitch bias tape invisibly to the front and then to the back of the chimney all around the edges.

Pin the chimney in place on the top center back of the potholder so the roof overlaps the chimney by ¼″. On the front, invisibly stitch the edge of the tape at the roof top to the chimney fabric. On the back, stitch the lower bound edge of the chimney to the teflon-coated fabric.

5. Finishing touches—Add lace trim to the roof edges and the door top, if desired. Stitch on the button door knob or satin stitch a circle in its place.

Tack a hanging ring to the chimney top or make a bias tape loop for hanging and tack it onto the chimney top.

SMALL SQUARE HOUSE PILLOW

Materials

A 9″ × 20″ rust floral fabric scrap

A 4″ × 12″ brown fabric scrap

A 3½″ × 3½″ brown-and-rust floral stripe fabric scrap

A 2″ × 3″ ecru fabric scrap

A 3″ × 4″ rust fabric scrap

A 4½″ length of ⅛″-wide brown grosgrain ribbon, optional

Sewing thread: brown and ecru; rust and tan thread, optional

A 10″ × 10″ piece of thin quilt batting

A ¼″- to ⅜″-diameter brass or ecru button

Polyester stuffing

1. Making the patterns and cutting the fabric—Follows the General Directions for the Small Square House Patchwork, Steps 1 and 2, to make the patterns and cut the fabrics for the pillow using the fabrics as follows:

a) Cut a 9″ × 10″ piece from the rust floral fabric and reserve it for the pillow back.

b) From the rust floral fabric, cut one roof peak (A), one top end (C) piece, two side (D) pieces, two bottom end (E) pieces, and two windows (G) for fillers. Copy all matching dots.

c) From the brown fabric scrap, cut one roof (B) and one door (F). If desired, lightly mark the position of the door panels on the right side of F.

d) From the brown-and-rust floral stripe fabric, cut two shutters (G).

e) From the ecru scrap, cut one window (G) and transfer the mullion lines, if desired.

f) From the rust scrap, cut two chimney pieces (H).

2. Assembling the house—Join the pieces for the house as explained in the General Directions for the Small Square House, Step 3.

3. Quilting the house—If you want to quilt the house, follow the General Directions for the Small Square House, Step 4. Also stitch a quilting line ⅛″ inside the seam line all around the outside edge of the house.

4a. Making the chimney for an unquilted house—Pin and stitch both chimney (H) pieces, right sides together, leaving one long side open. Clip the corners, turn the chimney right side out, and press it lightly. Stuff the chimney and baste the lower edge closed along the seam line without turning under the seam allowances.

4b. Making the chimney for a quilted house—Back one chimney (H) piece with batting and join them by quilting ⅛″ inside the seam lines. Now, pin and stitch the backed chimney piece to the other chimney piece, right sides together, leaving one long side open. Clip the corners, trim the excess batting almost to the seam line, turn the chimney right side out and press it lightly. Stuff the chimney and baste the lower edge closed along the seam line without turning under the seam allowances.

5. Completing the pillow—Pin and stitch the house front to the matching reserved fabric for the house back, right sides together, leaving open the entire top edge of the roof. Trim the backing fabric to match the house shape. Clip the corners, trim the batting outside the seam line, if used, and turn the house right side out, poking out all the corners. Press the edges lightly to flatten them.

Mark the seam lines of the roof top front and back with basting stitches. Tuck under and baste the front and back seam allowances separately, leaving the top edge open.

Stuff the house with batting, maintaining some flatness and pushing the batting into the corners.

Insert the chimney into the top opening, referring to Figure 1 for its position, pin, and stitch the opening closed invisibly, along both the front and back of the chimney.

GENERAL DIRECTIONS FOR THE RECTANGULAR HOUSE PATCHWORK

(to be used with specific directions for place mat or pillow)

1. Making the patterns and cutting the fabric—Trace the roof peak (A), making sure to mark the corner dots. Trace the left and right pattern sections of the roof (B) with the corner dots, butting them together along the dotted line to make a complete roof pattern as shown in Figure 3. The pattern lines include ¼" seam allowances.

Draw and label the following pattern pieces on graph paper according to the dimensions given. All the dimensions include a ¼" seam allowance.

- Upper door border and side filler (C): 1½" × 3½"
- Side (D): 3½" × 12½"
- End (E): 2" × 9½"
- Door (F): 3½" × 6½". Also, draw in two 1¾" × 2⅛" door panels, if desired, for quilting.
- Side window and shutter (G); 2" × 3½". Also, mark ⅛"-wide horizontal and vertical window mullions, if desired.
- Chimney (H): 2½" × 3½"
- End window and shutter (I): 1½" × 2½". Also, mark ⅛"-wide horizontal and vertical window mullions, if desired.

Trace around the patterns on the wrong side of the specified fabrics, but make sure to flip the roof pattern so it faces in the opposite direction from that in the book before tracing its outline. Cut out the fabric pieces along the pattern outlines.

2. Trimming the windows—Cut the ribbon into the following lengths: one 1½" strip, two 2" strips, one 2½" strip, and two 3½" strips. Hand stitch the 1½"- and 2½"-long strips to the end window (I) piece to create mullions. Similarly, stitch one 2"-long and one 3½"-long strip to each side window (G) piece.

3. Assembling the house—Referring to Figure 4, arrange the pieces in order on a flat surface.

Join the pieces as follows, pressing open the seam allowances as you work:

a) Join the roof peak (A) to the roof (B).

b) Stitch an end shutter (I) to each side of the end window (I).

c) Join the end window unit to the upper door border (C).

d) Add the door (F) along the bottom of the upper door border (C).

e) Join an end (E) piece to each side of the door unit.

f) Stitch a side shutter (G) to each side of the side windows (G). Then stitch a side filler (C) between the side window units and at each end of the side window strip.

g) Join a side (D) piece to the top and bottom of the side window unit.

h) Join the end and side units of the house.

i) Stitch the house to the roof unit.

4. Quilting the house—If quilting for a pillow top, place the house right side up on a piece of batting, and pin and baste them together ¼" from the edge. Trim away any excess batting and reserve the scraps for the chimneys. Hand or machine stitch on or next to the seam lines illustrated in Figure 8. If you wish, add other decorative lines of stitching such as door panels.

If making the place mat, the quilting should be done after the back and front are joined (see the directions for the Rectangular House Place Mat, Step 4).

——— seam line

Rectangular House Roof Peak (A)

ACTUAL SIZE

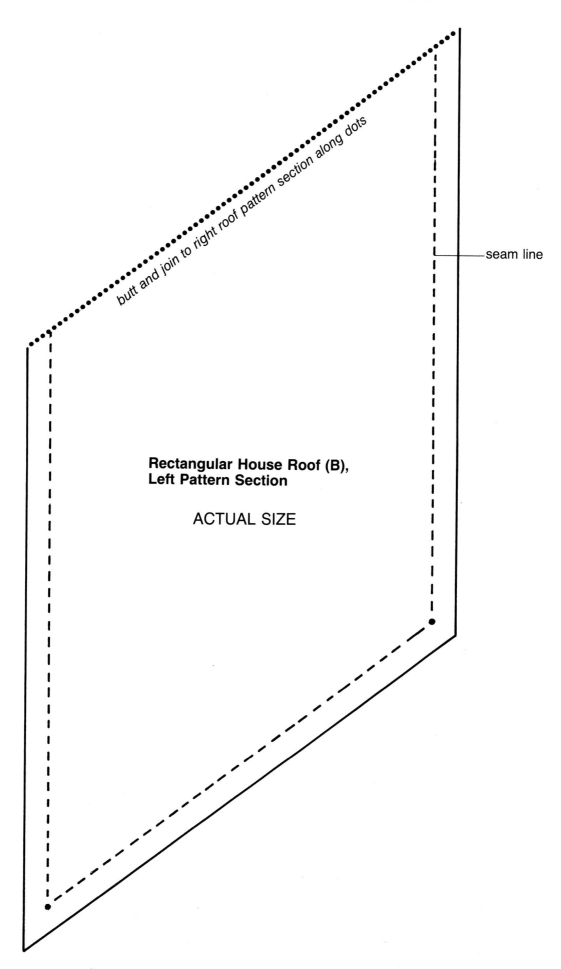

butt and join to right roof pattern section along dots

seam line

**Rectangular House Roof (B),
Left Pattern Section**

ACTUAL SIZE

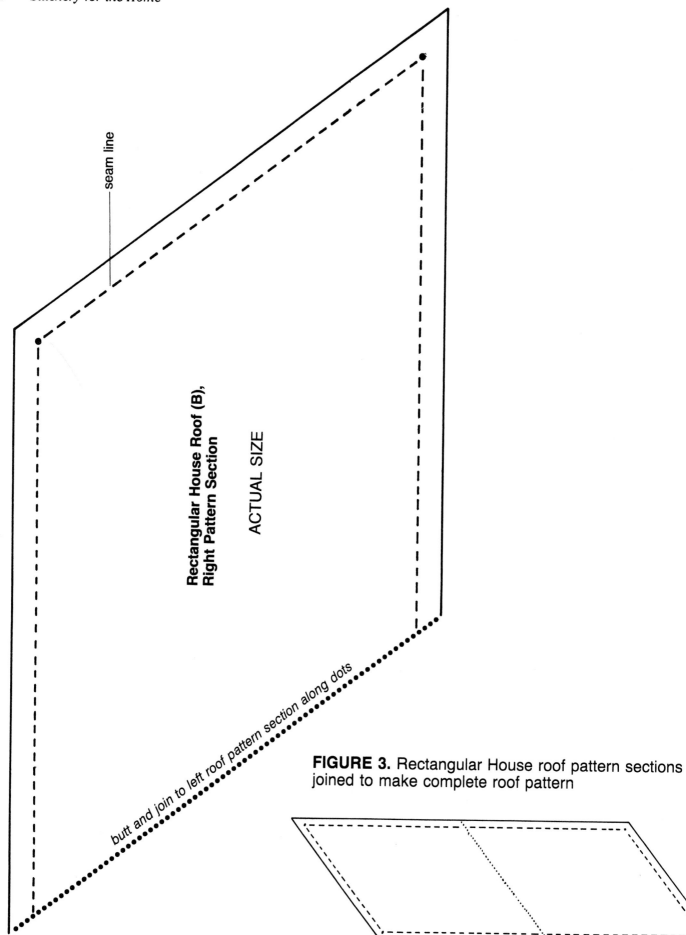

seam line

**Rectangular House Roof (B),
Right Pattern Section**

ACTUAL SIZE

butt and join to left roof pattern section along dots

FIGURE 3. Rectangular House roof pattern sections joined to make complete roof pattern

RECTANGULAR HOUSE PILLOW

Materials

A 12″ × 14″ piece of graph paper with ⅛″ or ¼″ squares, optional

A 16″ × 27″ rust-and-white ¼″-check fabric scrap

A 5″ × 17″ rust-colored fabric scrap

A 4″ × 7″ brown fabric scrap

A 6½″ × 7½″ tan-with-white-dot fabric scrap

A 4½″ × 5½″ ecru fabric scrap

A 3¼″ × 8″ brown-and-rust floral fabric scrap

Sewing thread: brown and ecru; rust and tan thread, optional

½ yard of ⅛″-wide brown grosgrain ribbon, optional

A ¼″- to ⅜″-diameter brass or ecru button

A 14″ × 22″ piece of thin quilt batting, optional

Polyester stuffing

1. Making the patterns and cutting the fabric

Follow the General Directions for the Rectangular House Patchwork, Step 1, to make the patterns and cut the fabrics, for the pillow, using the fabrics as follows:

a) Cut a 14″ × 19″ piece from the rust check fabric and reserve it for the pillow back.

b) From the rust-and-white check fabric, cut one roof peak (A), four (C) upper door border and side filler pieces, two side (D) pieces, and two end (E) pieces.

c) From the rust scrap, cut one roof (B) piece.

d) From the brown scrap, cut one door (F), and, if desired, lightly mark the position of the door panels on the right side of the fabric for quilting.

e) From the tan dot fabric, cut four shutter (G) pieces and two shutter (I) pieces.

f) From the ecru scrap, cut two window (G) pieces and one window (I). If desired, transfer the mullion lines.

g) From the brown-and-rust floral stripe fabric, cut four chimney (H) pieces with the stripes horizontal to the long edges.

2. Assembling the house

Trim the window pieces with ribbon, if

FIGURE 4. Rectangular House pattern piece layout

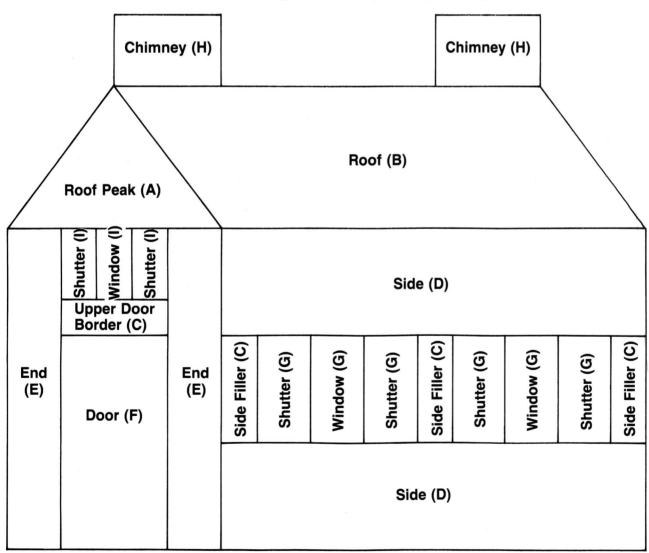

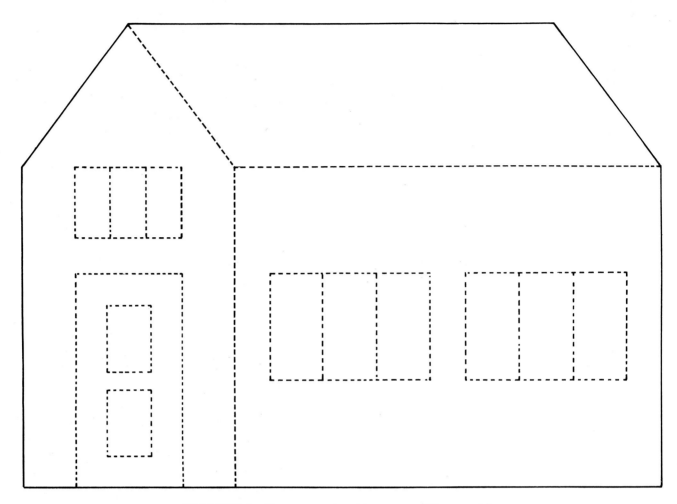

FIGURE 5. Rectangular House quilting guide

desired, and join the house pieces, following Steps 2 and 3 of the General Directions for the Rectangular House.

3a. Making the chimney for an unquilted house—Pin and stitch two of the chimney (H) pieces, right sides together, leaving one long side open. Clip the corners, turn the chimney right side out, and press lightly. Repeat to make the second chimney.

3b. Making the chimney for a quilted house—Back one of the chimney (H) pieces with batting and join them by quilting ⅛″ inside the seam lines. Pin and stitch the backed chimney section to another chimney section, right sides together, leaving one long side open. Clip the corners, trim any excess batting outside the seam line, turn the chimney right side out and press lightly. Repeat to make the second chimney.

4. Quilting the house—Quilt the house following the General Directions for the Rectangular House, Step 4, and referring to Figure 5. Also, stitch a quilting line ⅛″ inside the seam line all around the edge of the house.

5. Completing the pillow—Follow Step 5 under the directions for the Small Square House Pillow for completing the Rectangular Pillow, inserting the chimneys in the positions shown in Figure 4.

RECTANGULAR HOUSE PLACE MAT

Materials for One Mat and One Napkin

- A 12″ × 14″ piece of graph paper with an ⅛″ or ¼″ grid
- A 16″ × 27″ red-with-white-dot fabric scrap
- A 5″ × 17″ green-with-white-and-red floral fabric scrap for the mat, plus an 18″ square for the napkin
- A 9″ × 10″ solid green fabric scrap
- A 4½″ × 5½″ golden yellow fabric scrap
- A 3½″ × 8″ red-with-thin-white-stripe fabric scrap with the stripes horizontal to the long edges
- A 14″ × 22″ piece of polyester quilt batting
- ½ yard of ⅛″-wide, green grosgrain ribbon, optional
- A 24″ length of ⅜″- to ½″-wide white, flat, crochet-type lace trim
- A ¼″ to ⅜″-diameter white ball button

Sewing thread: white and green; red and yellow, optional

1. Making the patterns and cutting the fabric—Follow the General Directions for the Rectangular House Patchwork, Step 1, to make the patterns and cut the fabrics using the fabrics as follows:

a) From the red dot fabric, cut a 14″ × 19″ piece and reserve it for the place mat back.

b) From the red dot fabric, also cut one roof peak (A), four upper door border and side filler (C) pieces, two side (D) pieces, and two end (E) pieces.

c) From the green-with-white floral fabric, cut one roof (B).

d) From the solid green fabric, cut one door (F), four shutter (G), and two shutter (I) pieces.

e) From the yellow fabric, cut two window (G) and one window (I) pieces. Transfer the mullion lines, if desired.

f) From the red stripe fabric, cut four chimney (H) pieces.

2. Assembling the house—Trim the windows and join the house pieces following the General Directions for the Rectangular House Patchwork, Steps 2 and 3.

3. The chimneys—Cut two chimney (H) pieces from batting. Place two red stripe chimney pieces right sides together, insert a batting chimney piece between them, pin, and stitch the layers together leaving one long edge open. Clip the corners and trim any excess batting outside the seam line. Turn the chimney right side out, poke out the corners and press lightly. Baste the open end closed ¼″ from the edge without turning under the seam allowances. Repeat to make the other chimney. Set aside.

4. Quilting and joining the house—Place the house right side up on a piece of batting, and pin and baste them together ¼″ from the edge. Trim away any excess batting.

Pin the reserved red dot fabric and the house right sides together, and trim the excess red dot fabric to match the house shape. Stitch around three sides of the house leaving the entire roof top open. Clip the corners and turn the house right side out, poking out the corners. Press the edges lightly to flatten the house.

Mark the seam lines of the roof top front and back with basting stitches. Tuck under the seam allowances of the front and back separately and baste, leaving the top edge open.

Insert both chimneys into the top opening, placing one at each end. Pin. Stitch the opening closed invisibly.

Place many pins within the house shape, or baste the house layers horizontally, vertically, and diagonally to keep the layers from shifting during quilting.

Hand or machine quilt on or next to the design lines indicated in Figure 5. Use matching threads or use white thread for a decorative topstitched effect. Also, quilt all around the edges of the house and chimney to maintain the mat shape.

5. The finishing touch—If you wish, stitch lace trim along the roof edge.

The Napkin

Make the napkins following the directions for the napkins that accompany the Piglet Place Mats, page 113.

GENERAL DIRECTIONS FOR THE LARGE SQUARE HOUSE PATCHWORK
(to be used with specific directions for tote and pillow)

1. Making the patterns and cutting the fabric—Trace the roof peak (A), making sure to mark the corner dots. Trace the right and left pattern sections of the roof (B) with the corner dots, then butt and tape them together along the dotted line to make a complete roof pattern as in Figure 6. The pattern lines include ¼″ seam allowances.

Draw and label the following pattern pieces on graph paper according to the dimensions given. All the dimensions include ¼″ seam allowances.

a) End (C): 1½″ × 5½″
b) Upper and middle sides (D): 1½″ × 9½″
c) Lower side (E): 3½″ × 9½″
d) Door (F): 3½″ × 5½″, including two 1⅝″ × 1¾″ door panels, if desired, for quilting
e) Window, shutter, and filler sections (G): 1½″ × 2½″, including ⅛″-wide horizontal and vertical window mullions, if desired.
f) Chimney (H): 2½″ × 3″

Trace around the patterns on the back of the specified fabrics, but make sure to flip the roof pattern so it faces in the opposite direction from that in the book before tracing its outline. Cut out the fabric pieces along the pattern outlines.

2. Trimming the windows—Cut five 1½″-long and five 2½″-long ribbon strips to make mullions. Hand stitch one strip of each dimension to the right side of each of the five window pieces (G), within the guidelines.

3. Assembling the house—Referring to Figure 7, arrange the fabric pieces in order on a flat surface. Join the pieces, right sides together, as follows, pressing open the seam allowances as you work.

a) Join the roof peak (A) to the roof (B).
b) Center a window (G) between two shutters (G) and join them along the sides. Attach a filler (G) piece to each end of the window strip.
c) Attach an end (C) piece to the top and bottom of the window strip (Step b, above).
d) Attach an end (C) piece to each side of the door (F).
e) Join the bottom of the window unit completed in Step c to the top of the door unit.
f) Make two double window strips as follows. Stitch a shutter (G) piece to each side of the remaining four windows. Connect two of the windows with a filler (G) piece and add a filler at each end of the window strip. Repeat to make the second window strip.
g) Join an upper and middle side (D) piece to one of the window strips completed in Step f, above.
h) Attach the second window strip to the bottom of the window unit just completed.
i) Attach the lower side (E) piece to the free window strip bottom.
j) Join the end and side of the house.
k) Join the house to the roof unit.

4. Quilting the house—If quilting, place the house right side up on a piece of batting, and pin and baste them together ¼″ from the edge. Trim away any excess batting and reserve the scraps for the chimneys. Hand or machine quilt on or next to the seam lines illustrated in Figure 8. If you wish, add other decorative lines of stitching such as door panels.

— seam line

Large Square House Roof Peak (A)

ACTUAL SIZE

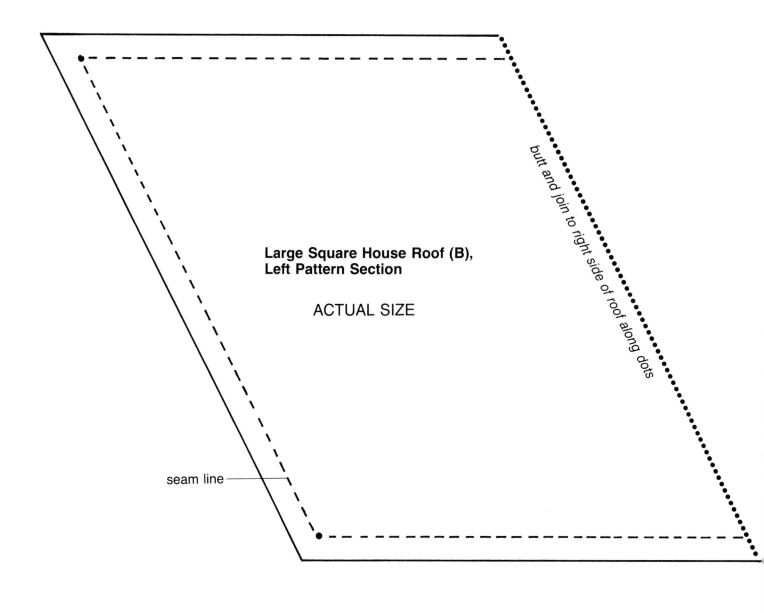

**Large Square House Roof (B),
Left Pattern Section**

ACTUAL SIZE

seam line

butt and join to right side of roof along dots

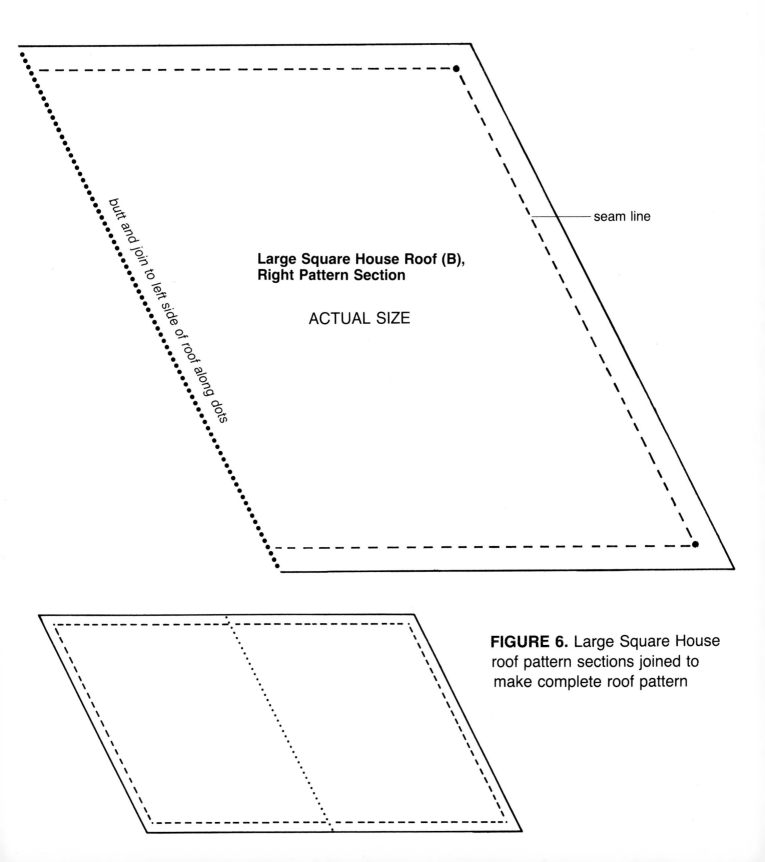

butt and join to left side of roof along dots

seam line

Large Square House Roof (B), Right Pattern Section

ACTUAL SIZE

FIGURE 6. Large Square House roof pattern sections joined to make complete roof pattern

LARGE SQUARE HOUSE PILLOW

Materials

A 10" × 11" piece of graph paper with a ⅛" or ¼" grid

A 15" × 29" tan-with-white-dot fabric scrap

A 6" × 12½" brown-and-rust floral stripe fabric scrap with the stripes horizontal to the long edges

A 7" × 10" rust fabric scrap

A 5½" × 9" brown-and-white geometric fabric scrap

A 2½" × 7" ecru fabric scrap

A 22" length of ⅛"-wide brown grosgrain ribbon, optional

Sewing thread: brown and ecru; rust and tan, optional

A 15" × 15" piece of thin batting, optional

A ¼"- to ⅜"-diameter brass or ecru button

Polyester stuffing

1. Making the patterns and cutting the fabric—Follow the General Directions for the Large Square House Patchwork, Step 1, to make the patterns and cut the fabric for the pillow, using the fabrics as follows. Be sure to flip the roof pattern before tracing it onto the fabric.

a) Cut a 15" × 15" piece from the tan dot fabric and reserve it for the pillow back.

b) From the tan dot fabric, cut one roof peak (A), four end (C), two upper and middle side (D), one lower side (E), and eight window/shutter/filler (G) pieces.

c) From the brown-and-rust floral stripe fabric, cut one roof (B).

d) From the rust fabric, cut one door (F) and four chimney (H) pieces. If desired, lightly mark the position of the door panels on the right side of the door (F) fabric.

FIGURE 7. Large Square House pattern piece layout

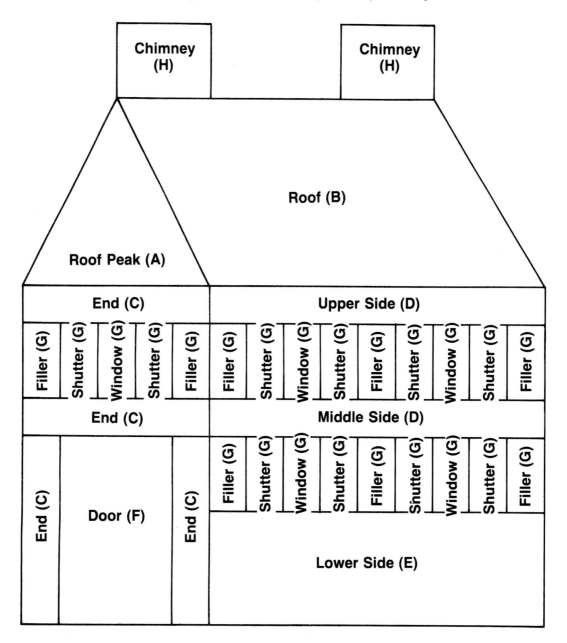

e) From the brown-and-white geometric fabric, cut ten shutter (G) pieces.

f) From the ecru fabric, cut five window (G) pieces, and, if desired, transfer the mullion placement lines.

2. Assembling the house—Trim the window pieces with ribbon, if desired, and join the house pieces following Steps 2 and 3 of the General Directions for the Large Square House Patchwork.

3a. Making the chimney for an unquilted house—Pin and stitch two of the chimney (H) pieces, right sides together, leaving one long side open. Clip the corners, turn the chimney right side out, and press it lightly. Repeat to make the second chimney.

3b. Making the chimney for a quilted house—Back one of the chimney (H) pieces with batting and join them by stitching ⅛″ inside the seam lines. Pin and stitch the backed chimney piece to another chimney piece, right sides together, leaving one long side open. Clip the corners, trim the batting outside the seam line, turn the chimney right side out, and press it lightly. Repeat to make the second chimney.

4. Quilting the house—Quilt the house following the General Directions for the Large Square House Patchwork, Step 4, and referring to Figure 7.

5. Completing the pillow—Follow Step 5 under the directions for the Small Square House Pillow to complete the Large Square House Pillow, inserting a chimney at each end of the roof opening.

FIGURE 8. Large Square House quilting guide

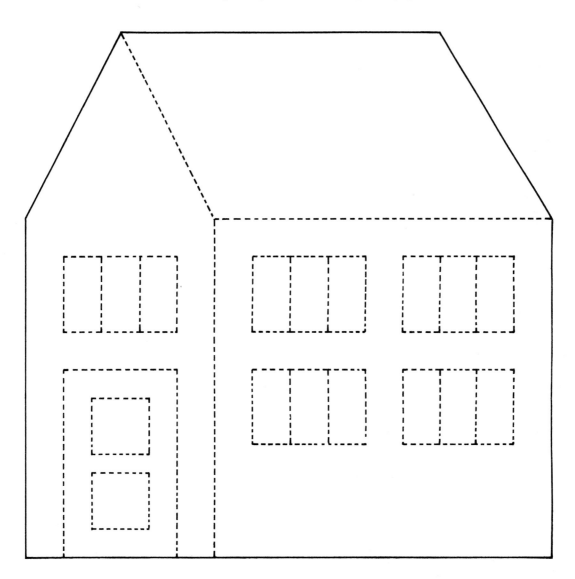

LARGE SQUARE HOUSE TOTE

Materials

A 10″ × 11″ piece of ⅛″ or ¼″ grid graph paper, optional

A 15″ × 19″ black-with-narrow-white-stripe fabric scrap

A 15″ × 34″ white-with-black-dot fabric scrap

A 9″ × 14″ golden yellow fabric scrap

A 6″ × 12½″ black-with-white-and-yellow floral print fabric scrap

A 15″ × 45″ piece of thin quilting batting

A ¼″- to ⅜″-diameter black ball button

Sewing thread: black and white; golden yellow thread, optional

A 22″ length of ⅛″-wide black grosgrain ribbon

3¾ yards of ¼″-wide white double-fold bias tape

A 22″ length of ⅜″-wide white crocheted-type lace

1. Making the patterns and cutting the fabric—Follow the General Directions for the Large Square House Patchwork, Step 1, to make the patterns and cut the fabric for the tote, using the fabrics as follows and making sure to flip the roof pattern before tracing it onto the fabric.

a) Cut a 15″ × 15″ piece from the black striped fabric and reserve it for the tote back. Then cut one roof peak (A), four ends (C), one upper and one middle side (D), one lower side (E), and eight filler (G) pieces.

b) From the white-with-black-dot fabric, cut ten shutter (G) pieces.

c) From the black floral fabric, cut one roof (B).

d) From the golden yellow fabric, cut five window (G) and four 1¼″ × 9″ handle pieces.

2. Assembling the house—Trim the windows, if desired, and join the house pieces as directed in Steps 2 and 3 of the General Directions for the Large Square House Patchwork page 99.

3. Quilting the house—Place the house right side up over two layers of batting; pin and baste the layers together ¼″ from the edge; trim away the excess batting.

Hand or machine stitch on or next to the seam lines as illustrated in Figure 8. If you wish, add other decorative lines of stitching such as door panels.

4. Making and attaching the lining and back—Using the completed house as a pattern, cut out two polka dot houses for the lining. Also cut one black stripe house and one batting house for the bag back. Reserve the batting scraps for the handles.

Pin and hand baste the polka dot piece right side out to the batting side of the quilted bag front. Stitch ¼″ from the edge to provide a placement guide on the front for the bias tape. Machine stitch ⅛″ from the edge.

Place the black stripe back piece and the polka dot back piece, wrong sides together, on a flat surface. Insert the layer of batting between them, pin and baste them together. Machine stitch ⅛″ from the edge.

5. Attaching the roof binding—Invisibly stitch the white double-fold binding to the top and ends of the roof on both the front and back of the bag, mitering the corners.

6. Joining the front and back and finishing the trim—Pin the front and back, lining sides together. Machine stitch around the unbound sides and bottom ⅛″ from the edge. Bind the unbound edges with bias tape. Stitch lace along the under edges of the roof and roof peak. Stitch on a button for the door knob.

7. The handles—From the batting scraps, cut two 1¼″ × 9″ strips. Place two handle strips, wrong sides together, sandwiching a batting strip between them, and baste the layers together ¼″ from the edge. Machine stitch ⅛″ from the edge. Encase the handle edges in bias tape. Repeat to make the second handle.

Center and pin a handle to the bag front, placing each end about 2″ from a roof corner. Stitch the handle in place on both the front and on the lining side. Repeat to attach the other handle to the bag back.

Piglet Place Mats and Potholder

I would not advise using Piglet Place Mats for all your dinner guests, but there must certainly be a few folks you can count among your friends who will not take offense. Our family happens to be quite fond of pigs, so we use these mats fairly often. It is always nice to see a smile at breakfast even if it's chainstitched onto a piece of fabric!

I recommend using "piggy pink" fabric and preshrinking it so that you avoid the unhappy experience of seeing your plates grow bigger with every washing of the placemats. The finished size of the mats and napkins will be 14" × 19½" and 17" × 17",

respectively, and that of the potholder about 7½" × 10".

If your fabric is only 42" wide, there will be little to spare because the edges of

your patterns will probably touch when you lay out and draw the pieces. Also, reversible quilted fabric is quite expensive, so plan carefully and don't waste an inch.

The mats are reversible, but of course the napkin doesn't look correct on the right side, so place it above the plate or fluff it into a goblet when the piglet faces to the left.

As an after thought, I included an extra pattern so you can make some piggy potholders. These are super-simple and super-quick to stitch in quantity and would look cute grouped together in a "pig pen" wooden box or basket at a bazaar.

Materials for 4 Mats and 4 Napkins

1 yard 42"-wide, or wider, dusty rose reversible print quilted fabric

White and dusty rose sewing thread

12 yards of ¼"-wide white double-fold bias tape

6-ply embroidery thread: 3 yards brown, 2 yards white

Polyester stuffing scraps for cheeks, optional

1 yard pale dusty rose napkin-weight fabric

THE PLACE MATS

1. Preparing the fabric—Secure the quilting stitches on the fabric by machine stitching across both cut ends of the fabric. Preshrink the fabric by machine washing and machine drying if those are the methods that you will eventually use.

2. Making the patterns—Trace the four quarter sections of the place

mat pattern, butting them together on the dotted lines to make a complete pig shape (see Figure 1). Copy the placement lines for the mouth, eye, and both ears. The appliquéd heart cheek is optional. Use a large needle to pierce the eye, mouth, and ear lines.

Trace the patterns for the ear and, if you wish, the heart cheek.

3. Marking and cutting the fabric—Pin the pig pattern to the quilted fabric and trace around the shape with a sharp soft pencil. Using the same pencil, transfer the mouth, eyes, and proper ear placement line to one side of the piglet. Repeat to mark three more piglets. Trace eight ears on the fabric also.

Before cutting the fabric, secure the quilting threads on all the individual pieces by sewing long machine stitches slightly less than ¼" inside the penciled pattern lines. Make a second row of stitches ⅛" inside the pattern lines. These stitches will be covered later by the trim.

Cut out all the shapes along the pattern lines. Repin each place mat pattern to the unmarked side of its corresponding fabric part and mark the piglet mouth and eyes and the proper ear placement line for that side.

4. Attaching the bias tape trim—Bind all the cut edges of the pigs' bodies and ears with bias tape, using the trim placement lines as guides. Invisibly handstitch the tape first to one side and then to the other side of each piece.

5. The pigs' features—Using two strands of brown embroidery thread, carefully embroider the facial details of each pig making sure that the stitches do not show on the reverse side of the fabric. Chain stitch brown mouth and eye lines, and use lazy daisy stitches to make brown ³⁄₁₆"-long eyelashes.

If you want to appliqué cheeks, make sure to cut out the napkins first, (see below), then trace eight heart shapes from the remnants of

(continued)

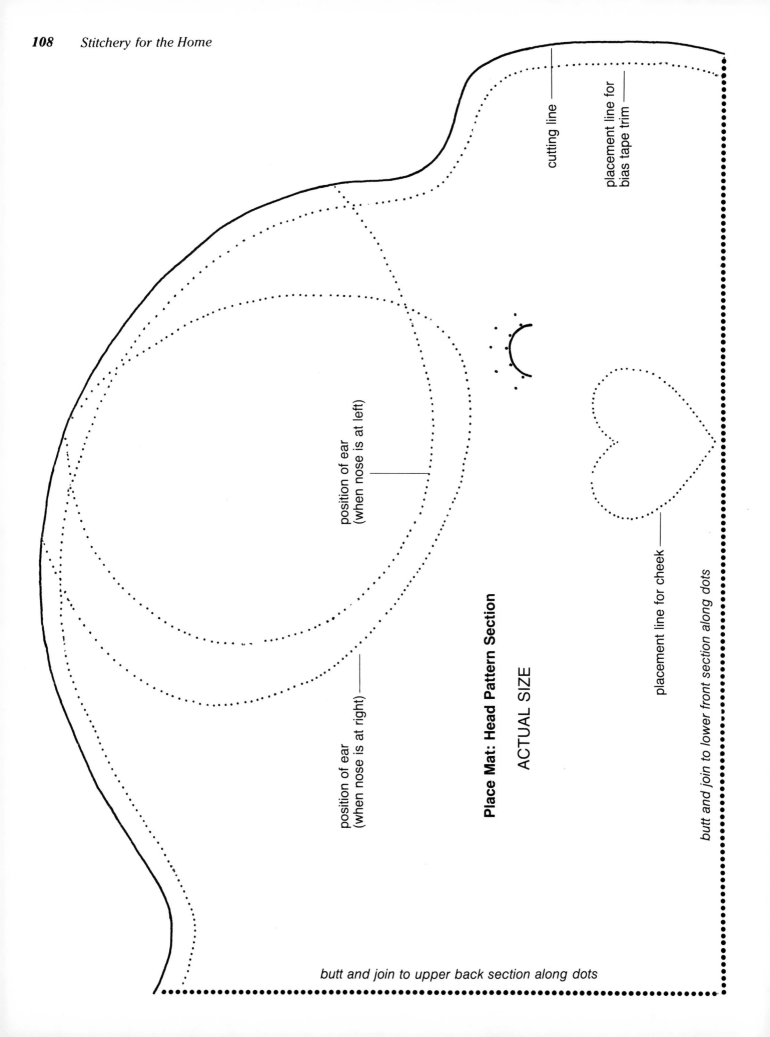

cutting line

placement line for
bias tape trim

position of ear
(when nose is at left)

position of ear
(when nose is at right)

Place Mat: Head Pattern Section

ACTUAL SIZE

placement line for cheek

butt and join to lower front section along dots

butt and join to upper back section along dots

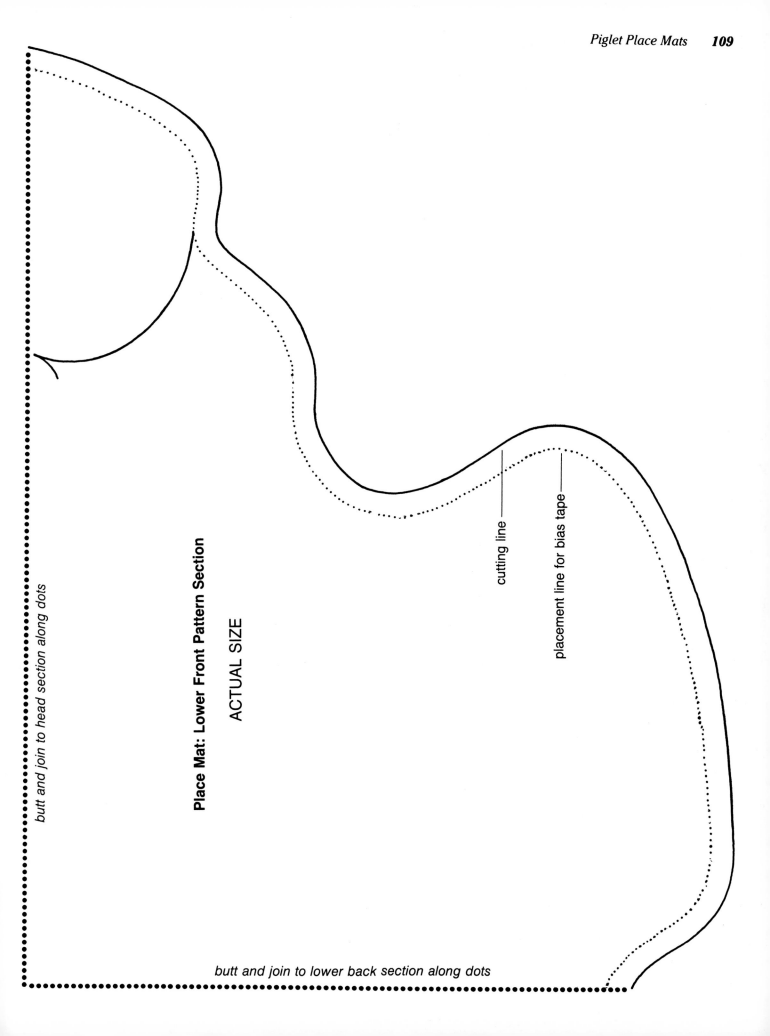

butt and join to head section along dots

Place Mat: Lower Front Pattern Section

ACTUAL SIZE

cutting line

placement line for bias tape

butt and join to lower back section along dots

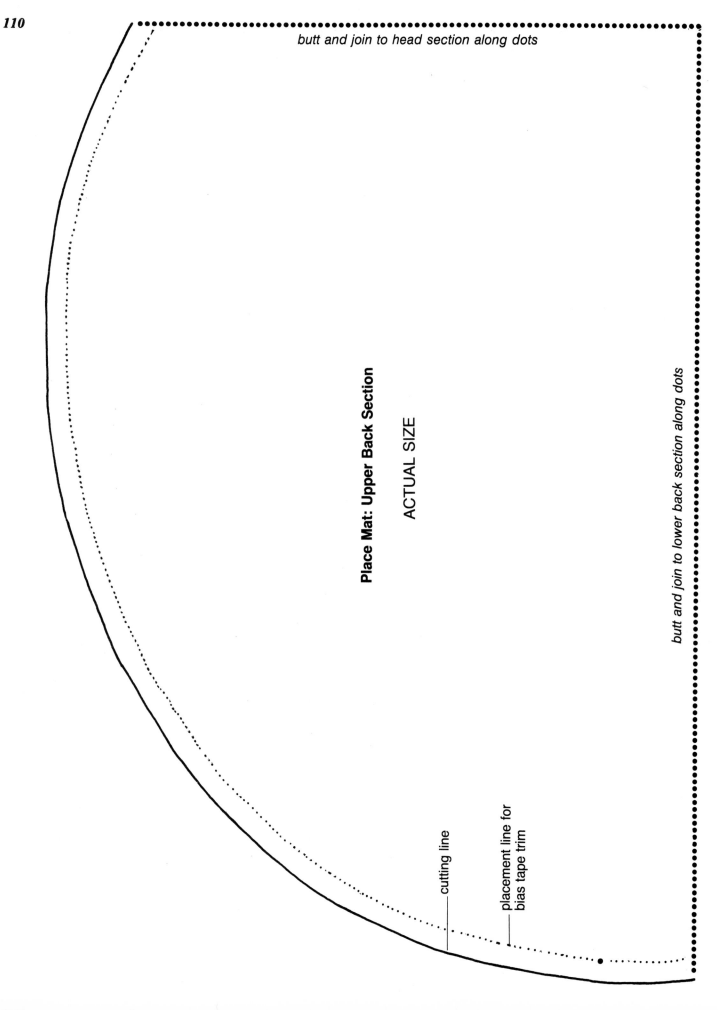

butt and join to head section along dots

Place Mat: Upper Back Section

ACTUAL SIZE

butt and join to lower back section along dots

cutting line

placement line for
bias tape trim

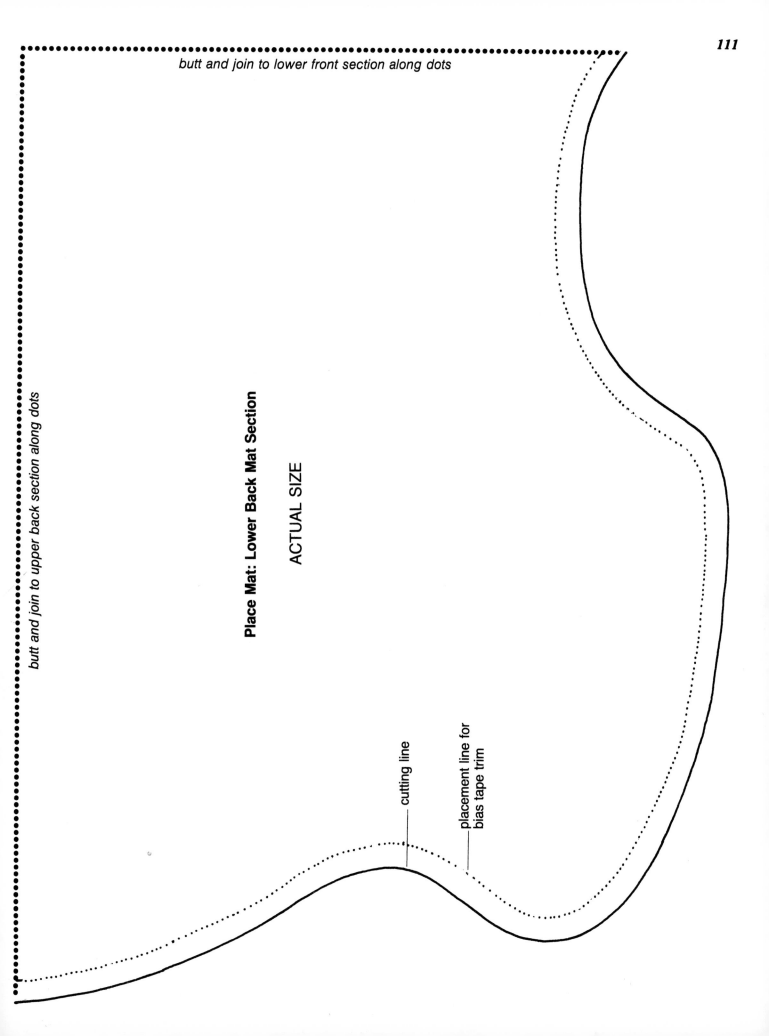

butt and join to lower front section along dots

butt and join to upper back section along dots

Place Mat: Lower Back Mat Section

ACTUAL SIZE

cutting line

placement line for
bias tape trim

FIGURE 1. Pig pattern sections joined to form complete place mat pattern

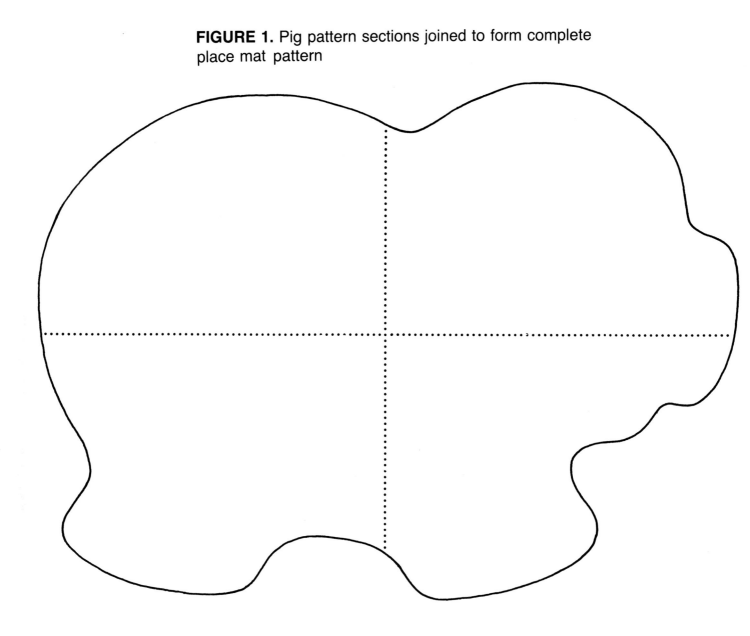

FIGURE 2. Hemming and mitering the corners of the napkin

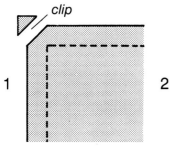 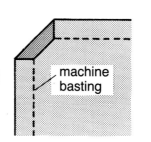 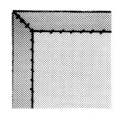

1. Machine baste ½" from the edge of the napkin and clip the corners.

2. Press the corners down to the stitching line.

3. Press down the sides along the stitching line. Fold under ¼" along the cut edge and then another ¼" to make a double hem and stitch by hand or machine.

the napkin fabric. Using very tiny stitches, hand baste the hearts along the seam line. Clip along the seam allowance of each heart to the basting line. Finger press the seam allowance to the back and hand baste it. Pin and baste a cheek in position on both sides of each placemat. Using blanket stitches and two strands of white embroidery thread, appliqué the hearts. If desired, just before the stitching is completed, push a little polyester stuffing under the cheek.

6. The tails and ears—Cut four 17″ lengths of bias tape, one for each pig, and invisibly handstitch together the open lengthwise edges. Knot the ends of the tape, and securely stitch a length of tape across the middle to the edge of the bias tape at the tail dot on each pig's back side.

Pin an ear in place on the front and back of each place mat along each ear placement line and invisibly handstitch it, leaving the front of the ear free and floppy.

THE NAPKINS

Draw four 18″ × 18″ squares on the wrong side of the napkin fabric. Machine baste ½″ from the cut edges to provide a guideline for the hem. Hem the edges as shown in Figure 2. Fold each napkin in quarters, then roll, and tie a pig's tail around each one.

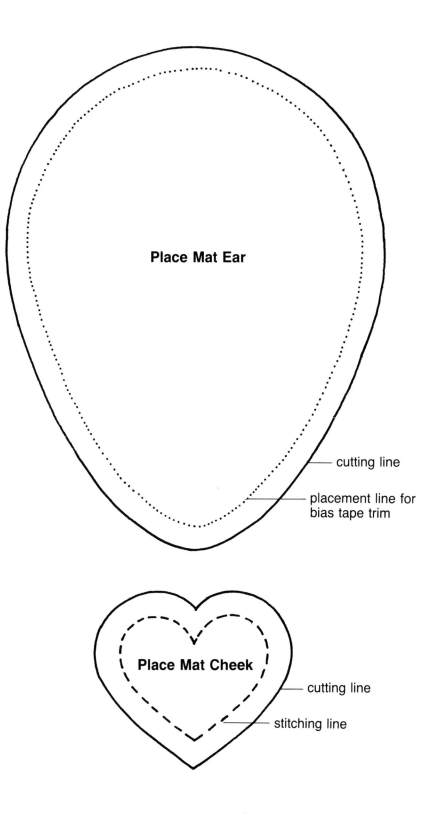

Place Mat Ear

— cutting line

— placement line for bias tape trim

Place Mat Cheek

— cutting line

— stitching line

ALL PATTERNS ACTUAL SIZE

PIGLET POTHOLDER

Materials

An 8″ × 11″ quilted dusty rose fabric scrap, preferably pre-shrunk

An 8″ × 11″ teflon-coated ironing-board scrap or another quilted fabric piece of the same size

An 8″ × 11″ piece of traditional polyester quilt batting or two layers of thin batting

1½ yards of ¼″-wide white, double-fold bias tape

White thread

6-ply embroidery thread: ½ yard each dusty rose and brown

1. Preparing the fabric—Secure the quilted stitches on the fabric by machine stitching around the edges.

2. Making and transferring the patterns—Trace the pattern for the pig's body and ear, copying the placement lines for the mouth, eye, and ear. Using a large needle, pierce the pattern along the eye, mouth, and ear lines. Cut out the patterns.

Pin the patterns to the right side of the quilted fabric and, using a sharp soft pencil, trace around each pattern once. Transfer the mouth, eyes, and ear line to the fabric.

3. The features—Using one strand of brown embroidery thread, chain stitch the mouth and eye lines and make ³⁄₁₆″-long lazy daisy eyelashes.

Using two strands of rose embroidery thread, satin stitch the cheek.

4. Cutting the fabric—Before cutting the fabric, secure the quilting threads again by machine stitching just inside the cutting line of each shape.

Cut out the pig's body and ear. Hand baste ¼″ from the cut edge around each shape to provide a guideline for the bias tape placement.

Trace and cut out one batting pig. Turn the pig's body pattern in the opposite direction from that used to trace on the quilted fabric, and trace and cut out one teflon-coated pig.

5. Stitching and trimming the potholder—Place the quilted and teflon-coated fabric pigs wrong sides together, and insert the batting pig between them. Pin and baste the layers together close to the edges. Trim away any extra batting or teflon-coated fabric, if necessary. Overcast the edges to flatten them. Bind the edges of the pig's body and ear with bias tape using the basting stitches as a guide and invisibly hand-stitching the tape first to the front and then to the back of the pig. Pin the ear in place and invisibly handstitch it.

Cut a 3″ length of bias tape and invisibly handstitch its lengthwise edges closed. Tuck under the ends and stitch them in place between the dots on the back of the pig to form a tail and hanging loop.

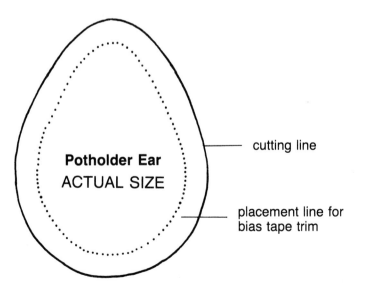

cutting line

placement line for bias tape trim

Potholder Ear
ACTUAL SIZE

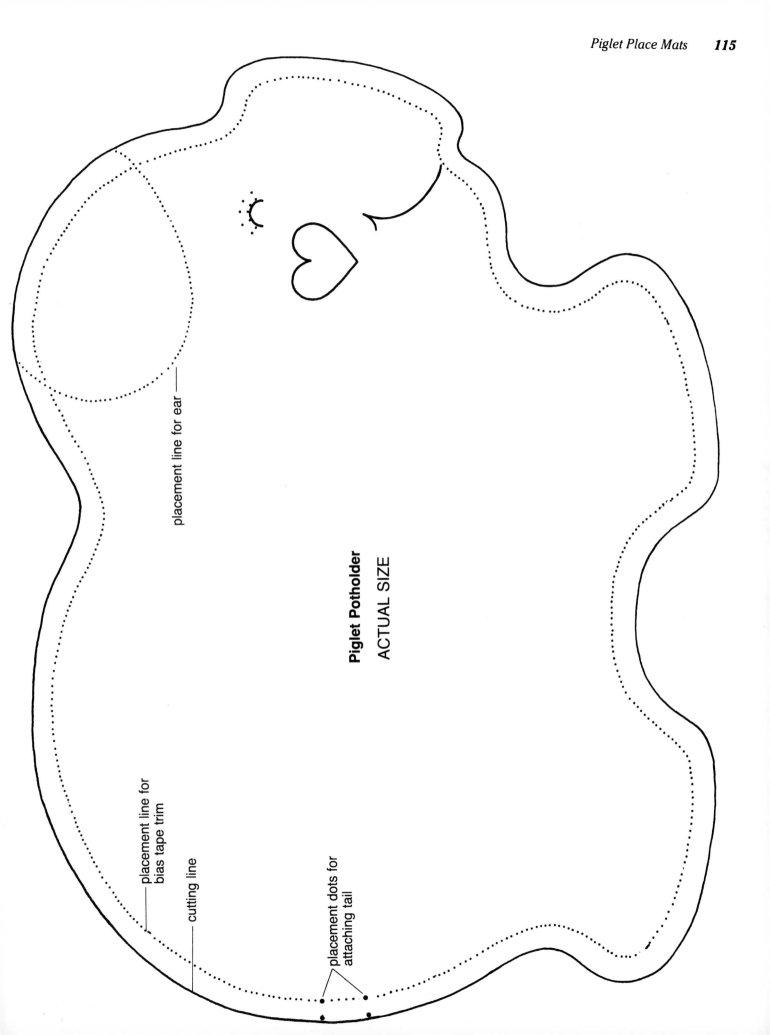

placement line for ear ——

placement line for
bias tape trim

cutting line

placement dots for
attaching tail

Piglet Potholder ACTUAL SIZE

Though simple to do, the three differently-colored triangles that make up these potholders should keep you busy for a while! Each block contains 24 pieces, but the same three pattern pieces are always used to form a basic triangle unit. Sometimes turned and sometimes reversed, these units can be arranged in a surprising variety of ways. As you work, you'll discover many more possibilities. Some of the patterns resemble the parquet floor blocks one sees in lovely old homes.

Parquetry Potholders

To make the designs more versatile, you can easily enlarge the patterns to make pillows, a tote bag, or a picnic cloth, or you can combine them to make a quilt. To enlarge the patterns, start by drawing the size square you want, but make sure it is easily divisible by three. Then divide it, referring to the Figure(s) you want to use.

If you make the potholders, it's best to cut up an inexpensive teflon-coated ironing board cover to make the backing pieces. The plastic rings I used for hangers are sometimes called "bone rings," and they are sold with knitting supplies. If you would rather use bias binding hangers, allow about 5" extra binding for each potholder.

General Materials and Equipment for each Potholder
(additional materials listed under individual directions)

Tracing paper

Heavy paper

Sewing thread: white, yellow, medium pink, purple, orange, turquoise, and bright green

Two or more 8" squares of traditional polyester quilt batting

An 8" × 8" fabric scrap, preferably teflon-coated

1 yard ¼"-wide double-fold white bias binding

A ¾"-diameter plastic curtain ring

DESIGN 1

Materials (plus general materials listed above)

A 3" × 6" medium green fabric scrap

A 3" × 6" light magenta fabric scrap

A 4½" × 6½" turquoise fabric scrap

A 4½" × 6½" orange fabric scrap

A 4½" × 8½" light purple fabric scrap

A 4½" × 8½" dark yellow fabric scrap

Design 1   (r) = reverse

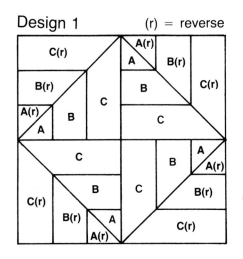

1. Making the patterns—Trace patterns A, B, and C onto tracing paper. Then paste the tracing paper onto very heavy paper. Cut out the patterns. Also make an 8" square pattern for the batting and backing. All the patterns include ¼" seam allowances.

2. Cutting the fabric—Hold the patterns against the right side of the fabrics specified below, lightly trace around the shapes, using a soft sharp pencil, and cut out the fabric along the pattern lines.

From the green fabric, cut four A pieces. From the magenta fabric, cut

four reverse A pieces. To reverse the pattern, simply flip it over. From the turquoise fabric, cut four B pieces. From the orange fabric, cut four reverse B pieces. From the purple fabric, cut four C pieces. From the yellow fabric, cut four reverse C pieces. Also cut one teflon-coated square and two batting squares.

3. Assembling the patchwork—Referring to the color photograph opposite and Design 1, arrange the pieces in order on a flat surface. Join the pieces as follows, leaving ¼" seam allowances and pressing them open as you work. Referring to Figure 1, make a triangle unit by stitching a green A to a turquoise B to a purple C. Repeat to make four triangles.

Make a triangle unit by stitching a magenta reverse A to an orange reverse B to a yellow reverse C. Repeat to make four triangles.

Make a square joining a green/turquoise/purple triangle to a magenta/orange/yellow reverse triangle. Repeat to make a total of four squares.

To complete the block, join the four squares together referring to the colored photograph and Design 1.

4. Joining the front and back of the potholder—Pin the completed

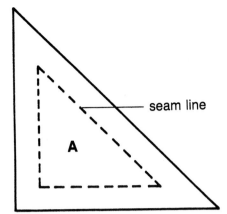

seam line

A

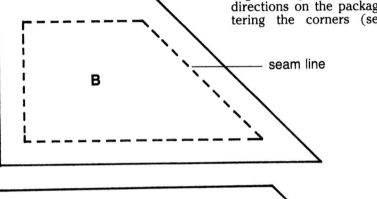

seam line

B

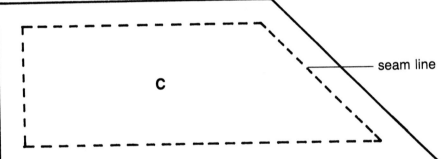

seam line

C

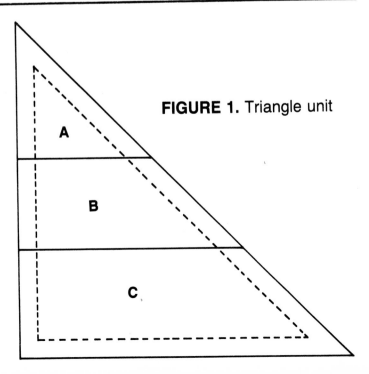

FIGURE 1. Triangle unit

A

B

C

block on top of a layer of quilt batting and baste close to the edge. If desired, machine or hand quilt along the seam lines between each major color area, not necessarily along every seam line, to emphasize the block patterns.

Pin the teflon square, right side out, to the second layer of batting. Then pin the teflon square and patchwork square batting sides together, and baste close to the edge around the entire square.

5. Trimming and finishing the potholder—Open one fold of the binding and baste it along the front edge of the potholder, following the directions on the package and mitering the corners (see *Sewing Techniques*, page 162). Machine stitch along the fold line of the tape. Fold the free edge of tape over the edge of the potholder and invisibly hand stitch it to the back of the potholder.

Tack a ring hanger to a corner of the potholder.

Tack all the layers of the potholder together at the center of the potholder, either tieing the thread or backstitching an unknotted thread several times to make the tack invisible.

DESIGN 2

Materials (plus general materials)

A 4½" × 6½" light purple fabric scrap

A 4½" × 8½" light magenta fabric scrap

A 4½" × 8½" orange fabric scrap

A 4½" × 6½" dark yellow fabric scrap

A 3" × 6" medium green fabric scrap

A 3" × 6" turquoise fabric scrap

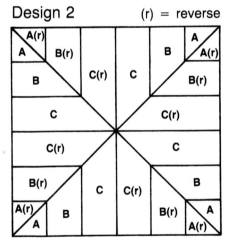

Design 2   (r) = reverse

1. Making the patterns and cutting the fabric—Make the patterns and mark the fabrics following the techniques explained in Steps 1 and 2 for Design 1, but use the following fabrics.

From the green and turquoise fabrics, cut two A and two reverse A pieces from each color. To reverse a pattern, simply flip it over.

From the yellow and purple fabrics, cut two B and two reverse B pieces from each color. From the magenta and orange fabrics, cut two C and two reverse C pieces from each color.

2. Assembling the patchwork—Referring to the color photograph on page 117 and Design 2, arrange the pieces in order on a flat surface. Join the pieces as follows, leaving ¼″ seam allowances and pressing them open as you work. Make a triangle unit by stitching a green A to a yellow B to an orange C. Then stitch a reverse green A to a reverse yellow B to a reverse orange C. Join these two triangular units together to make a square. Repeat this process with the remaining green, yellow, and orange pieces to make another identical square.

Make a triangle unit by stitching a turquoise A to a purple B to a magenta C. Then stitch a reverse turquoise A to a reverse purple B to a reverse magenta C. Join these triangles units together to make a square. Repeat this process with the remaining turquoise, purple and magenta pieces to make another identical square.

To complete the block, join the four squares together, referring to the colored photograph and Design 2.

3. Completing the potholder— Join the front and back and trim and finish the potholder following Steps 4 and 5 under the directions for Design 1.

DESIGN 3

Materials (plus general materials)

A 3″ × 6″ light purple fabric scrap
A 3″ × 6″ turquoise fabric scrap
A 4½″ × 6½″ medium green fabric scrap
A 4½″ × 6½″ light magenta fabric scrap
A 4½″ × 8½″ dark yellow fabric scrap
A 4½″ × 8½″ orange fabric scrap

Design 3   (r) = reverse

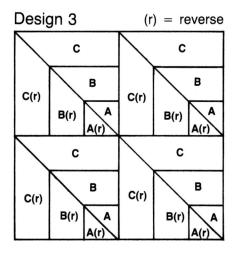

1. Making the patterns and cutting the fabric—Make the patterns and mark the fabric following the techniques explained in Steps 1 and 2 for Design 1, but use the following fabrics.

From the purple and turquoise fabrics, cut two A and two reverse A pieces from each color. From the green and magenta fabrics, cut two B and two reverse B pieces from each color. From the yellow and orange fabrics, cut two C and two reverse C pieces from each color. To reverse the patterns, simply flip them over.

2. Assembling the patchwork— Referring to the color photograph on page 117, and Design 3, arrange the pieces in order on a flat surface. Join the pieces as follows, leaving ¼″ seam allowances and pressing them open as you work. Make a triangle unit by stitching together a purple A to a magenta B to an orange C. Make a reverse triangle by stitching together a reverse purple A to a reverse magenta B to a reverse orange C. Join the triangles to make a square. Repeat the process with the remaining purple, magenta, and orange pieces to make another square.

Make a triangle unit by stitching together a turquoise A to a green B to a yellow C. Make a reverse triangle by stitching together a reverse turquoise A to a reverse green B to a reverse yellow C. Join the triangles to make a square. Repeat the process with the remaining turquoise, green, and yellow pieces to make another square.

To complete the block, join the four squares together referring to the colored photograph and Design 3.

3. Completing the potholders— Join the front and back and trim and finish the potholder following Steps 4 and 5 under the directions for Design 1.

DESIGN 4

Materials (plus general materials)

A 3″ × 6″ light purple fabric scrap
A 3″ × 6″ dark yellow fabric scrap
A 4½″ × 6½″ orange fabric scrap
A 4½″ × 6½″ turquoise fabric scrap
A 4½″ × 8½″ medium-green fabric scrap
A 4½″ × 8½″ light magenta fabric scrap

Design 4

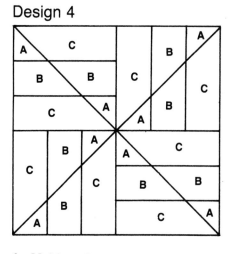

1. Making the patterns and cutting the fabric—Make the patterns and mark the fabric following the techniques explained in Steps 1 and 2 for Design 1, but use the following fabrics.

Cut four A pieces each from the purple and yellow fabrics. Cut four B pieces each from the orange and turquoise fabrics. Cut four C pieces each from the green and magenta fabrics.

2. Assembling the patchwork— Referring to the color photograph on page 117 and Design 4, arrange the pieces in order on a flat surface. Join the pieces as follows, leaving ¼″ seam allowances and pressing them open as you work. Make a triangle by stitching a yellow A to an orange B to a magenta C. Repeat to make a total of four triangle units.

Stitch a purple A to a turquoise B to a green C to make a triangle. Repeat to make a total of four triangle units.

Make a square unit by joining a yellow/orange/magenta triangle to a purple/turquoise/green triangle along the diagonal edges. Repeat to make a total of four square units.

To complete the block, join the four squares together, referring to the color photograph and Design 4.

3. Completing the potholder— Join the front and back and trim and finish the potholder following Steps 4 and 5 under the directions for Design 1 and quilting only the center horizontal, center vertical and the diagonal lines of the block to emphasize the pinwheel motif.

Diagonal rows of squares and triangles line up to create these patched heart aprons. I chose a spectrum of brilliant colors to make one apron look like a rainbow of hearts, but if you use a different color or print for each heart, your apron will be charming and you'll use up many of your smallest scraps as well. In order to use the cutting layouts, however, the background and backing fabrics must be 44" wide.

The red heart Christmas apron is reversible because a holly print was used for the

Patched Heart Aprons

backing fabric. The layers can be stitched and tied together, with or without a layer of thin quilt batting between them.

The Christmas apron in the photograph was made with batting, tied, and then each heart was quilted along the seam line. I chose heavier fabric for the rainbow apron, so I omitted batting, but I did tie the front and backing together.

The patched heart motif can also be used as a starting point for stitching potholders, place mats, pillows, and quilts. Enlarge or reduce the patch size to suit your needs and change the width of the binding to relate to the patch size.

PATCHED HEART RAINBOW APRON

Materials

1¼" yards white opaque fabric

A 3" × 39" brilliant pink fabric scrap

A 3" × 31" lavender-blue fabric scrap

A 3" × 24" green fabric scrap, or ⅛ yard green fabric

A 3" × 24" orange fabric scrap

A 3" × 8" yellow-orange fabric scrap

A 28" × 34" piece of thin quilt batting, optional

Sewing thread: white and green

6 yards green quilt binding or folded and pressed hem facing

1½ yards 6-ply white embroidery thread

1. The backing—If you are using the same fabric for the backing as well as for the A patches, cut a 28" × 34" piece from the fabric, referring to the layout in Figure 1, and reserve it for the backing.

2. Making the patterns and marking the fabrics for the patches Trace patterns A and B and cut them out, or, alternatively, draw 2½"

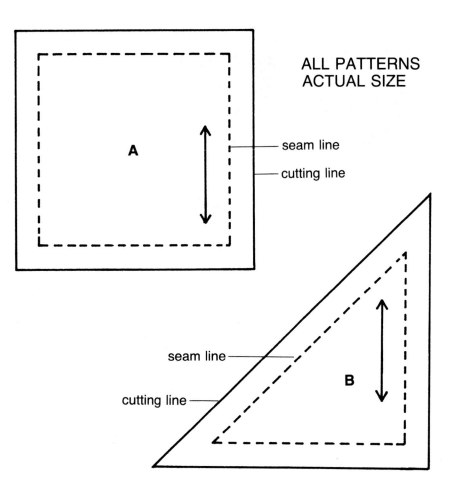

ALL PATTERNS ACTUAL SIZE

seam line
cutting line

seam line
cutting line

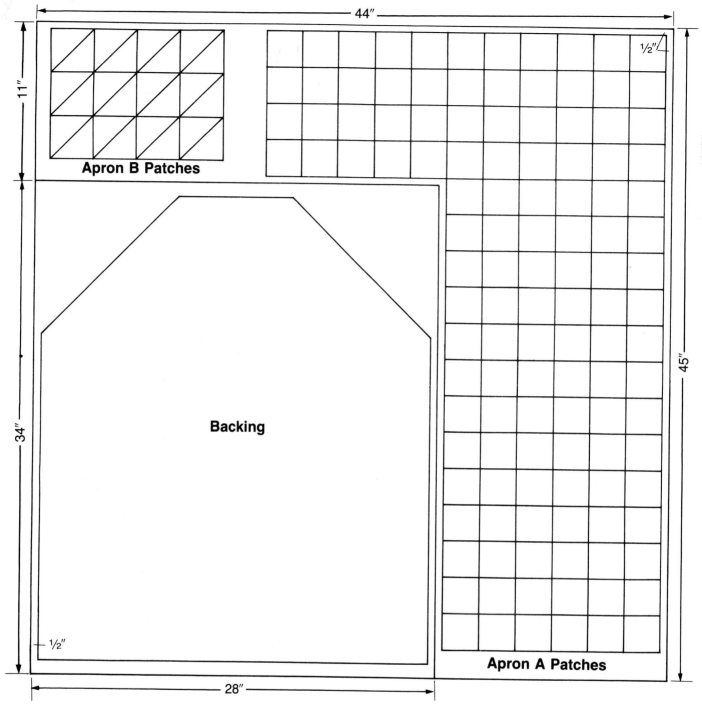

FIGURE 1. Cutting layout for the Patched Heart Rainbow Apron

squares for the A patches and 2⅞″ squares (divided diagonally) for the B patches directly on the backs of the appropriate fabrics. Don't mix the two techniques, because patch sizes will vary.

For the rainbow apron, mark the following A patches: 121 white, 15 brilliant pink, 12 lavender-blue, 9 green, 9 orange, and 3 yellow-orange. Also mark 23 white triangle B patches. Cut out the patches along the pattern lines. Both patterns include ¼″ seam allowances.

3. Joining the patches—On a large flat surface, lay out the patches in rows, referring to the photograph on page 121 and to Figure 2. Since the patches will be placed on the bias, the fabrics may reflect light differently, depending on the direction of the grain. Patches turned one way may appear darker than those turned

another way, so arrange them very carefully.

Starting at the lower left hand corner of the apron and referring to Figure 2, stitch the patches together in rows. There is no need to pin the fabric before stitching. As you work, press open the seam allowances or press them toward the darkest fabric.

Row 1: Join one white B to two white A's to one white B.

(continued)

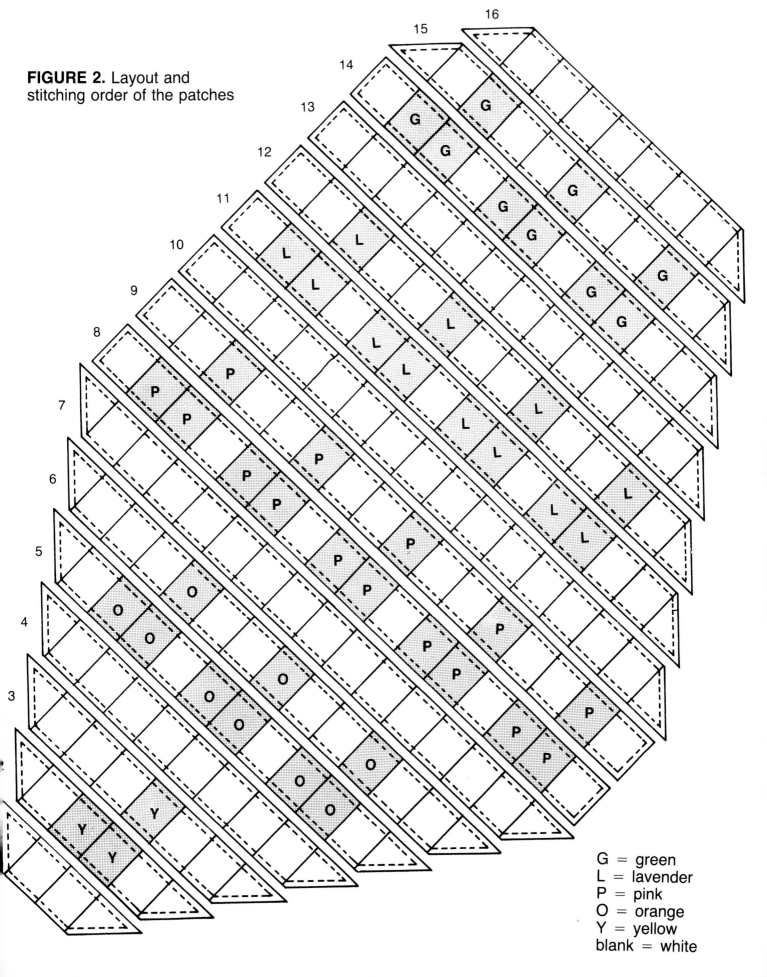

FIGURE 2. Layout and stitching order of the patches

G = green
L = lavender
P = pink
O = orange
Y = yellow
blank = white

tie placement dot

FIGURE 3. Quilting tie placement

Row 2: Join one white B to one white A to two yellow A's to one white A to one white B.

Row 3: Join one white B to three white A's to one yellow A to two white A's to one white B.

Row 4: Join one white B to eight white A's to one white B.

Row 5: Join one white B to one white A to two orange A's to one white A to two orange A's to one white A to two orange A's to one white A to one white B.

Row 6: Join one white B to three white A's to one orange A to two white A's to one orange A to two white A's to one orange A to two white A's to one white B.

Row 7: Join one white B to fourteen white A's to one white B.

Row 8: Join one white A to two pink A's to one white A to two pink A's to one white A to two pink A's to one white A to two pink A's to one white A to two pink A's to one white A.

Row 9: Join two white A's to one pink A to two white A's to one pink A to two white A's to one pink A to two white A's to one pink A to two white A's to one pink A to one white A.

Row 10: Join fifteen white A's to one white B.

Row 11: Join one white A to two lavender A's to one white A to two lavender A's to one white A to two lavender A's to one white A to two lavender A's to one white A to two lavender A's to two white A's to one white B.

Row 12: Join two white A's to one lavender A to two white A's to one lavender A to two white A's to one lavender A to two white A's to one lavender A to one white A to one white B.

Row 13: Join twelve white A's to one white B.

Row 14: Join one white A to two green A's to one white A to two green A's to one white A to two green A's to two white A's to one white B.

Row 15: Join one white B to one white A to one green A to two white A's to one green A to two white A's to one green A to one white A to one white B.

Row 16: Join one white B to seven white A's to one white B.

4. Joining the rows of patches—Pin and stitch the rows of patches together, starting with Rows 1 and 2 and working to Row 16. Match the seam lines carefully and, as you work, press open the seam allowances or press them toward the darkest color. Trim the threads on the back, and clip off the triangular tips that extend beyond the apron's shape.

5. Attaching the backing—Place the apron front and backing wrong sides together, with a layer of batting between them, if you wish. Then, using matching thread, machine stitch ¼" from the edges to secure the layers and provide a guideline for the binding.

6. Binding the apron—Encase the edges of the apron in quilt binding by hand (because of the corners), mitering the corners (see *Sewing Techniques,* page 162) and using invisible stitches.

7. The ties—Cut two 24" lengths of quilt binding for the neck ties and two 30" lengths for the waist ties. Turn under ¼" at both ends of each tie. Stitch the ends and lengthwise edges closed with invisible stitches and then stitch a neck tie securely in place on the back of the apron top at each corner and stitch a waist tie in place on the back of each waist corner.

8. Tieing together the apron layers—Referring to Figure 3 and using the full 6-ply strand of white embroidery thread, take a very tiny stitch and tie and knot the apron layers together at the position shown by each dot. The thread ends of the ties can be left on the front or back of the apron, as desired. If you wish, stitch around each heart by machine or by hand.

PATCHED HEART
CHRISTMAS APRON

Materials

⅝ yard 44″-wide green fabric

A 6″ × 44″ red fabric scrap

A 28″ × 34″ Christmas print

A 28″ × 34″ piece of thin quilt batting, optional

Sewing thread: green and red

6 yards red quilt binding or folded and pressed hem facing

1½ yards 6-ply green embroidery thread

To make the Patched Heart Christmas Apron, follow the directions for making the Patched Heart Rainbow Apron, with the following exceptions. Use green for all the white patches and red for all the colored patches. Referring to Figure 4, cut 121 square A patches and 23 triangular B patches from the green fabric, and cut 54 square A patches from the red fabric. Referring to Figure 3, assemble the patches.

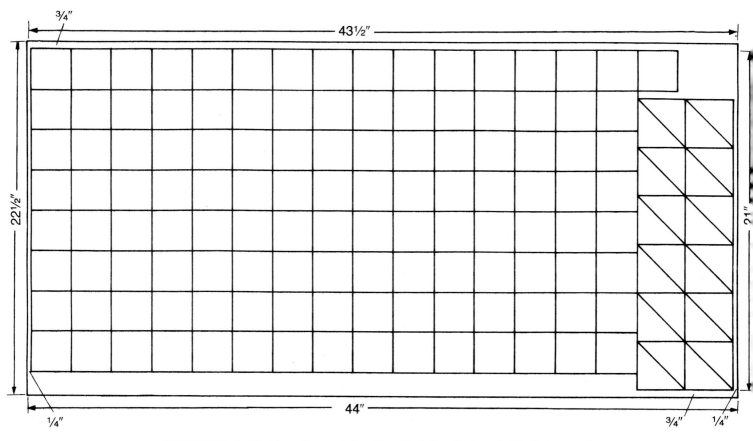

FIGURE 4. Cutting layout for the Patched Heart Christmas Apron

Christmas
Presents

Santa lovers, here's a stocking just for you! It is appliquéd with ten smiling Santas and ten puffy little hearts, and its ample size (11⅞" long and 9" wide at the top) provides lots of room for all kinds of wonderful stocking surprises.

If you don't have time to appliqué the figures by hand, substitute running stitches or machine straight or zigzag stitches for the blanket stitches I've used. You can also glue everything in place, but the result will be less attractive.

To create a trapunto effect, I pushed little puffs of stuffing under each heart and head as I appliquéd it, but that's

I-Love-Santa Stocking

an optional touch. If you are stitching by machine, the process is more difficult. Complete the stitching and then carefully cut a small slit

behind each appliqué, push in a little stuffing and close the opening with whip-stitches.

If you are making the stocking for a child under three, substitute white embroidered circles for the bells; bells, ball fringe, or buttons can always be added at a later, safer time.

One more thought. Individual Santa heads make delightful tree or package trimmers. Simply join a completed head/hat front piece to a single back piece of the same size and stuff it lightly. Knot a loop for hanging at the peak of the hat before stitching on the bell or the ball fringe.

Materials

A 13" × 17" piece of green felt
An 8½" × 11" piece of white felt
A 7" × 8½" piece of red felt
A 4" × 7½" piece of light pink felt
6-ply embroidery thread: 1 skein each of white and red, 2 yards medium pink, 1 yard black
Polyester stuffing, optional
2 yards red corded piping
Green sewing thread
A 19" length of 2"-wide green hem facing
A 4½" length of ³⁄₁₆"-wide red velvet ribbon
Ten ⁵⁄₁₆"-diameter bells

Equipment

A 14" × 17" piece of tracing paper
Rubber cement or white glue
A 4" × 5" piece of heavy paper
An X-acto knife
A white pencil or white dressmaker's carbon and tracing wheel
Zipper foot sewing machine attachment

1. Making the patterns—Trace the actual-size figures for the hat, face, and beard from the book. All the pattern lines are cutting lines for this project. Glue the patterns to heavy paper and cut them out, making an opening for the face in the beard pattern. Cut out the cheeks and nose of the face with an X-acto knife and pierce the eye dots and make a line of dots along the mouth with a needle.

Trace the stocking pattern sections and placement lines for the Santas and hearts from the book. Join the sections together along the heavy dotted lines to make the complete stocking pattern (see Figure 1). Cut out the shape. If you are using a white pencil to transfer placement lines, pierce the outlines of the Santas and hearts with a needle just enough to help you with placement.

2. Cutting the fabric—To cut out the stocking front, pin the pattern to the right side of a single layer of green felt. Trace around the pattern very lightly with a white pencil and cut out the stocking. Transfer the

placement lines of the Santas and hearts with a white pencil or a tracing wheel and dressmaker's carbon.

To make the back, trace and cut out one plain green stocking.

On the wrong side of the white felt, trace ten beards. Cut them out.

On the wrong side of the red felt, trace ten hats and ten hearts. Cut them out.

3. Making the faces—On the right side of the pink felt, trace ten faces, transferring the dotted features with a sharp, soft pencil. Cut out the faces.

Baste a face in place behind each beard. Use one strand of thread for all the embroidery in this project. Appliqué the beards to the faces using white blanket stitches. Using red embroidery thread, satin-stitch a dot for each nose and backstitch each mouth. Using pink embroidery thread, satin-stitch pink dots for the cheeks, and using black embroidery thread, satin-stitch or make French knots for the eyes.

4. The appliqués—Pin all the felt pieces in place on the stocking front, referring to the stocking pattern.

Blanket-stitch the pieces in place, matching the color of the embroidery thread to the appliqué figures. If you want a trapunto effect, push bits of stuffing under the figures as you work.

5. Stitching the stocking—Attach the piping to all edges except the top by pinning it to the right side of the stocking front so the seam allowances are together and the cording is just outside the seam line. If the seam allowances are not equal, trim the widest one to make them so. With green thread, hand baste the piping to the stocking just below the cording, then machine stitch over the basting to hold the piping in place.

Pin the stocking front to the back, right sides together. If the stocking front has shrunk a little because of the appliqué work, trim the back to fit the front. Machine stitch, clip the seam allowances along the curves, and turn the stocking right side out.

Hand baste and then machine stitch piping along the entire top, right side edge of the stocking, aligning the piping and stocking as before and starting and ending the piping at an inconspicuous place on the stocking back, preferably where the hanging loop will be placed and not at a side seam.

6. Finishing touches—Open the seam allowance of the hem facing, align the edge with the stocking top, right sides together, and hand baste to the stocking top. Machine stitch. Fold the facing to the inside of the stocking and invisibly stitch.

Softly fold the velvet ribbon in half, wrong sides together, to make a loop and stitch the ends together. Insert the stitched end of the loop into the top right side of the stocking and tack it in place through both sides.

Securely stitch a bell to the peak of each hat.

FIGURE 1: Stocking sections joined to make complete stocking pattern

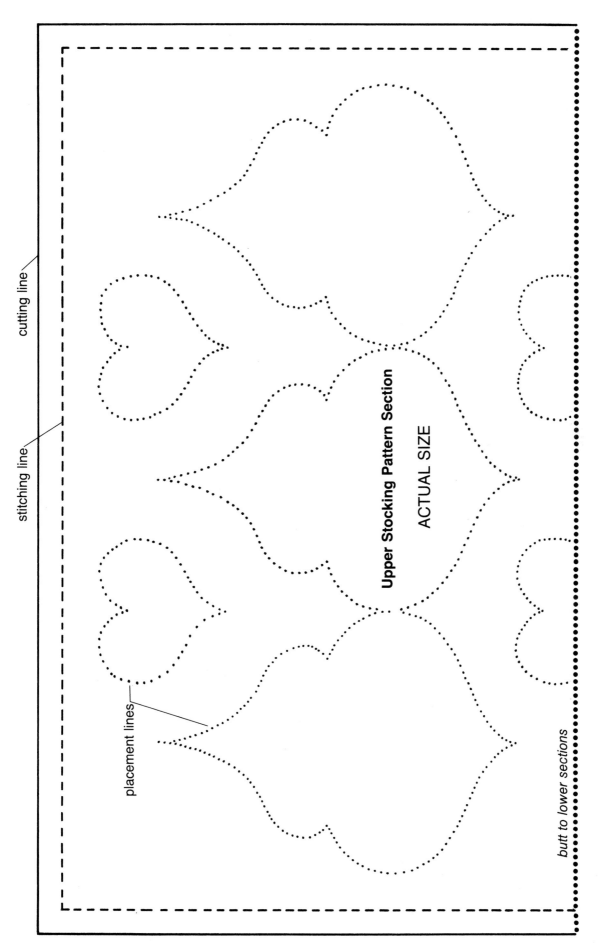

cutting line

stitching line

placement lines

Upper Stocking Pattern Section

ACTUAL SIZE

butt to lower sections

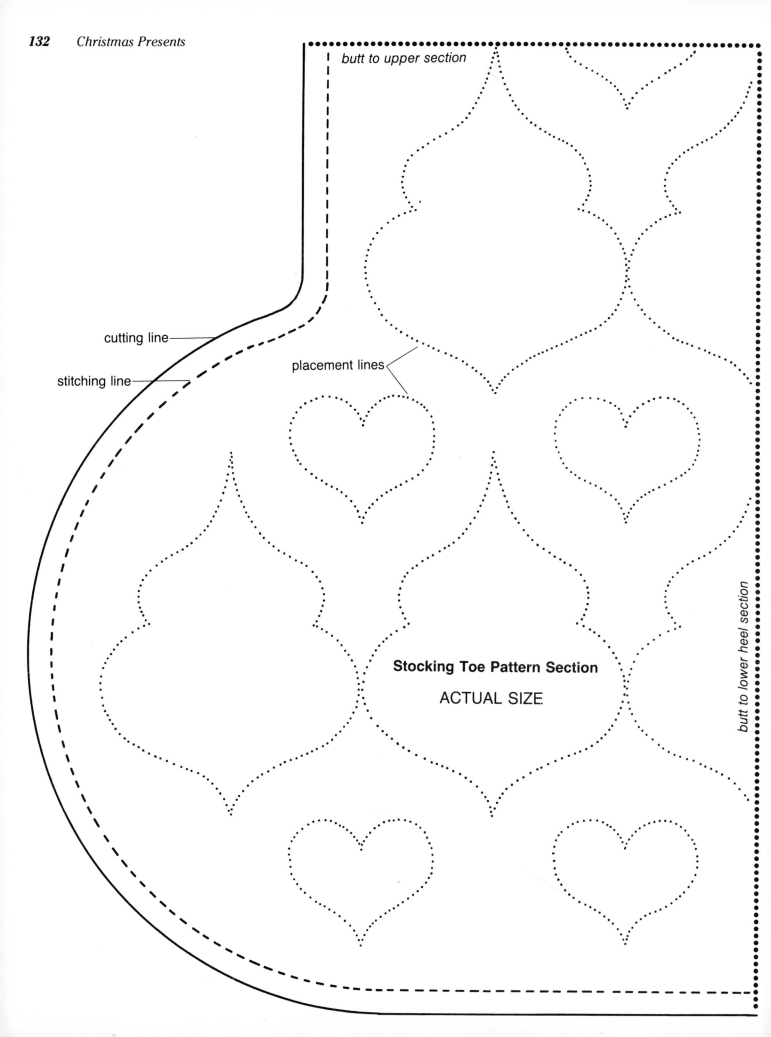

butt to upper section

cutting line

stitching line

placement lines

Stocking Toe Pattern Section

ACTUAL SIZE

butt to lower heel section

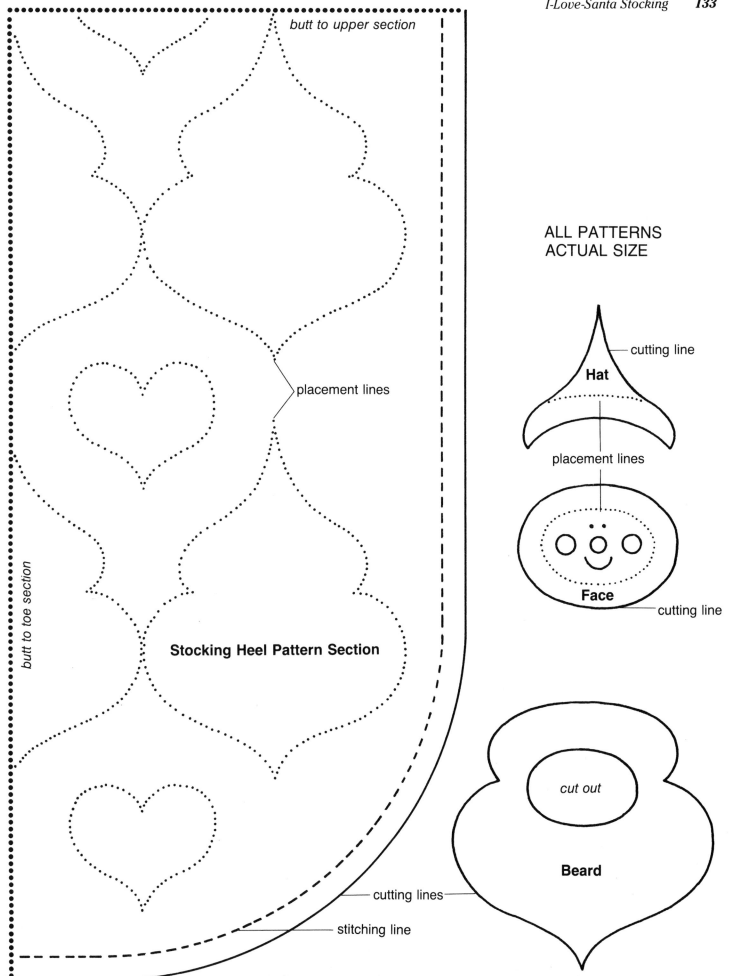

butt to upper section

placement lines

butt to toe section

Stocking Heel Pattern Section

cutting lines

stitching line

ALL PATTERNS
ACTUAL SIZE

cutting line

Hat

placement lines

Face

cutting line

cut out

Beard

Neatly tailored, crisply striped, or softly ruffled, this stocking design can be varied to suit the personality of any or all of your Christmas loves. You can simply blanket stitch the felt stocking, by far the easiest to make, or you can select elegant fabrics and trims and embellish the design to your heart's content.

If it's a case of making every minute count, the sim-

Heart Top Stockings

ple felt stocking can be made entirely on the sewing machine, using white or matching threads. The finished

stocking measures about 12" by 17", with a 7" opening. There are only slight variations in size between the designs.

To make a quick and convenient gift envelope or a tiny baby stocking, don't enlarge the pattern; just trace the pieces directly from the stocking on the grid. Embroider a name on the top of the finished design, and you're all set!

FELT HEART STOCKING
Materials
An 8½" × 11" red felt scrap
An 18" × 20" green felt scrap
3-ply crewel yarn: 2½ yards red, 2 yards green
A 6" length of ³⁄₁₆"-wide green velvet ribbon
An 8½" × 11" piece of thin polyester quilt batting

1. Making the patterns—Trace the patterns for the heart (together with the dots), the heel, and the toe. Make a grid of 1" squares to match the grid in the book, and enlarge the stocking pattern on your grid following the directions on page 163. Use the heart, heel, and toe patterns as aids in shaping the stocking and omit the broken lines. Use a large needle to make a small hole in the stocking pattern at the tip of the heart and corner of the heel. The pattern lines are cutting lines for felt.

2. Marking and cutting the fabric—On the wrong side of the red felt, draw one heart, heel, and toe, and cut them out along the pattern lines.

On the wrong side of the green felt, draw one stocking and one reverse stocking. To reverse the stocking, simply flip over the pattern. Mark the placement for the heart tip and the heel corner with a dot on the stocking front. Cut out both pieces along the pattern lines.

3. Assembling the stocking—Pin the heart, toe, and heel in place on

the right side of the stocking front.

Using one strand of red crewel yarn and blanket stitches, appliqué the pieces in place. Stitch completely around the heart, but stitch only along the straight edges of the heel and toe.

Pin the stocking front and back wrong sides together and blanket stitch around the edges, using yarn to match the felt.

Finish the top open edge of the stocking back with green blanket stitches.

Tack a ribbon hanging loop inside the stocking at the top right seam.

PRINT STOCKING WITH EYELET RUFFLES
Materials
A 9" × 15" piece of red-with-white print fabric
An 18" × 24½" piece of green-with-white print fabric
An 18" × 24½" piece of white batiste
An 18" × 24½" piece of traditional polyester quilt batting
Sewing thread: white and red
2³⁄₈ yards of 1"-wide (including binding) white eyelet ruffle
A 6" length of ³⁄₁₆"-wide red velvet ribbon

1. Making the patterns—Trace patterns for the heart (with the dots), the heel, and the toe. Make a grid of 1" squares to match the grid in the

book, and enlarge the stocking pattern on your grid following the directions on page 163 and omitting the dotted lines. Use the heart, heel, and toe patterns to help shape the stocking pattern. Using a large needle, pierce the stocking pattern at the tip of the heart and corner of the heel. On the stocking front, mark the dots at the top of the stocking and at the toe and heel.

2. Marking and cutting the fabric—On the wrong side of the red-and-white print fabric, trace one heart (with the dots) and the toe, and heel. Cut them out, adding ¼" seam allowances.

On the wrong side of the green-and-white print fabric, trace one stocking (the front) and one reverse stocking (the back). (To reverse the stocking, simply flip over the pattern.) On the batiste, also trace one stocking and one reverse stocking for the lining.

Cut out the stocking and lining, adding ¼" seam allowances to the pieces. On the right side of the stocking front, mark the placement of the heart tip and heel corner with dots, and within the seam allowance, mark the dots at the stocking sides, toe, and heel.

3. Attaching the batting—Pin and baste each lining piece, wrong side down, to batting. Trim the batting to the shape of the lining.

Pin the stocking front to its corresponding lining, right sides together along the top edge. Machine stitch along the top curves between

the side dots, securing the stitching at the start and finish. Trim the batting just outside the seam line. Clip almost to the seam line at each side dot and clip the seam allowances all around the curves and into the V-shaped area. Repeat for the stocking back.

Turn the stocking front and back right side out, and very lightly press them along the top curves, if necessary. Pin and baste all the layers

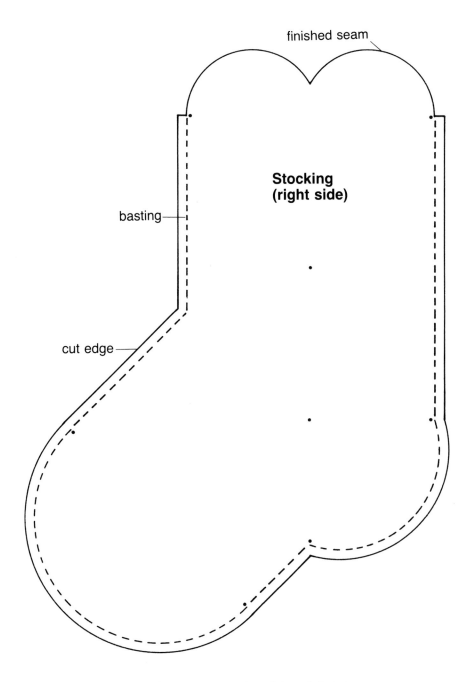

FIGURE 1. Right side of Print or Bandana Stocking front or back with lining attached

of each section together around the remaining edges. The stocking sections should resemble the drawing in Figure 1.

4. Attaching the toe and heel appliqués and the ruffle—Press under and baste the seam allowances along the straight edge of the toe section and both straight edges of the heel. Baste eyelet ruffle to the back of the heel and toe sections along the straight edges.

Pin the toe and heel in place on the stocking front and invisibly appliqué them, passing the needle through to the lining side to quilt the stocking at the same time. Baste the curved edges of the heel and toe pieces to the seam allowances of the stocking.

Place the remaining eyelet ruffle, right side down, along the sides and bottom of the stocking front, starting and ending at the side dots, so the ruffle faces in and the bound end of the ruffle is aligned with the cut edge of the stocking. Fold under both cut ends of the ruffle at the dots at a 45° angle and pin. Machine baste 1/4" from the edge, catching the folded ruffle ends.

5. Joining the stocking front and back—Pin the stocking front and back, right sides together, and stitch 1/4" from the edges, beginning and ending at the side dots and securing the stitches at the start and finish. Grade the seam allowances (see *Sewing Techniques*) and clip them along the curves. Turn the stocking right side out.

6. Attaching the heart—Baste along the seam line of the heart to transfer the outline to the front of the fabric. Slightly trim the seam allowance with pinking shears or clip around the outside edge. Clip deeply into the V-shaped area at the top. Fold the seam allowance under and baste. Cut a 22½" length of eyelet ruffle and baste it to the back of the heart edge mitering the binding at the heart tip.

Pin the heart in place and invisibly appliqué and quilt it at the same time to the stocking.

7. The finishing touch—Attach a ribbon hanging loop inside the stocking at the top right seam.

Each sq. = 1 in.

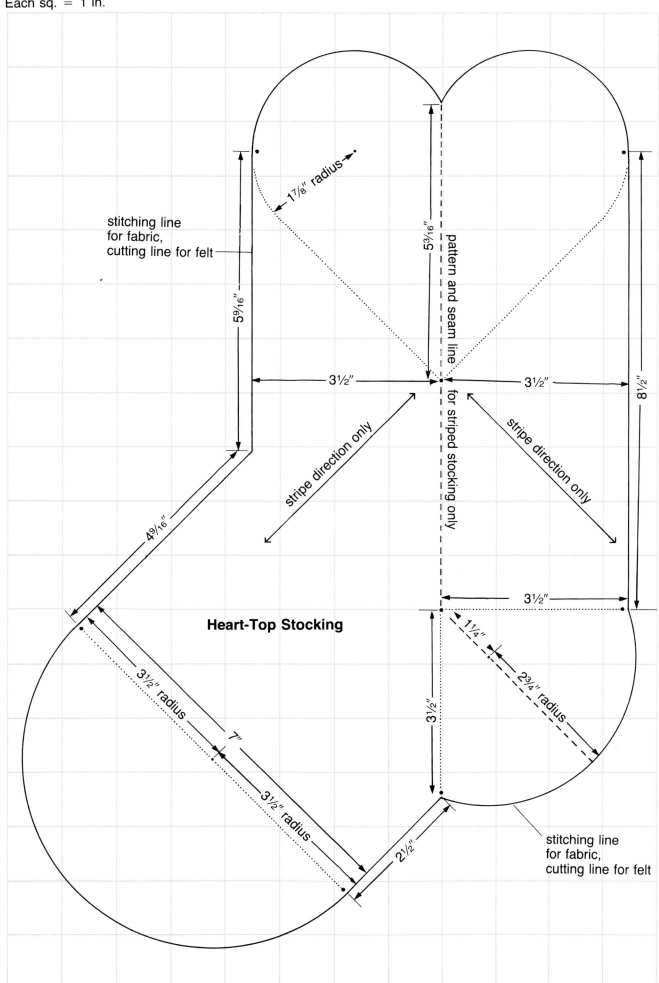

Heart-Top Stocking

stitching line
for fabric,
cutting line for felt

1⅞" radius

5³⁄₁₆"

pattern and seam line

5⁹⁄₁₆"

3½"

3½"

8½"

stripe direction only

for striped stocking only

stripe direction only

4⁹⁄₁₆"

3½"

3½" radius

7"

3½" radius

2¾" radius

1¼"

3½"

2½"

stitching line
for fabric,
cutting line for felt

BANDANA PRINT HEART STOCKING

Note: When choosing the bandana for this design, avoid those with a central medallion and select one that has a large center field and a wide border. Use tracing paper patterns so you can find the best area of the handkerchief from which to cut each part of the stocking. Place the heart tip and heel corner in two of the corners of the bandana. Also, you'll need a zipper foot attachment for your sewing machine in order to stitch the piping.

Materials

A 21″ × 21″ red bandana handkerchief

An 18″ × 34″ piece of dark green fabric

An 18″ × 24½″ piece of traditional polyester quilt batting

Sewing thread: red and green

2½ yards dark green piping

A 6″ length of ³⁄₁₆″-wide dark green velvet ribbon

1. Making the patterns, cutting the fabric, and attaching the batting—Follow the directions for making the Print Stocking with Eyelet Ruffles Steps 1 through 3, with the following exceptions. Cut the heart and heel from the bandana corners, the toe from the border, and the stocking front from the center. Cut the stocking back as well as the front and back lining pieces from the green fabric.

2. Attaching the toe and heel appliqués and the piping—Press under and baste the seam allowances along the straight edge of the toe piece and the straight edges of the heel. If necessary, trim the pip-

ing seam allowance to ¼″. Baste a strip of piping to the back of the heel and toe along the straight edges, clipping and mitering the piping seam allowance at the heel corner.

Pin and baste the toe and heel in place on the stocking front and invisibly appliqué them along the straight edges, passing the needle through to the lining side to quilt the stocking at the same time. Baste the heel and toe pieces along the curved edges to the seam allowances of the stocking.

Baste a strip of piping along the edge of the right side of the stocking front so that the seam allowance of the piping is flush with the edge of the stocking and the ends of the piping extend ½″ beyond the side dots. Carefully open the bias cover of the piping and trim off ½″ of the cord at each end. Close the bias tape and fold and pin the ends down along

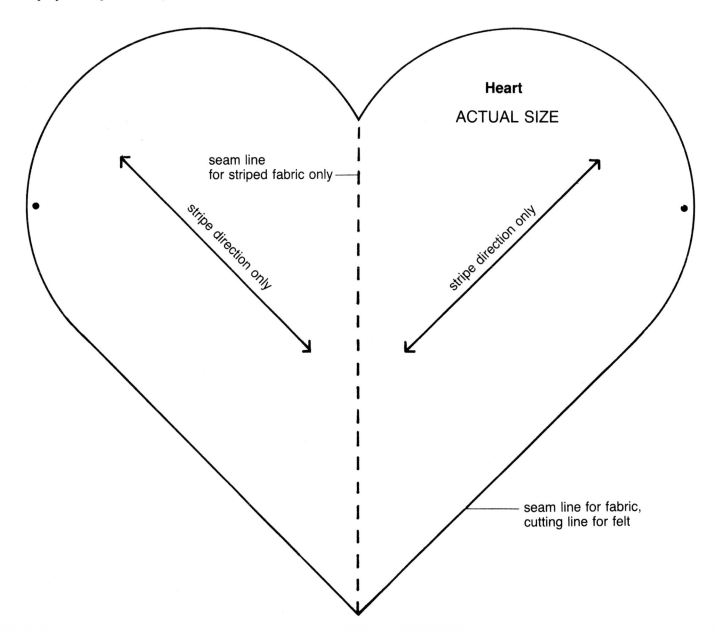

seam line
for striped fabric only

stripe direction only

stripe direction only

Heart
ACTUAL SIZE

seam line for fabric,
cutting line for felt

the seam line. Clip the seam allowance of the piping at the angles created where the foot joins the heel and leg part of stocking.

Machine stitch the piping along the seam line.

3. Joining the stocking front and back and attaching the heart and ribbon loop—Join the stocking front and back and attach the heart and hanging loop following the directions for the Green Stocking with Eyelet Ruffles, Steps 4, 5, and 6, substituting piping for the ruffle as follows. Trim the seam allowance of the piping to ¼". Cut a 22½" length of piping and baste it along the back edge of the heart, clipping and mitering the piping seam allowance at the heart tip. If the piping puckers at any point around the stocking shape, make a little tuck pulling the excess to the stocking back and tack it with a few tightly pulled stitches.

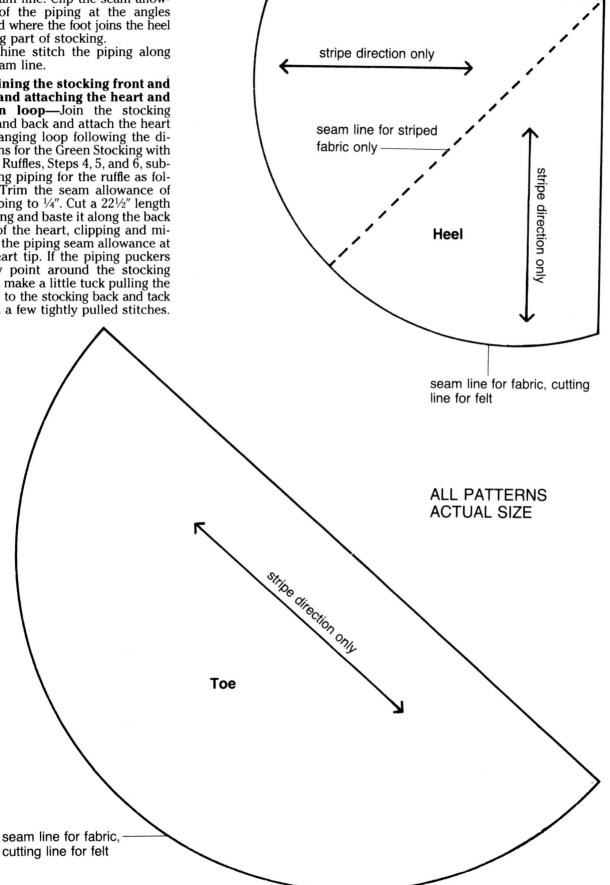

stripe direction only

seam line for striped fabric only

Heel

stripe direction only

seam line for fabric, cutting line for felt

ALL PATTERNS
ACTUAL SIZE

stripe direction only

Toe

seam line for fabric, cutting line for felt

STRIPED HEART STOCKING WITH BIAS BINDING

Materials

An 18″ × 25″ piece of red-and-white striped fabric with the stripes parallel to the 18″-long edge.

An 18″ × 34″ piece of red fabric

An 18″ × 24½″ piece of traditional polyester quilt batting

1⅞ yards of red bias binding

1. Making the patterns—Refer to Step 1 of the Print Stocking with Eyelet Ruffles to enlarge the stocking pattern. Trace the patterns for the heart, toe, heel, and stocking, and cut the patterns in half along the broken lines for all except the toe section so they resemble the shapes in Figure 2.

2. Cutting the fabric—Referring to Figure 3 for the cutting layout, trace the patterns for the heart, toe, heel, and stocking on the wrong side of the striped fabric and cut them out, adding ¼″ seam allowances. On the wrong side of the red fabric, mark one complete stocking front for the lining and two reverse complete stockings, one for the stocking back and one for the lining. To reverse the pattern, simply flip it over. Cut out the pieces, adding ¼″ seam allowances.

3. Attaching the batting—Pin and baste each lining section, wrong side down to batting. Trim the batting to the shape of the lining.

Pin the striped front halves of the stocking, right sides together, stitch, and press open the seam allowance.

Place the stocking front wrong side down against the batting side of the lining and baste ³⁄₁₆″ from the edge. Repeat to join the stocking back and lining layers.

4. Attaching the heart—Stitch the heart halves right sides together along the center line, and clip the seam allowance at the dot on each side. Press the center seam allowances flat.

Baste along the seam line to transfer it to the fabric front. Slightly trim the seam allowance, below the dots only, with pinking shears or clip it. Fold under the seam allowance below the dots only, to make a hem, and baste.

Pin and baste the heart in place at the stocking front top. Invisibly appliqué it through all layers, to quilt it as well, below the dots only. Machine stitch ¼″ from the top curved

FIGURE 2 Striped Stocking pattern pieces

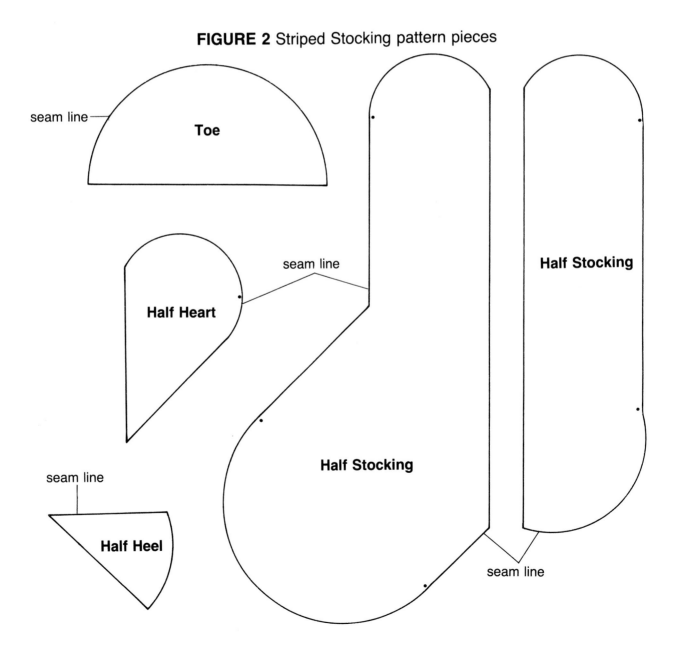

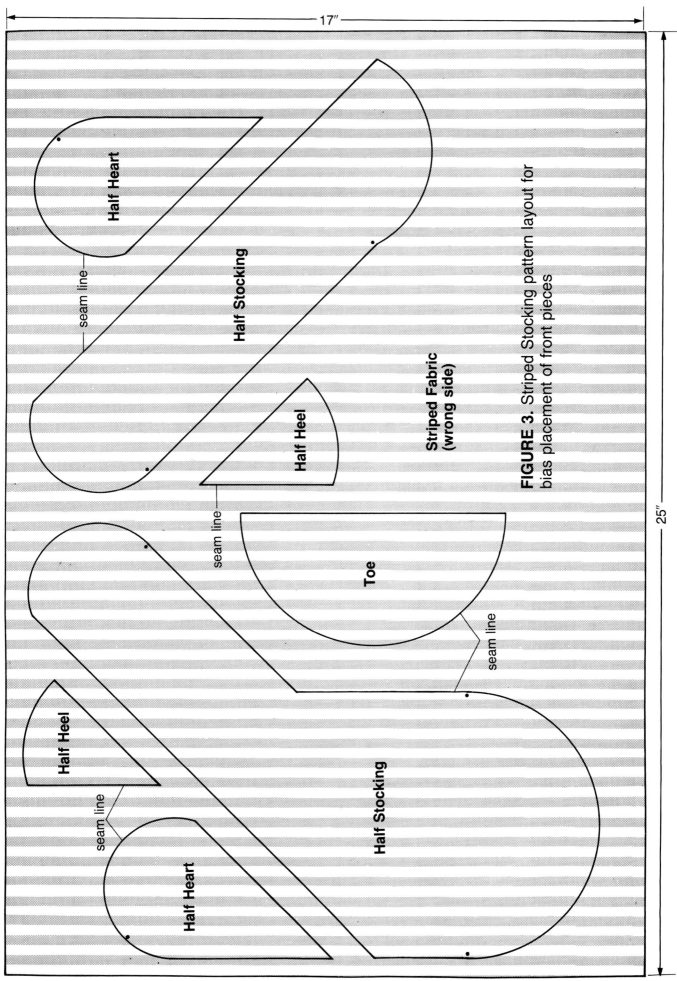

17"

25"

Half Heart

seam line

Half Stocking

Half Heel

seam line

Striped Fabric
(wrong side)

Toe

seam line

Half Heel

seam line

Half Heart

Half Stocking

FIGURE 3. Striped Stocking pattern layout for bias placement of front pieces

edges of the stocking front and back, starting and finishing the stitches ½" below the dots on the stocking sides. Trim away almost ⅛" of the seam allowance along the curved edges, starting and finishing ½" below the dots on the stocking sides. Overcast or zigzag stitch along the cut curved edges to eliminate bulk.

5. Attaching the toe and heel— Pin the heel halves right sides together along the center line and stitch. Press open the seam allowance. Attach the toe and heel appliqués following Step 4 of the direc-

tions for the Print Stocking with Eyelet Ruffles.

6. Attaching the binding and joining the stocking front and back—Cut two 12½" lengths of bias binding, and using invisible hand stitches, bind the top curved edges of the stocking front and back, starting and finishing ½" below the dots on the stocking sides.

Cut a 6" length of binding for a hanging loop. Close the open edges with invisible stitches, and tack it in place on the lining side of the stocking back.

Pin and baste the stocking front and back lining sides together. Machine stitch exactly ¼" from the edge. Trim away almost ⅛" of the seam allowances, then overcast or zigzag stitch along the cut edges to eliminate bulk.

Bind the unfinished edges of the stocking with bias binding, hand stitching invisibly and tucking under the cut ends at start and finish. Apply the binding first to the stocking front, placing the binding edge just over the machine stitched line. Then stitch the binding to the stocking back.

Some of these heart orna-ments can be put together in a matter of minutes. Others will take quite a bit longer, but regardless of the time spent, making the designs is an enjoyable way to use lots of your felt, lace, and ribbon scraps. I really loved making them, myself. The puffy

Christmas Heart Ornaments

hearts can be used as pin-cushions or sachets and the heart baskets will hold tiny presents, candy, or love notes. And, when you want to send someone just a little more than a card, some of the flat ornaments are the perfect size to include with your holiday greetings.

General Equipment
Heavy-weight paper
X-acto knife
Small, sharp scissors
Glue

RUFFLED POLKA DOT HEART

Materials
A 4″ × 8″ red or green dotted fabric scrap
A 1⅞″ × 22″ strip of white bias hem facing or bias fabric
A 22″ length of red or dark green baby rickrack
6-ply embroidery thread: 27″ dark green or red
Polyester stuffing
White sewing thread

1. Making the pattern and cutting the fabric—Trace and label only pattern A in Figure 1 and glue the tracing to heavy-weight paper. Using an X-acto knife, cut out the heart.

On the wrong side of the dot fabric, trace the heart pattern twice. Cut out the hearts, adding ¼″ seam allowances.

2. Making the ruffle—To make a ruffle from the hem facing, trim off each ¼″ folded edge, making the strip about 1⅞″ wide. Now, whether using hem facing or a strip of fabric cut on the bias, stitch the ends together, leaving a ¼″ seam allowance. Press open the seam allowance and press the fabric in half lengthwise to make a circular strip about 1″ wide. Mark the center point of the strip, opposite the seam, with a dot.

Machine baste ¼″ from the open

lengthwise edges of the strip to join them. Stitch a row of red rickrack (if you are making a green heart) or green rickrack (if you are making a red heart) invisibly by hand along the folded edge of the ruffle strip. Pull the basting thread to make an 11″-long ruffle and secure the thread.

3. Attaching the ruffle—Pin the ruffle on the right side of one heart piece, rickrack side down, so the rickrack-trimmed edge faces toward the center of the heart, the edge of the ruffle is aligned with the edge of the heart, the seam line of the ruffle is at the center top, and the dot on the ruffle edge touches the tip of the heart. Baste by hand, easing in any extra fullness at the heart tip, then machine stitch along the seam line.

4. Assembling the heart—If necessary, flatten and temporarily baste the rickrack edge of the ruffle to the heart front to hold down the fullness. Pin the heart front and back, right sides together, and machine stitch leaving an opening between the dots on one side. Clip into the V-shaped area at the heart top, and cut off the tip of the seam allowance close to the stitching. Trim the remaining seam allowances with pinking shears or clip along the curves.

Remove the basting stitches that held the ruffle flat, and turn the heart right side out. Stuff the heart maintaining flatness with your hand, and close the opening with invisible hand stitches. Also remove the gathering on the ruffle, if it shows.

5. The hanging loop—To make a hanging loop cut three 9″ lengths of the embroidery thread (red if you

are making a green heart, green if you are making a red heart). Knot them together at one end, tape the knot to the edge of a work surface and braid. Knot the end of the braid. Tack both ends of the braid to the center top of the ruffle behind the rickrack. Fold and invisibly stitch the ruffle at the V-shaped area of the heart to hide the ruffle seam and the end of the hanging loop.

Overleaf: *Brightening a Christmas tree are, clockwise from lower left, a Flower-trimmed Felt Basket, a Felt Heart Wreath with a Star-shaped Center, a Puffy Segmented Heart, a Ruffled and Embroidered Heart, a Felt Heart Wreath with a Circular Center, a Ruffled Polka Dot Heart, an Overlapping Felt Heart Basket, and a Grosgrain Ribbon Loop Heart. In the center, from left to right, are another Ruffled Polka Dot Heart, a String of Felt Hearts, and two Cross-stitch Hearts.*

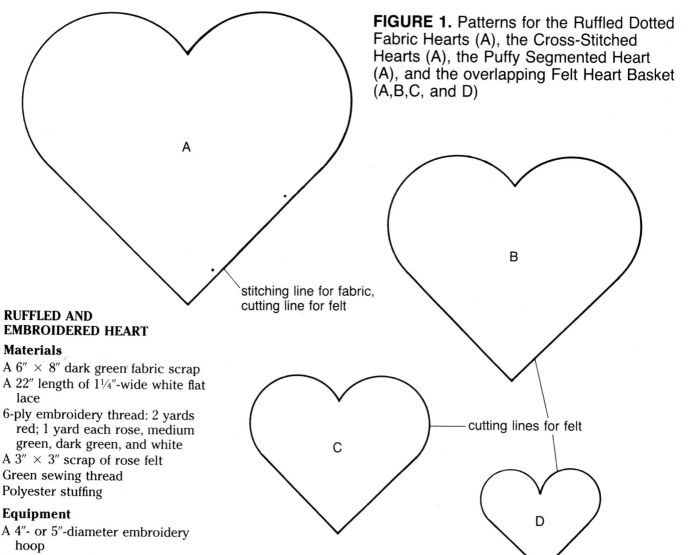

FIGURE 1. Patterns for the Ruffled Dotted Fabric Hearts (A), the Cross-Stitched Hearts (A), the Puffy Segmented Heart (A), and the overlapping Felt Heart Basket (A,B,C, and D)

stitching line for fabric, cutting line for felt

cutting lines for felt

RUFFLED AND EMBROIDERED HEART

Materials

A 6″ × 8″ dark green fabric scrap

A 22″ length of 1¼″-wide white flat lace

6-ply embroidery thread: 2 yards red; 1 yard each rose, medium green, dark green, and white

A 3″ × 3″ scrap of rose felt

Green sewing thread

Polyester stuffing

Equipment

A 4″- or 5″-diameter embroidery hoop

White dressmaker's carbon

1. Making the pattern and marking the fabric—Trace heart pattern E in Figure 2 and cut it out. Pin the pattern to the right side of the green fabric with a piece of white dressmaker's carbon under it. Trace over the embroidery design lines with a sharp pencil to transfer the floral motif to the fabric, but don't trace the heart outline and don't cut the fabric yet.

2. The embroidery—Using a single strand of embroidery thread, stitch the design as follows: satin stitch red outer petals and pink center petals; straight stitch white stamens on the side flowers, and top them with white French knots; and chain stitch white stamens on the center flower and medium-green stems and leaves.

Trace heart pattern F in Figure 2, cut it out, and if you wish, write the year on it. On rose felt, trace around the pattern shape and transfer the date, if desired, using a very sharp

FIGURE 2. Patterns for the Ruffled and Embroidered Heart

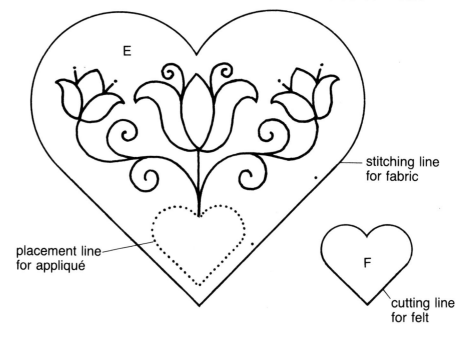

E

placement line for appliqué

stitching line for fabric

F

cutting line for felt

pencil and punching through the pattern. Don't cut out the heart. Using one strand of white embroidery thread, chain stitch the date. Cut out the felt heart along the pattern line and, using two strands of white embroidery thread, blanket stitch it in place on the green heart.

3. Cutting the fabric—Center the large heart pattern (E) from Figure 2 over the embroidery on the wrong side of the fabric and mark the heart outline. Cut out the heart adding a ¼" seam allowance. Similarly, mark and cut out another plain green heart for the back.

4. Making the ruffle—Stitch the ends of the lace right sides together, leaving a ¼" seam allowance. Press open the seam allowance and mark the center point of the lace, opposite the seam, with a dot.

5. Attaching the ruffle and assembling and finishing the heart—Finish the heart following the directions for the Ruffled Polka Dot Heart, Steps 3, 4, and 5, using green embroidery thread for the hanging loop.

OVERLAPPING FELT HEART BASKET

Materials

A 5" × 9" piece of red felt

A 3" × 7" piece of rose felt

3 yards of 6-ply white embroidery thread

1. Making the patterns and cutting the fabric—Trace patterns A, B, C, and D from Figure 1 onto tracing paper, paste them to heavy paper, and cut them out.

Trace around the patterns directly onto the wrong side of the felt and cut the pieces out along the pattern lines as follows. From the red felt, cut two A and two C hearts, and two ⅜" × 7" handle pieces. From the rose felt, cut two B and two D hearts.

2. Assembling the front and back of the basket—To make the basket front, pin a small rose D to a red C aligning the hearts at the bottom. Using two strands of white embroidery thread, appliqué the rose D heart along its curved edge to the red C heart. On the wrong side, trim away the lower overlapping part of the larger heart C, about ⅛" from the stitching.

Pin this section to a rose B heart, aligning the bottoms of the hearts, and appliqué the red C heart along its curved edge to the rose B heart. On the wrong side, trim away the lower overlapping portion of the rose B heart, about ⅛" from the stitching.

In a similar manner appliqué this section to a red A heart, but don't trim away the overlapping portion of the red A heart.

Repeat the above procedure to make a duplicate heart back.

3. Finishing the basket—Pin the completed front and back basket

sections wrong sides together and join the straight sides with blanket stitches. Leave the curved basket top open and finish the front and back edges separately with blanket stitches.

Baste the red handle strips together, one on top of the other, and finish the entire edge with blanket stitches. Tack one end of the handle inside the center front of the basket and the other end of the handle inside the center back.

FLOWER-TRIMMED FELT BASKET

Materials

A 5" × 8" white felt scrap

A 2" × 2" red felt scrap

A 1½" × 2" rose felt scrap

A 1½" × 3" medium green felt scrap

6-ply embroidery thread: 3 yards medium green, 18" white, 18" rose, 18" red

1. Making the patterns—Referring to Figure 3, trace heart pattern G, transferring all the design placement lines. Trace over the design lines on the back of the pattern with a soft pencil and cut out the heart. Trace and cut out patterns H, I, J, K, and L.

2. Marking and cutting the appliqués—Pin heart G to white felt and rub off the design lines with a

FIGURE 3. Patterns for the Flower-trimmed Felt Basket

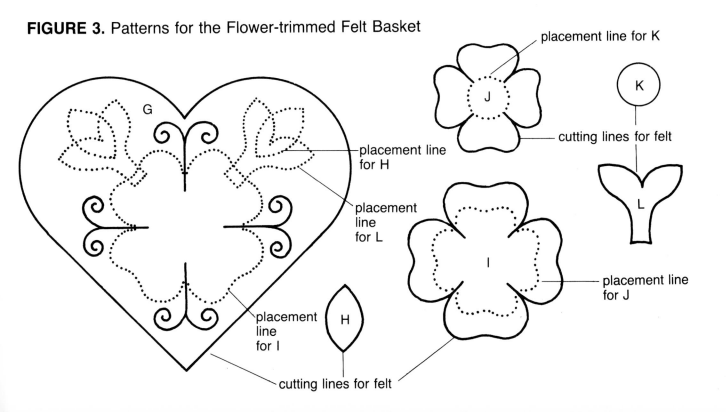

firm, blunt object, but don't trace around the heart shape yet. If the design doesn't rub off well, use a very sharp pencil to punch through the pattern and mark the design lines with a series of fine dots.

Trace the other patterns as follows and cut them out along the pattern lines. From the rose felt cut two H buds and one J flower. From the red felt, cut one I flower. From the white felt, cut one K flower center and two ⅜"-wide by 7"-long handle pieces. From the green felt cut two L leaf pieces.

3. Embroidering and appliquéing the basket—Using one strand of green thread, chain stitch the curved vine lines at the top, bottom, and sides of the flower marked on the white felt.

Using one strand of matching embroidery thread and blanket stitches (see *Embroidery Stitches,* page 164), appliqué the flower sections in place as follows. Tack each rose bud H in place on the white felt and appliqué it. Then overlap and tack the green leaf L pieces in place and appliqué them.

Tack the white center K to the rose flower J and appliqué it. Tack the rose flower J to the red flower I and appliqué it.

Tack the completed red flower in place on the white felt and appliqué it. Remove all visible tacks.

4. Cutting out and joining the hearts—Center the tracing paper pattern G on the wrong side of the completed appliquéd area. Trace the heart shape and cut the felt along the pattern line. Mark and cut a plain white heart for the basket back.

Pin the heart front and back, wrong sides together, and using two strands of green embroidery thread, join the straight sides with blanket stitches. Leave open the curved heart top and edge the front and back separately with blanket stitches.

5. The handle—Baste the white handle strips together, one on top of the other, then, using two strands of green embroidery thread and blanket stitches, stitch around the entire edge of the handle. Tack one end of the handle inside the center front of the basket and the other end of the handle inside the center back.

CROSS-STITCH HEART ORNAMENTS

Materials and Equipment for Each Heart

6-ply embroidery thread: 3 yards red and 1 yard dark green for the Tiny Heart Design; or 1 yard rose, 1 yard red, and 3 yards dark green for the Floral Heart Design.

A 4"- × 5"-diameter embroidery hoop

A 6" × 6" piece of 14-squares-to-the-inch white Aida embroidery cloth

A 4¼" × 4¼" white fabric scrap

White sewing thread

Polyester stuffing

1. Cross-stitching the design—Using one strand of embroidery thread and an embroidery hoop and referring to Figure 4 for the Tiny Heart Design chart or Figure 5 for the Floral Design chart, complete the cross-stitch embroidery on the Aida cloth (see *Embroidery Stitches*).

2. Making a heart pattern and cutting the fabric—Trace a pattern A heart from Figure 1. Center the tracing paper pattern over the wrong side of the embroidery, and trace the pattern outline around it. Trace the pattern again on the white fabric scrap to make the heart ornament back. Cut out both hearts, adding ¼" seam allowances.

3. The hanging loop—To make a hanging loop, cut three 8" lengths of red embroidery thread for the Tiny Heart Design or green embroidery thread for the Floral Design, and knot them together at one end. Secure the knotted end to the edge of a work surface with tape, then braid the strands and knot the free ends together.

Tack both ends of the hanging loop to the center top on the right side of the heart front, so the loop faces the center of the heart and the ends are aligned with the seam allowance.

4. Assembling the heart—Pin the heart front and back right sides together. Machine stitch along the seam line, leaving an opening between the dots for turning.

Clip into the V-shaped area at the heart top. Cut off the tip of the seam allowance close to the stitching. Clip the remaining seam allowance or trim it with pinking shears but do not trim or clip the seam allowance between the dots.

Turn the heart right side out, stuff it firmly, but maintain some flatness. Close the opening with invisible stitches.

5. Trimming the heart edge—To make the trim for the edge, cut three 14" lengths of red embroidery thread for the Tiny Heart Design, or green for the Floral Design and knot them together at one end. Braid the strands together and knot the free ends. Trim excess thread ends close to the knot. Starting at the center top, hand stitch the braid to the heart exactly along the seam line.

Each sq. = $\frac{1}{8}$ in.

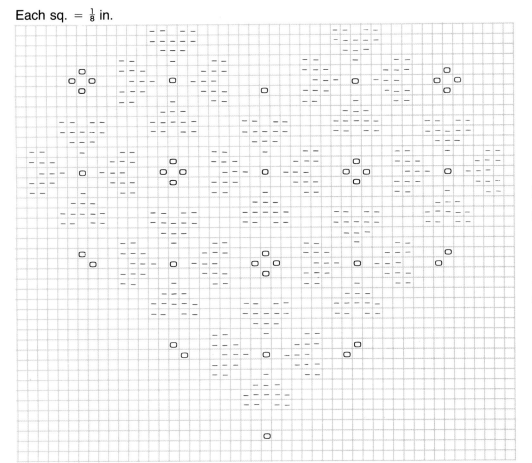

FIGURE 4. Tiny Heart cross-stitch chart

Color Key:
− Red
○ Green

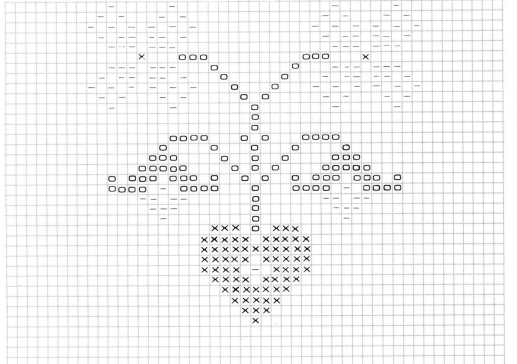

FIGURE 5. Floral cross-stitch chart

Color Key:
− Red
○ Green
X Rose

FELT HEART WREATHS

Materials

A 4″ × 8″ felt scrap: red for pattern M, white for pattern N

6-ply embroidery thread: 3 yards dark green for pattern M, red for pattern N

Polyester stuffing

1. Making the pattern—If you want to make the Red Heart Wreath with the Circular Center, trace pattern M, Figure 6. If you want to make the White Heart Wreath with the Star-Shaped Center, trace pattern N, Figure 7. Paste the pattern to heavy paper and cut out using an X-acto knife.

2. Marking and cutting the fabrics—If you are using pattern M, trace the pattern twice on the back of the red felt. If you are using pattern N, trace the pattern twice on the back of the white felt. Cut out both pieces along the pattern lines.

3. The hanging loop—Cut three 8″-long strands of embroidery thread, green for pattern M, or red for pattern N, and knot the ends together at one end. Braid the strands and knot the free ends. Tack both ends of the braid to the wrong side of the wreath back piece at either a heart tip or a V-shaped area, depending on which wreath you are making.

4. Assembling the wreath—Pin the front and back of the wreath wrong sides together. Using two strands of embroidery thread, green for pattern M or red for pattern N, edge each individual heart in the wreath with blanket stitches, tucking a bit of stuffing into each heart before stitching it closed.

GROSGRAIN RIBBON LOOP HEART

Materials

A 14″ length of 1″-wide white grosgrain ribbon

A 12″ length of 1″-wide red grosgrain ribbon

A 10″ length of 1″-wide green grosgrain ribbon

Sewing thread: white, green, and red

A 27″ length of 6-ply dark green embroidery thread

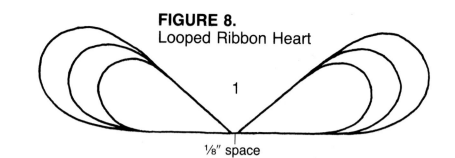

FIGURE 8.
Looped Ribbon Heart

1

⅛″ space

1. Marking and joining the ribbons—Mark the midway point on each length of ribbon with basting stitches. This will be the heart tip. Aligning the center bastings, layer the white, red, and green ribbons in that order. Join the layers with bastings, again at the midpoint. Align the three cut edges of ribbon at one end and join them with overcast stitches. Repeat at the other end.

2. The hanging loop—Cut three 9″ lengths of dark green embroidery thread and knot them together at one end. Tape the knot to the edge of a work surface, braid the threads and knot the free ends. Set aside.

3. Forming the heart—Referring to Figure 8, Drawing 1, fold both overcast ends toward the center basting line, leaving a ⅛″ gap between the two ends, and securely stitch them in place. The finished heart will be neatest if the stitches

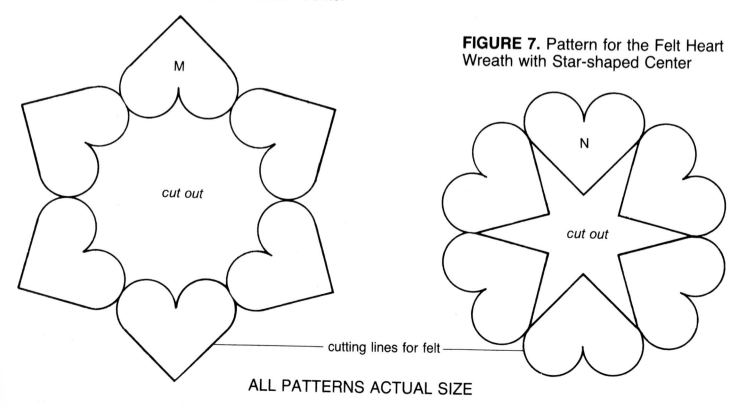

FIGURE 6. Pattern for the Felt Heart Wreath with Circular Center

M

cut out

FIGURE 7. Pattern for the Felt Heart Wreath with Star-shaped Center

N

cut out

cutting lines for felt

ALL PATTERNS ACTUAL SIZE

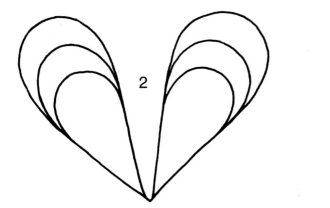

don't show on the white ribbon.

Referring to Figure 8, Drawing 2, fold at the center basting line to make the heart tip. Secure the tip by hand, stitching across the width of the ribbon about ⅛″ from the fold. Pass the needle completely through all the ribbon layers, making neat and even stitches on both sides of the tip within one of the grosgrain ridges.

Bring the loops together to complete the heart shape (Figure 8, Drawing 3), inserting the hanging loop in the center between them and tacking it in place through all the layers of ribbon at the center with green thread. If the center area doesn't lay flat, tack the center ribbon layers at the front and back edges about 1″ up from the tip.

PUFFY SEGMENTED HEART

Materials

A 4″ × 8½″ red-with-white-dot fabric scrap

A 4″ × 8½″ red floral print fabric scrap

Red sewing thread

Polyester stuffing

3 yards of 6-ply white embroidery thread

1. Making the pattern and marking the fabric—Trace heart pattern A onto tracing paper and cut it out.

Trace around the pattern twice on the back of each fabric. Cut out the hearts, adding a ¼″ seam allowance around each shape.

2. Assembling the hearts—Pin a dot heart to a floral print heart, right sides together. Using small stitches, machine stitch along the seam line, leaving an opening between the dots. Repeat to make another identical heart.

Clip into the V-shaped area at each heart top, and cut off the tip of the seam allowance close to the stitching. Clip the remaining seam allowance or trim it with pinking shears, except between the dots.

Turn each heart right side out and press it flat to straighten out its shape. Lightly draw a center line from top to tip on the floral print side of one of the hearts. Stuff the hearts very lightly.

3. The hanging loop—To make a hanging loop, cut three 8″ lengths of embroidery thread and knot them together at one end. Secure the knotted end to the edge of a work surface with tape, then braid and knot the free ends.

Stitch the ends of the loop together securely just above the knots. Cut off the knots and tack both ends of the hanging loop neatly to the top of one dotted heart.

4. Finishing the ornament—Pin the hearts, dotted sides together, and machine stitch along the center line marked earlier on one of the floral print hearts.

Using two strands of white embroidery thread, blanket stitch around the edges of both hearts.

STRING OF FELT HEARTS

Materials

A 2″ × 6″ red felt scrap

A 2″ × 6″ white felt scrap

6-ply embroidery thread: 2½ yards red, 2 yards white

Sewing thread: white and red

1. Making the pattern and marking and cutting the fabric—Trace heart pattern O in Figure 9, and paste the tracing to heavy paper. Cut it out. Lightly draw around the pattern four times on the red felt and four times on the white felt. Cut out each heart along the pattern line.

2. Embroidering the hearts—Using two strands of embroidery floss, blanket stitch completely around each of the eight hearts, making red stitches on the white hearts and white stitches on the red hearts.

3. The hanging loop—To make a hanging loop, cut three 8″ lengths of red embroidery thread and knot them together at one end. Secure the knotted end with tape to the edge of a work surface, braid the strands together, and knot the ends. Stitch the ends together securely just above the knots. Cut off the knots and tack the hanging loop neatly to the top of one white heart.

4. Joining the hearts—Pin two hearts of the same color together and stitch down the center to join them, using tiny stitches and matching thread. Fold and then gently press along the stitching line to open the hearts. Repeat with the remaining pairs of hearts.

Nest the tip of the white heart with the hanging loop into the V-shaped area of a red heart and tack. Repeat with the remaining hearts, alternating the colors.

FIGURE 9. Pattern for the String of Felt Hearts

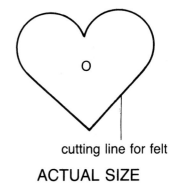

cutting line for felt

ACTUAL SIZE

This basic ruffle wreath design lends itself to as many variations as you can create, and the colors may be changed to suit any season or occasion. Each wreath is approximately 12" wide when completed and requires one yard of 44"-wide broadcloth or lighter fabric that will hold a crease well when pressed.

The wreath base is made in half sections that are hand-stitched together to make a doughnut shape. For

Ruffle Wreaths

best results when using several fabric colors, the front wreath base color should always match the color of the outside ruffle (A), and the

back wreath color should always match the color of the inside ruffle (F). After completing the initial work on your sewing machine, this project becomes very portable, provided you take along a lot of pins!

If you plan to hang one of these wreaths in an open doorway, you'll need extra fabric to make ruffles for both sides of it; a single A-sized ruffle around the outside will be enough, however.

General Materials

Sewing thread to match the fabrics
Polyester stuffing
Heavy duty (not carpet) thread to match the fabrics
A ¾"-diameter plastic curtain ring or bone-colored ring.

Equipment

A 4¼"-wide × 44"-long strip of cardboard, in one piece or pieced, to make a ruffle guide
Ruler
White dressmaker's pencil for dark fabrics
Dressmaker's carbon
Tracing wheel
Iron
Zipper foot attachment for attaching lace, where used.

LACE-TRIMMED FLORAL PRINT WREATH

Materials (plus general materials)

1 yard 44"-wide green floral print fabric
6⅞ yards of ¼"-wide, tatting type, flat white lace
¾ yard of 1½"-wide white grosgrain ribbon

1. Making the pattern and marking the fabric—Trace the wreath base pattern with the ruffle attachment lines, cut it out, and set it aside.

Mark and label the cardboard guide at the following intervals: 36" for the length of ruffle D, 32¼" for the ruffle A sections, 28" for the length of ruffle E, 26¼" for the ruffle B sections, and 20" for the length of ruffle F. Ruffle C will be 44", the entire length of the guide.

Using the ruffle guide and a ruler and referring to Figure 2, draw all the ruffles and ruffle sections on the wrong side of the green floral fabric so that one end of each ruffle and ruffle section falls along the selvage edge of the fabric.

On the wrong side of the remaining fabric and following the same cutting layout, trace four wreath base sections. All dimensions include ¼" seam allowances. Using dressmaker's carbon and a tracing wheel or pencil, transfer all the concentric placement lines on the base pattern to the right side of the fabric on two of the base sections. These will be used for the front of the wreath. The unmarked base sections will be used for the back of the wreath.

2. Cutting and joining the ruffle sections—Cut out the ruffles and ruffle sections along the pattern lines and label each piece.

Place the ruffle A sections right sides together and stitch them across one end, leaving a ¼" seam allowance. Repeat to join the ruffle B sections. Pin a label on each ruffle to identify it.

3. Cutting and assembling the wreath base—Cut out the four wreath base sections. To make one half of the base, take two base sections, one marked with concentric circles (front) and one unmarked (back) and turn under and press a ¼" seam allowance along both straight, short edges of each one. Then pin the pieces right sides together and join them along both curved edges, securing the stitches at the beginning and end of the seam lines. Trim the curved seam allowances, with pinking shears, or clip at frequent intervals almost to the stitching line. Turn the section right side out. Repeat to make the other base section, but this time do not turn under the seam allowances along the straight edges; simply join the pieces along the curved edges. (See Figure 1.)

Stuff both base sections firmly with polyester stuffing, but maintain the flatness.

Pin both base sections together with both marked sections on the same side, lapping the folded edges of one over the cut edges of the other and pushing in extra stuffing, if necessary, to make a solid flat wreath. Using doubled thread and overcast stitches, securely join the sections together, front and back. Set aside.

4. Finishing the ruffles—Press to the wrong side a ¼" seam allowance

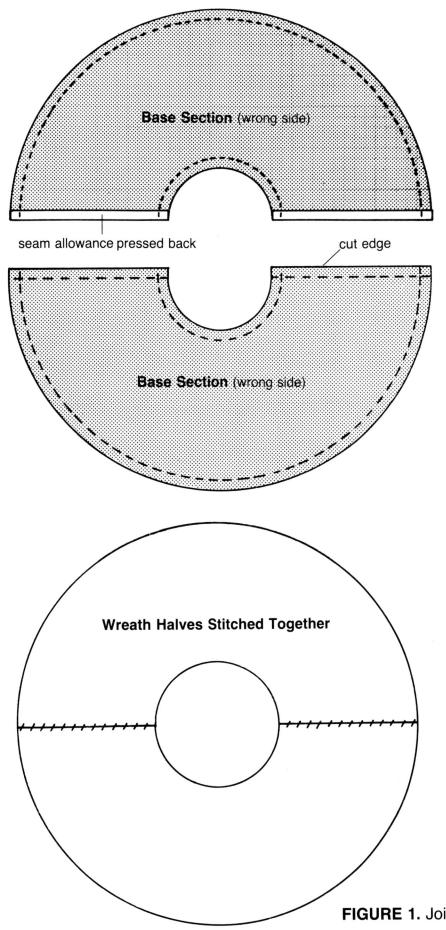

seam allowance pressed back

cut edge

FIGURE 1. Joining the base sections

along both lengthwise edges of each ruffle strip. Fold the ruffle in half lengthwise, wrong sides together, and press. Each ruffle strip should now be 1⅞" wide.

Using long machine stitches and heavy duty thread in the bobbin, stitch the open lengthwise edges of each ruffle strip together ⅛" from the edge. Pinning is usually not necessary. Mark the halfway point on each ruffle strip with a pin placed on the unstitched edge.

Stitch a row of lace along the folded edge of each ruffle strip, placing the straight, finished edge of the lace against the back of the ruffle. It is easiest to do this with a zipper foot attachment, placing the ruffle to the right, under the foot, and stitching the lace in place while guiding it with your free hand.

Starting with ruffle A, pull the bobbin thread to gather each ruffle, then temporarily secure the thread ends by wrapping them around a pin stuck into the ruffle end.

5. Attaching the ruffles—Pin ruffle A in place along the seam line on the outside edge of the wreath base, matching the pinned center of the ruffle with one of the seam lines on the wreath front and adjusting the ruffle fullness or length as necessary. Overlap the cut end of the ruffle with the selvage edge at the opposite end and pin. Overcast the gathered edge of the ruffle to the edge of the wreath base by hand exactly on the seam line. Invisibly stitch the overlapped ruffle ends together.

Repeat for all the ruffles, stitching each one to the base along its appropriate guideline and working in toward the center of the wreath. The gathered edge of each ruffle should just touch its respective circle on the wreath front, not overlap it, and the last ruffle should be exactly on the seam line along the inside of the wreath. It's easiest to stitch the final F ruffle from the back of the wreath. If it doesn't lay flat when you're done, tack it loosely and invisibly to ruffle E in a few places.

6. The finishing touches—Tie a white ribbon bow, trim the ends, and tack it to the wreath front on ruffle E. Stitch a curtain ring to the top of the wreath back.

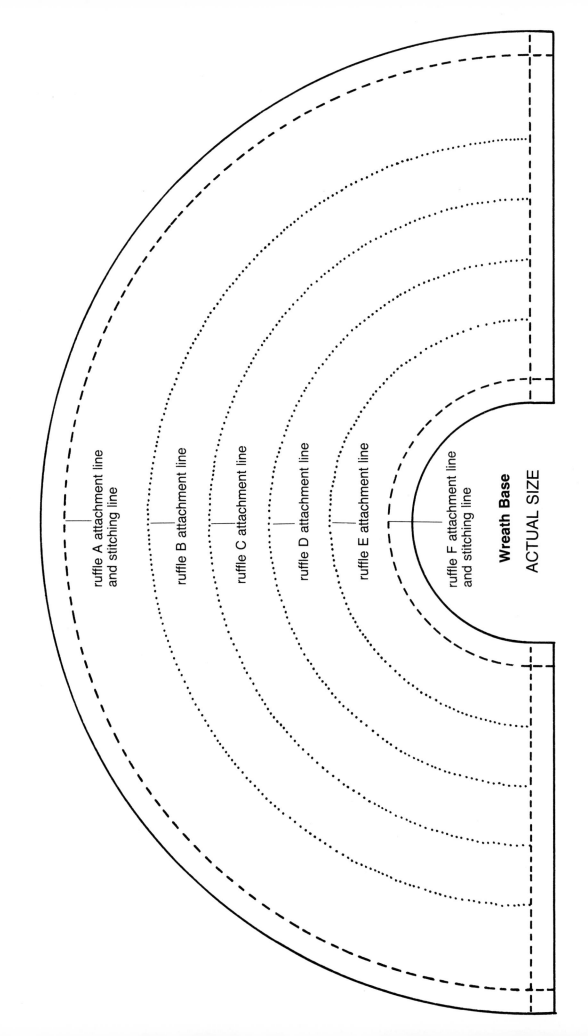

ruffle A attachment line
and stitching line

ruffle B attachment line

ruffle C attachment line

ruffle D attachment line

ruffle E attachment line

ruffle F attachment line
and stitching line

Wreath Base
ACTUAL SIZE

RED BANDANA WREATH WITH RICKRACK TRIM

Materials (plus general materials)

1 yard of 44"-wide red bandana print fabric

6⅞ yards green, medium-sized rickrack

¾ yard of 1½"-wide green grosgrain ribbon

Follow the directions for making the Lace-trimmed Floral Print Wreath, referring to Figure 2 for the cutting layout and substituting rickrack for the lace on each ruffle and green ribbon for white.

RED AND GREEN POLKA DOT WREATH

Materials (plus general materials)

½ yard of 44"-wide red-and-white polka dot fabric

½ yard of 44"-wide green-and-white polka dot fabric

¾ yard of 1½"-wide white grosgrain ribbon

Follow the directions for making the Lace-trimmed Floral Print Wreath, referring to Figure 3 for the cutting layout and making the following exceptions. From the green dot fabric, cut the wreath front (marked with concentric circle placement lines) and ruffles A, C, and E. From the red dot fabric, cut the wreath back and ruffles B, D, and F.

GREEN STRIPE WREATH

Materials (plus general materials)

1 yard of 44"-wide green-and-white striped fabric

¾ yard of 1½"-wide green grosgrain ribbon

Follow the directions for making the Lace-trimmed Floral Print Wreath, referring to Figure 4 for the cutting layout and substituting green ribbon for white. Note that the sections for Ruffle A are different lengths for this wreath and Ruffle C is cut in sections.

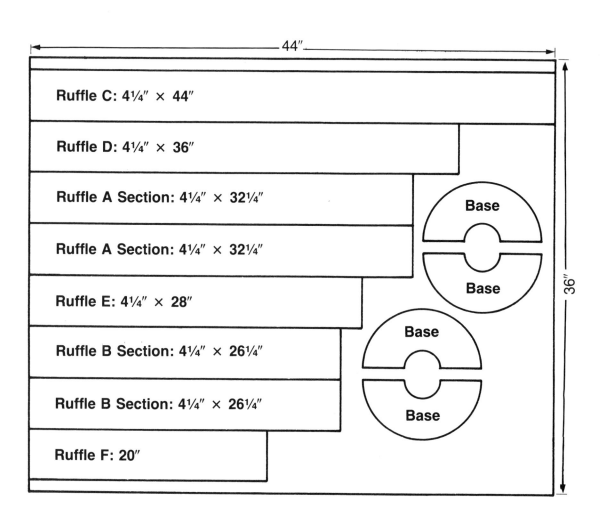

FIGURE 2. Cutting layout for the Lace-Trimmed Floral Print and Bandana Wreaths

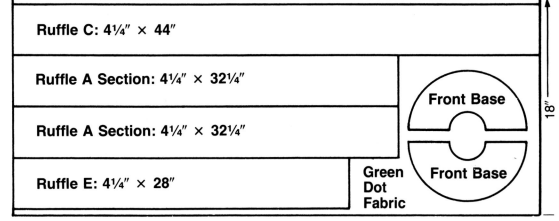

FIGURE 3. Cutting layout for the Red- and-Green Dot Wreath

Ruffle C: 4¼" × 44"

Ruffle A Section: 4¼" × 32¼"

Ruffle A Section: 4¼" × 32¼"

Ruffle E: 4¼" × 28"

Front Base

Front Base

Green Dot Fabric

18"

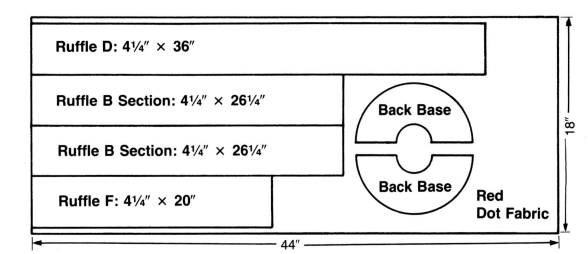

Ruffle D: 4¼" × 36"

Ruffle B Section: 4¼" × 26¼"

Ruffle B Section: 4¼" × 26¼"

Ruffle F: 4¼" × 20"

Back Base

Back Base

Red Dot Fabric

18"

44"

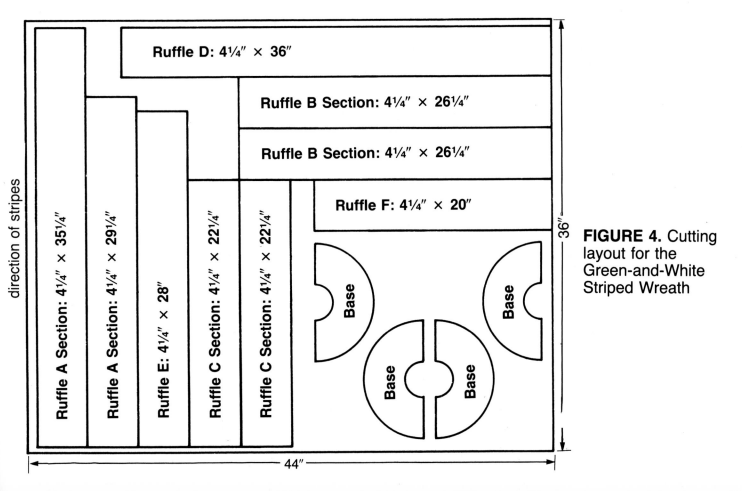

direction of stripes

Ruffle D: 4¼" × 36"

Ruffle B Section: 4¼" × 26¼"

Ruffle B Section: 4¼" × 26¼"

Ruffle F: 4¼" × 20"

Ruffle A Section: 4¼" × 35¼"

Ruffle A Section: 4¼" × 29¼"

Ruffle E: 4¼" × 28"

Ruffle C Section: 4¼" × 22¼"

Ruffle C Section: 4¼" × 22¼"

Base

Base

Base

Base

36"

44"

FIGURE 4. Cutting layout for the Green-and-White Striped Wreath

Basic Sewing Supplies, Tools and Techniques

Before you begin stitching, please sit down for a few moments and read through this section. It will be a wise investment of your time because it will give you a basic understanding of the terms and procedures used in this book, and it will probably

Basic Sewing Supplies, Tools and Techniques

help you to avoid some confusion and disappointments as well. Then, even before you look for your scissors, begin each individual project by first reading completely through the accompanying directions. This will alert you to any exceptional supplies or techniques required.

SUPPLIES AND TOOLS

Scissors—Scissors are a major and very important investment. Your grandmother was right! Don't use your good sewing shears on paper. Keep two pairs of scissors on hand, one for paper and one for sewing, and hide your sewing shears to protect them, if necessary. Mine, which I find to be the best, were relatively inexpensive. They have contoured plastic handles and very sharp, tapered stainless steel points. A pair of embroidery scissors is also indispensable for precision cutting of felt shapes and for clipping into small V-shaped areas of fabric.

Pinking shears are helpful, too, but they are not actually required for any project in this book. When trimming seam allowances, however, pinking shears eliminate the time-consuming clipping that is usually required along curves.

Hobby knife—Another important cutting tool to have on hand is a small hobby knife with a sharp point, such as an X-acto knife with a #11 blade. It's just right for cutting out template details in paper and lightweight cardboard. As long as you keep your fingers away from the blade, it's much safer and easier to use than a single-edge razor blade. As with scissors, it should be kept hidden from children.

Tracing and graph paper—Purchase a pad of transparent tracing paper at least 14″ wide by 17″ long so you can easily trace patterns from the book. A few projects require larger paper, but you can tape the smaller sheets together, if necessary. Graph paper is wonderful to have on hand for drawing straight-sided patterns. Purchase a pad with ⅛″ or ¼″ squares.

Rulers—You'll need a ruler for drawing straight pattern lines. I have two favorites. One is a very wide 15″-long transparent sewing ruler, which is available at most fabric stores. The other is a 39″-long metal straight edge that came from an art supply company, and I often use it as a cutting edge with the X-acto knife.

Pencils and drawing tools—Have on hand a few soft pencils, a white dressmaker's or drawing pencil, and a pencil sharpener.

Also helpful are a tape measure, a yardstick, and a compass for drawing accurate circles.

A T-square with a triangle or a right angle for making perfect 90° corners would be great, but these items aren't essential.

Thread—You can start a rainbow-colored collection of thread by taking advantage of sales that include unusual colors. Find a large shallow box, lay the spools on their sides, and organize them in rows of matching color. I often find sales that offer as many as six 225-yard spools for the usual price of one name-brand spool. I know there are thread purists, but I'm not one of them, and I've never had trouble with my bargain collection. I love having my own well-stocked thread store right on the premises!

Try to organize your embroidery threads, too. I never seem to find those threads on sale and they tangle up like spaghetti if you're not careful. I keep mine in candy sampler boxes and tie the color families together with ribbons.

Embroidery hoop—When you do decorative stitchery it's often helpful to use an embroidery hoop to keep the work neat. The ones I use the most are 4″ and 8″ in diameter.

Pins and needles—Other necessities are piles of pins, as well as a jumbo pin cushion studded like a porcupine. Having a box of extra-long (1¾″), super strong quilting pins on hand is a great help when working on quilts and comforters.

For needles, purchase an assortment card so you can determine your favorite size. The type I like best is rather fine and small and about 1½″ long, but you may favor another size. You'll also need some large-eyed embroidery needles that can accommodate multiple threads or yarn. Also purchase an assortment pack of sewing machine needles. You'll probably use numbers 11 and 14 most often, but it's a good idea to have the other sizes on hand as well.

Quilt batting—Polyester quilt batting comes in several thicknesses, and you can substitute multiple thin layers for one thick layer, if necessary. Save batting scraps for making potholders and stuffing toys and pillows. If you're working on a small project that requires batting and you don't have suitable scraps on hand, remember that it is available in a small, crib quilt size.

Pressing equipment—An iron is an essential piece of equipment for me. I can't imagine sewing without having one right next to the machine so I can press each seam as I work. Mine came from a garage sale. A small tailor's ham is also handy for pressing curved seams, but it isn't a necessity. Keep a good-sized scrap of lightweight, smooth, white fabric on hand to use as a pressing cloth when you want to protect your work.

Additional, miscellaneous equipment—Here are a few more tools that can be real timesavers. When you're turning and stuffing small forms, a crochet hook is a great aid, though a clean popsicle stick or a pencil with a broken and blunted point (no lead showing) works well too. To help pull out tiny corners and curves once shapes are turned right side out, use an extra long, very sturdy needle, but use great care to avoid snagging the fabric. A long ruler, wooden spoon handle, or a cafe curtain rod with the rough edges encased in tape are all useful when turning long, thin shapes inside out.

One more addition to your supply list should be a roll of masking tape. Do not use transparent tape of any kind, except for joining pattern sections. If you're careful and use a light touch, you can usually peel masking tape off of surfaces easily. It is ideal for anchoring tracing paper when you copy patterns from the book, although paper clips work, too. You can also position a piece of masking tape on the throat plate of your sewing machine to provide a guideline for making ¼″ or other width seams. Sometimes when you're machine stitching projects that have batting placed on the top layer, the presser foot catches the top fibers and slows you down. This won't happen if you first wrap a piece of masking tape around the toes of the presser foot.

And, speaking of sewing machines, you don't need a fancy one to make any of the projects in this book. You only need a straight-stitch machine, because after you've read the embroidery directions at the end of this section, you'll realize that those decorative stitch features built into many machines are also built into you!

Storage—In general, try to keep all your sewing equipment together in one area so that when you're ready to start a project you don't have to hunt all over the house to locate your supplies. In addition, collect a few portable containers to hold your work-in-progress. These might be anything from antique baskets to shopping bags or cardboard boxes from the supermarket. You'll work more efficiently and minimize clutter if all your necessary supplies and materials for each project are all together. At times, when I'm doing hand work I like to get away from my usual sewing area and sit on the sun-porch or in the kitchen. It's easy to do that when my work is folded away in a basket, ready to go.

Fabrics—When yardages are given, it is assumed that the fabric is at least 44″ wide, unless otherwise specified. I don't allow much extra length when I list fabric requirements because I lay out pieces very close together, with seam allowance edges touching at times. If this seems too close for comfort to you, always purchase at least ⅛ yard extra to be on the safe side.

Use light- to medium-weight fabrics, similar to broadcloth, for most of the projects in this book, unless otherwise specified. If fabric is too heavy or stiff, it's difficult to turn under seam allowances for appliqués or to turn small items right side out after stitching them. Also, I usually prewash the fabrics I use.

Avoid fabrics that fray easily. When you look at loosely woven fabrics, it's usually apparent that fraying will be a problem, but the same thing can happen with closely woven fabrics as well. To save yourself a lot of grief, always try to unravel a few threads of any fabric you've chosen before you buy it.

Where the grain of the fabric is important to a design, I've marked patterns with an arrow to indicate "straight-of-grain." Felt has no grain, so you can lay out pattern pieces any way you choose. If the felt is creased, steam press it before cutting because the moisture will make it shrink. Generally speaking, real felt is not washable, but a washable, felt-like craft material is now available.

SEWING TECHNIQUES

Making patterns—Don't underestimate the importance of making neat and accurate patterns. Most of the patterns in this book are actual size, ready for you to trace. When you start a project, always first check the pattern and directions for seam allowances. Most seam allowances are ¼″, but sometimes they vary, so it is critical to make sure of them from the beginning. Sometimes seam allowances are included in the patterns, but other times, when a very accurate stitching line is required, they are not included. Make a note of them on each pattern piece.

You may be tempted to use a photo copier to quickly duplicate the patterns, but I don't recommend it. Even the finest copiers slightly change the size of originals, in spite of assurances to the contrary. Photostats, on the other hand, are usually very accurate, but also very expensive, so trace!

Some of the designs are drawn on grids and need to be enlarged according to the accompanying directions (see page 163.). Alternatively, purchase large printed sheets of graph paper in a stationery or art supply store to make drawing the squares easier. It's costly to use a fresh sheet for each project that requires enlarging but you can make a master grid; draw 1″ squares on it, and tape tracing paper on top of it for each new project.

Another item that's useful for enlarging patterns and for several other purposes as well is a folding cardboard pattern-cutting board ruled in 1″ squares. When opened, the board provides a very large work surface as well as a master grid for tracing. Fabrics and patterns can be pinned to the board when necessary to protect your table or floor.

When you enlarge patterns or trace actual-size patterns from the book, always include all the features, matching dots, etc., and label each piece. This can save you much frustration later.

In trying to fit full-size patterns onto book-size pages, I've broken some patterns into sections. When a project has this type of pattern, directions are given for butting the sections together to make the complete pattern outline.

Sometimes, when both sides of a pattern are identical, I've drawn only half the pattern. When you trace a pattern of this sort, use folded tracing paper. Lay the paper fold along the "place on fold" edge of the pattern and trace half the pattern. Then, pin the layers of paper together in several places inside the pattern outline and cut out the pattern. Copy the features, dots, etc., on the unmarked side of the pattern, when necessary.

Tracing patterns on fabrics—Lay patterns face down on the wrong side of the fabric to be cut, pin them in place, and trace around them with a sharp soft pencil. If the pattern outlines are seam lines, leave enough space between the pieces to add seam allowances, usually ¼″ unless otherwise specified. Add the required seam allowances when cutting the fabric. I use this method most of the time because I like to have a precise seam line drawn on each fabric piece.

If no seam allowances are required, as with most felt appliqués or pieces that will have bound edges, pattern pieces can be placed much closer together on the fabric.

For greater durability, patterns that will be used a number of times can be glued onto lightweight cardboard or plastic before they are cut out.

Transferring embroidery details to fabrics—There are several ways, enumerated below, to mark the right side of a piece of fabric for embroidery or the placement of appliqués. Choose the one best-suited to your project, fabric, time, and standards.

1. Stencil and basting—I don't like to risk having pencil lines show on the front of the fabric, so when I have enough time I make a stencil or template. I trace the design lines of the interior details (eyes, cheeks, smiles, etc.) onto the pattern and cut them out with a razor-edged art knife. I then draw the lines lightly on the fabric back and baste along them with tiny stitches to transfer the details to the fabric front.

2. Direct stencil or dressmaker's carbon—When I am rushed, I cut out the fabric shape (unless the directions specify otherwise), position a stencil-cut pattern (see item 1 above) on the fabric front and lightly draw the details directly on it. Alternatively, I sometimes use dressmakers' carbon and a tracing wheel to transfer the outlines of large details.

3. "Rub-off" technique—On occasion, I go over the detail lines on the back of a pattern with a soft pencil. I then lay the pattern in position on the right side of the fabric and rub off the design with the end of a popsicle stick or something similar. This works most efficiently after the fabric pieces have been cut out.

4. Basting seam lines on small pieces—When I work on very small pieces that aren't cut out until after the seams are stitched, I first transfer the seam line marked on the fabric back to the front with bastings. Then I can accurately place the details on the fabric front. Actually, the technique described next is fastest for those very small pieces.

5. Lightbox technique—I don't have a lightbox, but if it's a sunny day, I get the same result by using a brightly lit window. After tracing the pattern outline on the fabric back, I tape the pattern in place on the fabric. I then tape both to my window, pattern down, and lightly trace the details on the fabric front.

6. Transferring details to felt—The stencil technique (#2 above) sometimes works well, but the best way to mark felt is to make dots along the detail line by first punching through the pattern with a fat needle and then marking the spots on the felt with a pencil. On dark felt, use a sharp-pointed white drawing pencil.

7. Marking and stitching features on stuffed toys—When making a toy, I usually mark the fabric before stitching using one of the methods discussed above, but often I don't embroider facial features until after the figure is stuffed because the filling can distort a face so much. You may even prefer to wait and transfer the features by means of a stencil after a figure is stuffed. You can then find the best position for them on the stuffed head.

Appliqués—Before cutting out appliqué pieces, decide whether you will attach them by hand or by zig-zag machine stitching. If you use the machine, cut out the fabric along the seam lines, omitting a seam allowance. Use fusible web to attach the cutout to fabric, then secure the edges with close zigzag stitches.

If you attach appliqués by hand, more of your sewing can be done in your lap as a take-along project. Add ¼″ seam allowances when cutting out the fabric, turn the edges under along the seam line, finger press or iron, and baste.

To make the handling of small fabric pieces easier, especially small circles, cut them out with pinking shears. Pinking trims away some of the fabric bulk so the edges will turn under smoothly. Alternatively, make tiny basting stitches along the seam line before cutting out the fabric. This gives you a precise folding edge. Then cut out the pieces, adding a ¼″ seam allowance to each one; clip or trim the seam allowance before you turn under the edge.

Pin the fabric pieces in position and baste them in place. Appliqué the figures with blind hemming and/or embroidery stitches, and remove the basting. I edge most of my appliqués with blanket stitches.

Stitching stuffed figures—In most cases, I recommend pinning and basting together any pieces that will be stuffed before sewing. This is time-consuming, but the results are well worth the extra effort. Line up the fabrics, and push a pin straight down through each pair of matching dots, checking for accuracy. Then pin along the seam allowance, placing the pins perpendicular to the edge.

To make seams smooth on the right side, it is often necessary to trim and clip them. With bulky seams, I grade or layer the seam allowance, cutting away each separate layer at a different distance from the stitching line. For instance, if the seam allowance is ½″ wide, I might trim the bottom layer to ⅜″ and the top layer to ¼″. If there is a third batting layer, it would be trimmed to ⅛″ or closer. This eliminates much of the bulk along the edges and makes a neater finish. Cut across the corners, trimming close to the stitching. On curves, make vertical clips into the seam allowance, almost to the stitching line.

Quilting—To quilt layers of fabric together, sew directly on top of the seam line or close to each side of it, using thread to match or blend with the fabric. Catch all layers with each stitch. For hand quilting, use a small running stitch. For machine quilting, use long straight stitches.

Machine basting—If you baste or sew gathering stitches on the machine, set the machine for a long stitch and loosen the tension slightly, if possible. Then pull the bobbin thread, either to gather the fabric or to remove basting threads after a seam has been completed.

Stuffing techniques—When you use stuffing, insert only a little at a time and start with the arms, legs, and head (the extremities). Using the blunt end of a crochet hook, really pack it in. You'll almost always use more stuffing than you estimate, so have an extra bag on hand. Sometimes I suggest maintaining a flat, softly stuffed appearance for a figure, but usually it's best to make the stuffing firm. Polyester stuffing is my favorite.

SOME WORDS OF CAUTION

Avoid the use of buttons, bells, fringe balls, and other "munchies" if a young child will be the recipient of your gift stitchery. Even if the item is not intended for a little one, a gift often receives a thorough inspection by small curious hands. I also strongly recommend that you pre-wash any materials that you use to make baby gifts.

Now pull out your scrap bag, find those scissors, and get busy!

MITERING DOUBLE-FOLD BIAS TAPE USED AS A BINDING

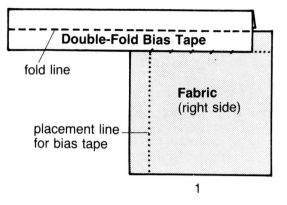

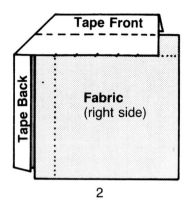

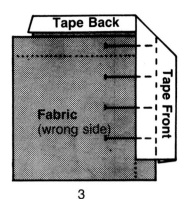

1

2

3

1. Open center fold of tape and place one edge of tape along placement line. Invisibly stitch tape to front of fabric.

2. At the corner, fold down loose end of tape at a 45° angle toward the back of the fabric.

3. Turn work to back and pin tape in position along placement line.

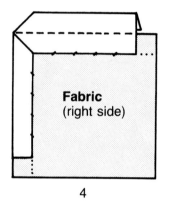

4

5

4. Turn work to the front. Fold flap of pinned tape forward toward front and invisibly stitch.

5. Turn work to back, fold down remaining tape and pin in position. Stitch tape to back of fabric.

MITERING SINGLE-FOLD BIAS TAPE USED AS FLAT TRIM.

Stitch the bias tape in place along both edges all the way to a corner, fold the tape back on itself, and, holding both layers of tape together at the outer tip of the corner, fold the loose end of tape straight down so the outer edge is aligned with the folded end of tape underneath it (Drawing 1). Pin and stitch (Drawing 2).

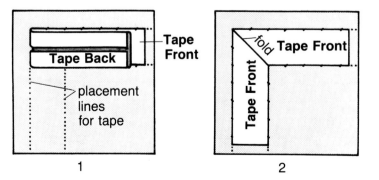

1

2

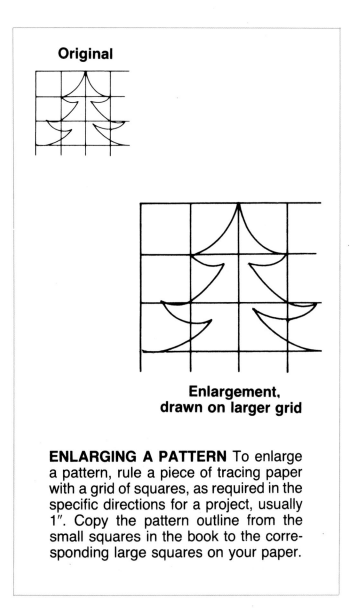

Original

Enlargement, drawn on larger grid

ENLARGING A PATTERN To enlarge a pattern, rule a piece of tracing paper with a grid of squares, as required in the specific directions for a project, usually 1″. Copy the pattern outline from the small squares in the book to the corresponding large squares on your paper.

Embroidery Stitches

BACKSTITCH. Working from right to left, bring the needle up on the guide-line. Take a stitch backward and bring the needle up an equal distance ahead of the first hole. Repeat, taking the needle back to the end of the last stitch.

RUNNING STITCH. Working from right to left, make stitches of the same size, with even spaces between them. Use running stitches for quilting, gathering several stitches on the needle before pulling the thread through the fabric.

CHAIN STITCH. Working from right to left, or top to bottom, depending on your preference, bring the needle and thread to the right side of the fabric. Make a loop with the thread and, holding it against the fabric, insert the needle again as close as possible to where the thread last came up. Take a short stitch ahead, drawing the needle over the loop.

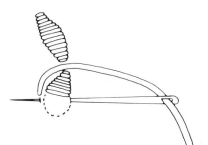

SATIN STITCH. Working from one end of a figure to the other, bring the needle up on one side and insert it on the opposite side. Carrying the thread behind the work, repeat from side to side, keeping the stitches parallel, smooth, and close together.

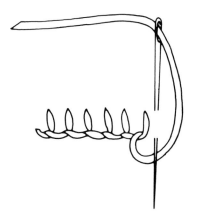

BLANKET STITCH. Bring the needle out along the edge of the fabric. Insert the needle above and to the right of the starting point and bring it out in line with the last stitch on the fabric edge, keeping the thread behind the needle point. Continue working from left to right and top to bottom.

BUTTONHOLE STITCH. Work exactly as for the blanket stitch, but keep the stitches close together.

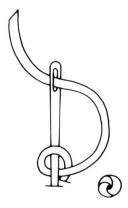

FRENCH KNOT. Bring the needle out on the right side of the fabric where you want an embroidered dot. Wrap the thread two or three times around the point of the needle. Insert the needle close to the spot where the thread emerged. Holding the knot in place, pull the thread to the wrong side.

PADDED SATIN STITCH. Work exactly as for the satin stitch, but make two layers of stitches perpendicular to each other.

LAZY DAISY STITCH.
Make a chain stitch loop, then insert the needle to anchor the end of the loop and bring the needle up at the beginning of the next loop.

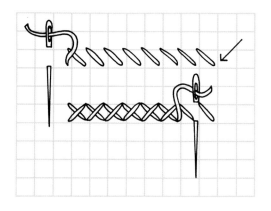

CROSS STITCH. Beginning at the arrow, bring the needle up from the back of the fabric and make parallel, evenly spaced slanted stitches along the rows to be worked, forming the first half of each cross. To cross the stitches, bring the needle out directly below the end of the last stitch and even with the beginning of that stitch. Insert the needle at the upper end of the prior stitch, completing the first cross stitch. Repeat across the row.

Index